Design for Performance | From Diaghilev to the Pet Shop Boys

205

A Centenary Publication by Central Saint Martins College of Art and Design   Edited by Peter Docherty and Tim White

Design for Performance | From Diaghilev to the Pet Shop Boys

Lund Humphries Publishers, London
in association with
The Lethaby Press, Central Saint Martins College of Art and Design, London

Lund Humphries Publishers, London
First published in Great Britain in 1996 by
Lund Humphries Publishers
Park House
1 Russell Gardens
London NW11 9NN
in association with
The Lethaby Press
Central Saint Martins College of Art and Design, London
Design for Performance: From Diaghilev to the Pet Shop Boys

British Library Cataloguing in Publication Data.
A catalogue record of this book is available from the British Library.

ISBN 0 85331 720 8
Distributed in the USA by
Antique Collectors' Club
Market Street Industrial Park
Wappingers Falls
NY 12590
USA

Designed by Chrissie Charlton & Company
Made and printed in Great Britain by
BAS Printers Limited, Over Wallop, Stockbridge, Hampshire

Cover illustration:
Ralph Koltai *Conflicts*
Music by Ernest Bloch
Choreography by Norman Morrice
Ballet Rambert, 1962
Photograph by Anthony Crickmay
The Theatre Museum, V&A

Contents

Acknowledgements

The Design for Performance Research Project is grateful to a large number of individuals and organisations without whom this book would not have been possible. Our sincere thanks must be given to all those who kindly lent works for the 1993 *From Diaghilev to the Pet Shop Boys* exhibition in The Lethaby Galleries, London which led to the commissioning of this book, to those who contributed additional designs, those who granted permission for these to be reproduced in this book and those who assisted in gathering information:

The Department of Prints and Drawings, Victoria and Albert Museum; Peter Farley; Marina Henderson; The Theatre Museum, Victoria and Albert Museum; Rambert Dance Company Archive; James Gordon; The Royal Opera House, Covent Garden; The Royal Ballet Benevolent Fund; Lord Snowdon; Madame Jean Hugo; Peter Williams; Peter Wilson; Peter Docherty; Elisabeth Dalton; English National Ballet Archives; Norman Morrice; John Chesworth; Ian Spurling; Peter Snow; Clarissa Dixon-Wright; Yolanda Sonnabend; Pamela Howard; Janet Eager; David Walker; Terry Bartlett; Mathilde Sandberg; Richard Hudson; Ann Curtis; Andrew Logan; Peter Logan; Antony McDonald; Jennifer Carey; Robin Don; Allen Jones; Brendan Thorpe; Paul Andrews; Lez Brotherston; David Fielding; Peter Whiteman; Richard Bridgland; John Macfarlane; Bernadette Roberts; Tim Hatley; Deborah, Lady MacMillan; Anthony Powell; Maria Bjørnson; Leslie E. Spatt; The Beaton Archive, Sotheby's; Ralph Koltai; Anthony Crickmay; John B. Read; Dance Unlimited; Philip Prowse; Nicholas Georgiadis; Bill Cooper; Hugo Glendinning; The Redfern Gallery; Karsten Schubert, London; Mrs Annette Armstrong; Desmond Corcoran, The Lefevre Gallery; Jack Carter; Thomas Elliot; Mrs H. Garnett; John Hurry Armstrong; Mrs Ann Rendall; Michael Werner; Professor Anthony Jones, Rector of the Royal College of Art; John Sibley, the Paul Nash Trust; Geoffrey Parton, Marlborough Fine Art; Prunella Clough; Muriel Large; Anthony Russell-Roberts; Francesca Franchi and Guy Baxter at the Royal Opera House Archive; Margaret Benton, Sarah Woodcock and Leelah Meinertas at The Theatre Museum; Jane Pritchard, Archivist at Rambert Dance Company, English National Ballet and London Contemporary Dance Trust; Graham Cruickshank, Archivist, Palace Theatre, London; John Percival; Noël Goodwin; Michael Merwitzer; Ann Nugent; Tanya Moiseiwitsch; Pegeret Anthony; Matthew Hamilton; Mary Clarke and Sue Merrett, *The Dancing Times*; Sylvia Backemeyer; Vijay Dhir; Gordon Taylor; the Stuttgart Ballet; the Royal Ballet Companies.

The editors and publishers thank all those who have given permission to reproduce works or who have provided photographs. Every effort has been made to trace the copyright holders or owners of works and photographs. We apologise if any institutions or individuals have been incorrectly credited, or if there are any omissions, and would be glad to be notified so that the necessary corrections can be made in any reprint.

Credit lines for copyright owners or those who have provided photographs are given in the last line of each caption. All copyright for illustrations remains vested with the artists, their heirs, or trustees.

Foreword | Professor Margaret Buck

Design for Performance: From Diaghilev to the Pet Shop Boys by Central Saint Martins College of Art and Design marks the centenary of one of its founding colleges, the Central School of Arts and Crafts, established by the architect, educationalist and conservationist, William Richard Lethaby. Central Saint Martins College of Art and Design was formed in 1989 through the merger of the then Central School of Art and Design and Saint Martin's School of Art which was founded earlier, in 1854. For more than 100 years, staff and students have made impressive contributions not only to art and design practice but also to education. The College is the largest of The London Institute art and design colleges and offers the most diverse and comprehensive range of disciplines in the country, from foundation and undergraduate to postgraduate studies and research degrees – it is, in essence, the complete art college.

The Design for Performance Research Project, established in July 1994 following the success of the Peter Williams Design for Dance Project, has, in this publication, brought together a unique collection of dance designs with essays and interviews by designers talking about design. From its beginnings in 1989, Design for Dance has enabled final year BA (Hons) Theatre Design students at Central Saint Martins to work with an ever increasing number of dance schools and companies as well as professional designers and choreographers, collaborating to produce performances at The Cochrane Theatre during the spring term. The Design for Dance Project was dedicated to Peter Williams in 1993 at the opening of the exhibition *From Diaghilev to the Pet Shop Boys*, held in The Lethaby Galleries. Conceived by Project Leader Peter Docherty and curated by gallery owner Marina Henderson and Theatre Design tutor Peter Farley, the Exhibition gathered together a wide range of designs for dance embracing the twentieth century. The Research Project has subsequently mounted a further exhibition, *The Designers: Pushing the Boundaries – Advancing the Dance*, celebrating the work of designers who have collaborated with four of the most innovative post-war choreographers and artistic directors of dance companies in Britain: Robert Cohen, Peter Darrell, Sir Kenneth MacMillan and Norman Morrice. Held in The Lethaby Galleries in November 1995, the Exhibition featured not only a large number of designs but also slides and photographs of productions, elements of the set from a number of pieces and videos of both performances and interviews with their creators.

Video plays an increasingly central part in the work of the Design for Performance Research Project. The project has conducted video interviews with leading designers, choreographers, directors, performers and critics that complement the assembling of other resource material on particular productions, which includes not only designs but music and choreographic scores, lighting plans, reviews and production photographs and videos. This provides a rich and diverse body of material that is a resource for both teaching and further research. This ongoing work is to be augmented by a practical enquiry into the nature of design-led performance. A collaboration between Project Director Peter Docherty and the artistic Directors of Dance Unlimited, Matthew Hamilton and Sue Nash, will take as its starting point a visual score and will culminate in a series of performances at The Cochrane Theatre in June 1997. The possibilities afforded by the move away from the literary or musical score will be documented by the Design for Performance Research team, for whom the collaboration provides a unique opportunity to access the process of creation from conception to performance. Additionally, in a new initiative, the research team are developing virtual reality models both as a means to explore existing designs interactively and to extend the possibilities of scenographic practice.

In documenting the annual Peter Williams Design for Dance Project and videoing the lectures and seminars given by visiting practitioners, Design for Performance contributes to a long term project established by Central Saint Martins five years ago to build up a substantial collection of current and past staff and student work. This work, some of which is on permanent exhibition in the College, will be of inestimable use for future generations of students and researchers. This resource relates to our exhibition policy which is increasingly taking on more of an international dimension; currently work from the College Collection is being shown in Budapest. This policy complements the many links the College is building abroad through international courses such as our MA in Scenography under its artistic director and contributor to this book, Pamela Howard. The Course offers students the opportunity to study at two of the four participating centres of London, Helsinki, Utrecht, and Prague. Additionally, the College has established a franchise arrangement with Malaysia.

As we reach the millennium, the College continues to build upon the success of its past by pushing the boundaries of art and design education and practice. Next year, the College will introduce a new, innovative combined studies undergraduate degree course where architectural studies, a prominent discipline in Lethaby's time, together with environment-related art and design, will play a major role. The Course will encourage collaboration across the College, from fashion and textiles, graphic and product design including furniture, to jewellery, ceramics, theatre design and fine art. Central Saint Martins will continue to provide an unrivalled opportunity for students to select the best career pathway, enabling them to realise their potential and make a significant contribution to the new millennium. Accordingly, the College envisages that its graduates will play a key role in determining the quality of life for all, whether in a learning or working environment, enjoying our leisure time or old age, or with disability.

The work of the Design for Performance Research Project has been made possible through funding from the Higher Education Funding Council for England. In particular I would like to express my gratitude to all those who have contributed to this valuable enterprise.

Professor Margaret Buck
Head of College
June 1996

Peter Williams (right) standing backstage with Kenneth MacMillan during a performance of *The Sleeping Beauty* by Sadler's Wells Ballet.

Introduction | Peter Docherty

In looking at the life and work of Peter Williams one is looking at design for dance this century and the parallel development of theatre design at Central Saint Martins College of Art and Design. The following pieces on Peter Williams by Peter Docherty and Sir John Drummond give some idea of Peter's importance to design and performance.

The book is divided into three sections. The first section, 'Designers on Design', presents some of the writings of Peter Williams, as valid today as when they first appeared in *Dance and Dancers*. The item on Philip Prowse's costumes for *Diversions* is just one of many in which Peter covered design from the designer's perspective, and we have followed this approach throughout the book, which includes the comments of a number of the most respected designers of recent times. The section opens with 'Stepping into the Twenties', the first chapter of Peter Williams's unfinished autobiography, in which he describes his first experience of dance, 'a world where it was possible to believe that fairies and magic were a natural part of daily life'. The less ethereal world where one learned how to create such visions is conveyed in Peter Farley's account of the instruction given by Jeannetta Cochrane to aspiring stage designers at the Central School of Arts and Crafts in his essay 'Draped Life'. Farley continues in 'A Stage of Creation', considering the revolution in dance at The Jeannetta Cochrane Theatre and the contributions of Ballet Rambert's Norman Morrice and his long-time collaborator, Ralph Koltai, a designer whose influence on both the theatre design course and scenography in general is immense. The interview with John B. Read then looks at the important role of the lighting designer and his innovative work in The Jeannetta Cochrane Theatre. This is followed by a look at the Peter Williams Design for Dance Project and at the aims and achievements of the Design for Performance Research Project, so energetically encouraged and supported by Professor Margaret Buck, Head of Central Saint Martins, and by Professor John McKenzie while he was Rector of The London Institute. Having provided an overview of the past, the section concludes with accounts by three current practitioners of their approach to design, once more allowing designers an opportunity to speak of their profession in their own words.

The second section of the book, 'Designing the Narrative', focuses on how different designers have treated a common theme. It begins with an introduction by Nicholas Georgiadis to the three full-length ballets of Tchaikovsky. As one of the very few designers to have designed all three ballets on at least two occasions, he is eminently qualified to speak of the challenge these works present. The section continues by illustrating how these ballets have been interpreted by a number of designers from Léon Bakst (1921) to Lez Brotherston (1995). Further comments on particular productions by their respective designers conclude with lighting designer Rick Fisher's notes on Adventures in Motion Pictures' *Swan Lake*. The second part of this section opens with Peter Williams's first editorial for *Dance and Dancers*, which invites the reader to embrace the diversity of dance, and continues by illustrating four distinct points of departure and how designers have responded to them. These include *Cinderella*, as the marrying of fairy-tale and twentieth-century score, *Coppélia*, the perennial Romantic ballet, 'Shakespeare', exemplifying the adaptation of literary source and, finally, the challenges of 'The Musical'.

The third section of the book takes its inspiration from the exhibition held in The Lethaby Galleries of Central Saint Martins, *From Diaghilev to the Pet Shop Boys*. The theme of the exhibition was Peter's life, those he had taught, those who were trained at Central Saint Martins and who have taught or continue to teach there. Of over ninety artists represented in this book, nearly half of them fall into one or more of these categories, and further details of their work can be found in this part of the book. As can be seen from the selection of designs from the exhibition reproduced here, it was both eclectic and vital, full of energy and love of dance and design – a perfect reflection of Peter's life.

Peter Williams Remembered | Peter Docherty

'Peter Williams 1914–95,
Writer, editor, designer, teacher and friend of dance', *Dance Theatre Journal*, Vol.12, No.2, November 1995, p.42.

I first met Peter Williams thirty years ago when I was a student at The Slade School of Fine Art. He had the most profound effect on my life, not only as tutor but also as promoter, critic and friend. His generosity in helping me as a future theatre designer was typical of the way he helped countless other theatre creators, including choreographers, composers, musicians, writers, artistic directors – even chairmen of boards.

His family came from Cornwall, which he always thought of as home, even though he lived in London for much of his life. He was educated at Harrow, and later went to the Central School of Arts and Crafts (now Central Saint Martins College of Art and Design) where he was taught theatre design by Jeannetta Cochrane, who was an important influence. After graduating he started his own fashion house in Belgravia, later becoming chief designer for Jantzen swimwear.

But long before that Peter's mother had begun introducing him to a wide range of theatrical fare, and he went to everything from music hall, variety and musical comedy to grand opera, ballet and drama. He was soon bitten by the theatre bug, and developed a taste that was catholic enough to take him on one night to Covent Garden and the next to a drag show in Battersea. However, he considered that the most significant performance he ever attended was in 1921, when he and his mother saw the Diaghilev production of *The Sleeping Princess*, with designs by Léon Bakst. (He recounted the experience in the first instalment of his memoirs, originally published in *Dance and Dancers*, and sadly unfinished.)

After World War Two, dance became a central part of his life. He designed John Taras's *Designs with Strings* for the Metropolitan Ballet, and was both librettist and designer for Andrée Howard's ballet *Selina*, made in 1949 for the Sadler's Wells Theatre Ballet.

In the late 1940s he began to assist Richard Buckle with the influential magazine *Ballet*, becoming assistant editor from 1949-50. In January 1950, at the invitation of the publisher Philip Dosse, he became founding editor of *Dance and Dancers*. This was to be the centre of his life for the next thirty years, and he gave it a reputation as a serious monthly that had a feeling both for tradition and for what was new and likely to be of lasting value.

In 1950 Peter also saw and wrote about the work of a young Greek designer from The Slade, Nicholas Georgiadis, who was working with a young British choreographer, Kenneth MacMillan. Georgiadis was to become a great friend, and a designer whom he admired all his life. This led Peter into teaching dance projects at The Slade, through which emerged a generation of designers for dance.

I was one of those designers, and I remember Peter smoking a Senior Service in a cigarette holder. At the time I was a non-smoker, and had never seen anybody chain-smoking before. I was later to become a nicotine addict myself, and it was Peter's courage in stopping smoking which encouraged me to do the same! The project he set us at The Slade was to create the designs for *Coppélia* – a truly awful project for progressive young art students. But Peter inspired not only me, but also Derek Jarman and Peter Logan, to love this ballet and to create exciting work for it.

Just as he was inspiring student designers, so he was influencing the course of dance in this country. He was closely involved in 1950 with the founding of Festival Ballet (as it was originally known), or English National Ballet (as it has since become). From the 1960s to the early 1990s he served on committees representing dance for the British Council, the Royal Ballet Benevolent Fund and the Arts Council, becoming chairman of the Arts Council's Dance Theatre Sub-Committee for several years. At the DTS-C's recommendation several key reports were commissioned that led to a major restructuring of British dance, in particular to the establishment of contemporary dance as a force, with the new-styled Ballet Rambert, and the founding of the London Contemporary Dance Theatre. Peter was behind Western Theatre Ballet's metamorphosis into Scottish Ballet, the founding of Northern Ballet Theatre and the establishment of both the Dancers Benevolent Fund and the Dancers Pension and Resettlement Fund (now the Dancers Trust). He also played a part in Peter Brinson's initiative in setting up what is nowadays known as the International Dance Course for Professional Choreographers and Composers.

In 1981 he published *Masterpieces of Ballet Design* (Phaidon). Two years ago an exhibition of dance design entitled *From Diaghilev to the Pet Shop Boys*, at the Central Saint Martins College of Art and Design, was dedicated to him. It was a celebration of his life, and his twin loves of dance and design. Out of this developed the annual Peter Williams Design for Dance Project, bringing together young designers, choreographers, dancers, musicians and composers in a truly 'Williamsesque' way.

Peter was always an avid party-goer, and giver, frequently inviting scores of people to Sunday soirées in his London studio. I will never forget his wit and fun. On my last visit to see him in the Chelsea and Westminster hospital he told, with a twinkle in his eye, how he was certain he had seen Mae West in a lift and the Dolly Sisters in Monte Carlo!

Philip Prowse Costume designs for *Diversions*
Music by Sir Arthur Bliss
Choreography by Kenneth MacMillan
The Royal Ballet, Royal Opera House, London, 1961
Reprinted by permission of Peter Williams from *Dance and Dancers*, Vol.12, No.11, November, 1961 p.13.

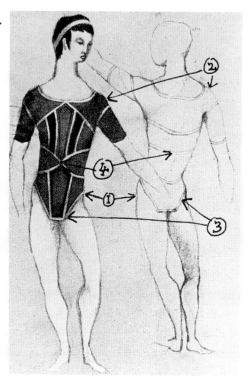

FOUR REASONS WHY PHILIP PROWSE'S COSTUMES ARE SO GOOD FOR THE MALE DANCER

1. Long leg line giving elegance and freedom of movement.

2. Clean shoulder line which does not obscure the arm line in any position.

3. Concealing and flattering line which serves its purpose admirably without obscuring the line of the dance.

4. All decoration kept within the internal lines of the silhouette. Decoration which pays heed to anatomical lines of the body — both flattering and elegant.

The basic features of these designs should point the way to how all male costumes ought to be designed in the future, both in classical and neo-classical works.

Peter Williams: An Appreciation | Sir John Drummond CBE

For those of us who knew him and worked with him, a very strong case can be made to suggest that Peter Williams was one of the half-dozen most influential people in the history of this country in making dance and its world relevant and significant, not only to a wide public, but to those who have the power to influence things by providing or denying the necessary funds.

Peter was a dance enthusiast from his early years, but he soon learned to question the complacent belief that everything in dance had already been achieved. For him, until his very last years, the future mattered quite as much as the past. Influenced as he was by the achievements of the Diaghilev ballet, he subsequently refused to accept that anything less than the reunion of all the arts was what was required from people working today. A designer by training, he became a publicist, then a journalist and eventually a crucial arbiter, through his membership of committees, of what was happening. Uniquely, in my experience, he could, as a friend, suggest to people what they might do, as an Arts Council Panel Chairman decide whether it should be funded and then as a critic review the success or otherwise of what had been achieved. Even more remarkably, no one ever questioned his right to occupy three roles, all normally thought to be impossibly contradictory. No one ever disputed his right to withdraw funding to something that he had suggested should be explored, or indeed to review unfavourably something over whose birth he had presided. It was a remarkable example of the original thinking behind the creation of the Arts Council; the belief that there were indeed village elders who knew a great deal, who could advise and help, but who retained the right to disagree with the result without losing their faith in the art form, and remaining deeply involved on a day-to-day basis with its practitioners. For those of us who were close to him, Peter's triple role was an inspiring example and one that we should fight to the final cut to maintain and reinforce.

It was tremendously appropriate that, as a former student, Peter Williams should lend his name to an important initiative from Central Saint Martins; not just to celebrate the achievements of design in dance, but to seek to underwrite its success through further exploration and achievement. The exhibition upon which this book is based was a tribute to Peter Williams's belief that design is as important as music or choreography in the total theatrical experience to which we should all aspire. The publication of this impressive record stands as a fitting memorial for all he stood for and fought for.

I

DESIGNERS ON DESIGN
1920-1996

John Craxton Donald MacLeary in *Apollo*
Music by Igor Stravinsky
Choreography by George Balanchine
The Royal Ballet, 1966
Photograph by Houston Rogers
The Theatre Museum, V&A

Originally created for Diaghilev in 1928 with scenery
by André Bauchant and costumes by Chanel. At each
revival Balanchine made the setting and costumes
sparer but the structure of the steps is an integral part
of the ballet and is included in one form or another
in all versions.

Stepping into the Twenties | Peter Williams

Dance and Dancers, Vol.31, No.2, February 1980, pp.18–23.

By the time I was six years old, my family decided that the time was ripe for my return to England; I had left there a few weeks after I was born near Nottingham, where my father had been stationed before the outbreak of the 14/18 war. All through my childhood in Cornwall the word 'London' kept cropping up in conversation, and it had sounded like some mysterious Utopian place; at last I was going to find out for myself. We set off, my grandfather driving us – my mother, my half-sister Jess, our nannie and myself – to Truro station in our De Dion Bouton, affectionately known as Bacchante. In those days a motor ride was quite an adventure, for not only did tyres puncture with amazing regularity, and at most inconvenient moments, but those Cornish hills often proved too much for a lady of French breeding. This meant that we would have to get out, push her up the last few yards of a hill; when we reached the top we would rush to get back in before she swooped down the other side, so as to give her enough impetus to carry us as far as possible up the next one. This prelude to my first London visit contained all these hazards, plus the fact that I fell between the train and the platform, grazing the back of my knees rather badly. Having been brought up with the strict instruction that boys never cried and that all pain must be endured in silence, I consoled myself by going to talk to the engine driver of the Cornish Riviera Express and to admire the beautiful 'Castle' class engine that would speed us towards London. In those days, for reasons that I still don't understand, it was just not done to eat in a public restaurant car; the guard would be tipped so that we got a carriage to ourselves and the huge meal, that had been prepared at home, could be eaten in peace. One of the courses was a raspberry jelly which unfortunately hadn't set properly and Jess, who had been charged with looking after it, had nursed the thing all the way from home and we were all terrified that it would spill out of its mould; it never did set and when we got down to eating it, somewhere between Plymouth and Exeter, it was a nasty sweet cordial that had to be drunk like soup. The only other impressions I have of that journey were the beauty of Brunel's Tamar Bridge, linking Cornwall with England, and the bitter disappointment at the approaches to London, which in no way seemed like the Utopia I had imagined.

We were staying with one of my many great-aunts; this one had been the daughter of a former Court physician at Sandringham, and in her youth had been known as the 'pocket Venus' who slapped the face of King Edward VII when he made a pass at her in a corridor. Now widowed (her husband had been an admiral), she occupied a spacious three-storey flat at the top of 14 Earl's Court Square. The flat was charming but the neighbourhood seemed the very essence of dreary middle-class respectability. On the day after our arrival we went by Tube, a great thrill, to Knightsbridge; walking back along Brompton Road I saw a building I took to be St Paul's. When told it was Harrods, my spirits rose, because I knew it was a shop where possibly I would be bought the Hornby train set (I was very much into trains in those days) I had been promised for my birthday. But before this transaction could take place, we had to spend ages in a boring little room where a rather abrupt lady kept telephoning and then referring back to my mother quoting a lot of meaningless numbers. The mystery of this room, actually Ashton & Mitchell's theatre ticket office, was solved a few days later when I was told that we were going to the theatre; no reaction from me, since it meant nothing at all.

We had luncheon at the Carlton Hotel in the Haymarket, and I caused certain consternation by invading the ladies' loo, since I was then unaware that in public places the sexes were segregated for these primary functions. That problem settled, we went to another building next door where a lot of people were struggling to get in. After we had pushed through the mob and were halfway up a staircase, I noticed a photograph on the wall. 'Who's that?' I asked, and was told that the man with the tremendously long fingernails was Oscar Asche as Chu-chin-chow. When we moved further into the building, we were shown to seats perched on the edge of a kind of shelf and it all seemed to be a rather more comfortable form of church; it was in fact the front row of the dress circle of His Majesty's Theatre. A curtain went up and in a flash I was transported to the fantastic world of Arabian nights – streets filled with exotic people, donkeys, camels and a potter (you could buy the pots and I treasured one for years), palm-fringed deserts, caves glittering with jewels, palace courtyards where oriental ladies danced. Some of the Norton music I knew since I had been taught the song about the man who cobbled all day and cobbled all night in our pre-bedtime singsongs at home. I suppose that *Chu-chin-chow*, which throughout the 14/18 war had been the mecca of troops on leave, was the ideal way of introducing a child to the theatre.

Anyway, from that afternoon on I was hooked on the theatre, which I imagined to be some sort of time machine which transported one, like on a magic carpet, to all kinds of wonderful places.

It was the following year, 1921, that I went to the theatre for the second time. We were in London on a Christmas shopping expedition and suddenly we were in Leicester Square, on one side of which was an oriental palace with onion domes of glistening gold. I was informed that it was the Alhambra Theatre and that a few nights later we were going

Marie Laurencin David Blair and
Georgina Parkinson in *Les Biches*
Music by Francis Poulenc
Choreography by Bronislava Nijinska
The Royal Ballet, 1964
Photograph by Houston Rogers
The Theatre Museum, V&A

there to see a ballet. 'What's a ballet?' I demanded. The explanation didn't make it sound exciting: no speaking or singing, music and dancing which I imagined to be a series of waltzes, fox-trots and tangos similar to what I was then laboriously learning from a dancing teacher at home. Far more exciting for me was that for the first time I was to be allowed to stay up as late as the grown-ups. In those days, Leicester Square at night was magical, with the old Empire Theatre, Daly's and, crowning it all, the Alhambra, whose Moorish interior made the perfect setting for a fairy-tale, *The Sleeping Princess*, which was in fact to change my life.

For a start, Tchaikovsky's score sets up the feeling that something wonderful is about to happen. From the moment the curtain rose on Bakst's setting for King Florestan's palace, with guards ranged on a staircase that appeared to rise up to infinity, I found myself in a world where it was possible to believe that fairies and magic were a natural part of daily life. By the time I saw *The Sleeping Princess* all the effects, which had caused havoc on the opening performances, were working properly; at the command of the Lilac Fairy (Lydia Lopokova, with whom I promptly fell in love) shrubbery grew and grew, totally obliterating the palace where Aurora slept, but just leaving a small arch which enframed the Lilac Fairy as she bourréed around continually, weaving her spell as the curtain fell on Act I.

Although I naturally knew nothing about ballet technique, or if anyone was dancing badly or well, I think I instinctively knew when I was faced by greatness, and there was no doubt whatsoever about this quality in Olga Spessivtzeva's Princess Aurora, which had a precision, delicacy and beauty of line that I have seldom seen since. Partnered by Vladimirov as her Prince, Spessivtzeva will always remain with me as the true meaning of *prima ballerina assoluta*. I often wonder how she compared with the first Aurora, Carlotta Brianza, who was terrifyingly evil as Carabosse in that production. It was pretty heady stuff for a young boy, all those great dancers, the sumptuousness of Bakst's designs combined with

Tchaikovsky's music, which I still think is one of the greatest ballet scores. Faced with such richness, it came as rather an anticlimax when I first saw Pavlova in divertissements at the Queen's Hall, about which I can remember very little apart from *The Dying Swan*, which was so moving that, even if boys weren't allowed to cry, I did. But I missed all those things that I had come to think of as theatre, though at later performances by Pavlova's company I changed my mind.

Shortly after *The Sleeping Princess* I began to see a lot of theatre in London. As well as the 'pocket Venus' great-aunt who was responsible for taking me to ballets, operas, concerts and art galleries, I had some cousins who lived in hotel suites – the Great Central, the Langham, the Kensington Palace; it was they who took me to plays, revues and musical comedies so that another side of theatre was opened up. When I went as a boarder to my prep school, on the Hog's Back near Guildford, I had to pass through London on my way to Cornwall for holidays, so I would stay with one or other relation for several days on the way and managed to see almost everything that was considered suitable, and a good deal that was not. While I was at the prep school I had a great friend who was the son of the singer Frederick Ranalow, the famous MacHeath in Nigel Playfair's production of *The Beggar's Opera*, and whereas most other boys talked about the cricketing feats of Hobbs, Sutcliffe and the body-line bowling of Larwood, Patrick Ranalow and I would discuss theatre endlessly. Through this friendship I got to see nearly all those famous productions at the Lyric, Hammersmith, including a revue, *Riverside Nights*, in which there was a ballet, *A Tragedy of Fashion*, by a Frederick Ashton who also danced in it with a chic little lady, Marie Rambert; it was designed by Sophie Fedorovitch (those Russians get everywhere, I thought). I remember it as charming and witty, but not perhaps on the level of what I had by then become accustomed to in ballets and Cochran revues.

The third theatre I went to was the London Coliseum, and it was here that I consider that I received most of my education. On that vast revolving stage appeared most of the great names in the performing arts – artists such as Mark Hambourg, Clara Butt, Grock, Harry Lauder, Harry Tate, Ruth Draper (her first appearances in England), Yvonne Arnaud, Gerald du Maurier, performing seals, bicycling monkeys, horse racing, table tennis, almost everything you could think of – all appeared in what would seem inappropriate juxtaposition, but it worked. The Coliseum was, and is, a wonderful theatre; in those days stalls seats cost about five shillings and there was an enormous amount of leg room, with a shelf to put one's feet up on, another for your tea cup or drink. Occasionally there was a system by which the curtain wasn't brought down between acts, but psychedelic lighting was played on the darkened stage as the next act came in on the revolve. The

Natalia Gontcharova *Les Noces*
Music by Igor Stravinsky
Choreography by Bronislava Nijinska
The Royal Ballet, 1966
Photograph by Houston Rogers
The Theatre Museum, V&A

Pablo Picasso *The Three-cornered Hat*
Music by Manuel de Falla
Choreography by Léonide Massine
London Festival Ballet (revival), 1973
English National Ballet

effect was magical and presupposed something we all thought was an invention of more recent years.

In 1924 it was announced that the Diaghilev Ballet would return to the Coliseum. I didn't think this was anything to do with *The Sleeping Princess*, since the name Diaghilev didn't mean anything to me then. Anyway, this 'Diaghilev' company seemed, as I looked at pictures in the *Illustrated Sporting & Dramatic*, to bear no relation to what I thought of as ballet – people in bathing dresses and tennis clothes in a very angular beach set. However, I was taken several times to that season, and on the first occasion it was *La Boutique Fantasque* with Nemchinova and Massine as the Can-Can dancers. It was a bit of a shock to find that ballet was not all fairy-tale, but within a few minutes of Derain's drop curtain, with its naïve painting of huge dolls, rising, I instantly took to this other side of ballet. I loved the Rossini/Respighi music, the clear colours of Derain's designs and the fact that the human characters in the shop were people I could relate to. Then the ballet about the bathing and tennis people, *Le Train Bleu*, didn't appear so extraordinary after all, since it seemed very like the second act of the musical comedies that I then had become addicted to. I was thrilled by a very acrobatic gentleman, Anton Dolin, who as Patrikeeff had appeared in *The Sleeping Princess*, listed as one of the 'Dignitaries of the Court'. Massine again, in *The Three-cornered Hat*, and with that started my deep love of Spanish dancing which has remained with me to this day. I was also thrilled with Picasso's Cubist décor. The only other ballet I saw during that 1924 winter season at the Coliseum was *Aurora's Wedding*, which saddened me as it seemed a travesty of my adored *Sleeping Princess*, but I think also that the modern ballets so excited me that the classics seemed boring and more than a decade was to pass before I again became interested in them.

Away from the ballet, dancing in the theatre was not particularly stimulating. In the variety theatres there were always pairs who did speciality acts, very graceful and virtually a theatrical form of ballroom dances, sometimes rather acrobatic. The hero and heroine of most musical comedies, people like Jack Buchanan and June, inevitably had one of these numbers, which reached a new level with Fred and Adele Astaire, whom I first saw in Gershwin's *Lady Be Good*, the last show at the old Empire before it was pulled down to make way for a new super-cinema. Fred was then part of a duo although he had a solo number, 'The Half of it Dearie Blues', in which he had a tap routine which must have been the first step in his progress to becoming one of the great dancers of the present century. About this same time Cochran brought the first all-black revue, *Blackbirds*, to the London Pavilion, and this not only introduced tap dancing in a big way but the music was to influence many young composers, Constant Lambert amongst others. But in all of Cochran's Pavilion revues, most of which I saw – from *On with the Dance*, when Massine created *The Rake* (to Roger Quilter music) and several other numbers in which he danced himself – there were always ballets and dance numbers of a quality and taste far above anything else in the lighter theatre, even today. The first example of immaculately drilled chorus dancing came with the Totem chorus in *Rose Marie* at Drury Lane. After that the previous somewhat languid chorus cavortings took on the precision and discipline of the Tiller Girls, a then very popular music-hall act. It was, though, in *Hassan*, yet another oriental spectacle at His Majesty's, that ballet first became properly integrated in theatre production. James Elroy Flecker's poetic drama was vastly superior to anything of its kind seen before, something that was underlined by Delius's score and Fokine's choreography.

It was also at His Majesty's that I next saw the Diaghilev Ballet, in a proper season rather than as part of variety. By this time I had moved on to my public school, Harrow, from where London was easily accessible; when ballet seasons didn't coincide with holidays I always invented excuses to get up to London for an afternoon or even a night. Since I had grown too fast, I had certain weaknesses in my limbs and joints, and therefore needed constant treatment, I said; it was accepted and mercifully this ruse was never discovered, otherwise I should have been expelled. It was in the 1926 season that I first saw Nijinska's *Les Noces,* which, though starker than anything I had seen before, completely fascinated me; I felt it to be a masterpiece and I still feel that way. The pianos in those days were on each side of the stage and were played by Auric, Dukelsky (Vernon Duke), Poulenc and Rieti, which was quite a line-up. In the same season I saw *Pulcinella* and was more fascinated by Picasso's set than by the ballet itself, although later I came to understand it better and still feel it to be one of Massine's more revivable ballets. Apart from *Les Noces,* what I remember most clearly was *The House Party* (as *Les Biches* was then called in England); it seemed to me to be the essence of chic sophistication, and Marie Laurencin's pastel set and dresses epitomised the haute couture, interior decoration and behaviour of the time. It was also in this ballet that I first became conscious of Serge Lifar, whose presence on stage was dynamic.

Lifar was the dominant personality in the 1928 season at His Majesty's, especially in Balanchine's *Apollo*, a work that, with Stravinsky's lyrical score and the quiet simplicity of the choreographic patterns, created a sense of divine mystery. This particular work stood out in a season that in every way was quite remarkable: it could be said to have epitomised everything that the Diaghilev Ballet stood for in bringing a form to ballet that involved all the other arts on an equal level. The works I saw reflected all the contemporary attitudes towards theatre production, choreography, music and painting. I was stunned by the fact that dance could represent the machine age, as in Massine's *Le Pas d'Acier* with Yakoulov's constructivist set of lathes and work benches. Constructivism again with Gabo and Pevsner's talc and American cloth vision of an Aesop fable with Lifar, borne on in triumph as the young man in love with a cat; in this work, *La Chatte*, Balanchine used a very different choreographic form from his *Apollo*. Different again in his *Triumph of Neptune*, with its English pantomime characters in a Pollocks's penny-plain-

tuppence-coloured toy theatre setting. Puzzling and beautiful was Massine's *Ode* with Tchelitchev's blue gauzes and mysterious lighting, a perspective of dolls dressed in imitation of live dancers; I didn't then realise that this was actually the first expression of multi-media in ballet.

It was in this season that I first saw *The Firebird*, with Felia Dubrovska in the title role and Massine as Ivan Tsarevich. She was wonderful, tall and strangely unearthly, but in spite of Stravinsky's shimmering magical score, it seemed to me, then deeply caught up in the excitement of the more modern works, that *The Firebird* was exotic but rather old-fashioned. Nor did *Les Sylphides* or a one-act version of *Swan Lake* interest me particularly. But after that season, which had a more varied repertory than probably any Diaghilev season since the war, I remember thinking that the world of ballet was the most wonderful thing that had ever happened and I only wished I could be a part of it. I realised that I had been supremely lucky to have had the opportunity to see and hear nearly everything of importance in the theatre during the 1920s, and a great deal that wasn't important but had been highly enjoyable. Those years, since *The Sleeping Princess* of 1921, had provided me with standards of assessment that were unique, although I was unaware of this at the time.

I missed Diaghilev's 1929 Covent Garden season, because by that time I was spending part of the summer in the south of France. My father, believing that cricket was better for the good of my soul than swimming and sunning in Monte Carlo or fishing off Cap Ferrat, insisted that I return to Cornwall in the middle of August. I can remember a very hot day at the end of that month when I came in sweaty and tired after an exhausting afternoon on the cricket pitch. I walked into the drawing-room to find my mother and Jess looking very serious; they had just heard the news on the wireless that Diaghilev had died in Venice. I said nothing, left and went up to my bedroom; then, possibly for the first time since Pavlova's *Dying Swan*, I cried. That, I thought, is the end of everything; it was in fact only the beginning.

Peter Williams, Designer, Talks to Peter Williams, Editor

Dance and Dancers, Vol.14, No.4, April 1963, pp.26–7 and Vol.14, No.5, May 1963, pp.29–31.

Alexandre Benois *Petrushka*
Music by Igor Stravinsky
Choreography by Michel Fokine
A photograph of the original 1911 production
The Theatre Museum, V&A

Peter Williams: So, you can draw, you can paint, you can cut materials and sew them, you know just everything about lighting. You also know everything about human clothing and about architecture, and therefore think you could pass all those idiotic tests which provide the key for entry into that union in America and join the privileged few who are allowed to decorate theatre pieces there. So, you are very clever and my admiration for you is boundless. Even so you possibly still wonder why ballet managements are not falling over each other in the scramble to avail themselves of your doubtless invaluable services.

Peter Williams: *I just cannot understand it. I was the prize pupil at every art school and they all said that a rosy future was assured, and here I am in the future and it's just not rosy at all – it's dim grey becoming black.*

PW: Why did you want to become a stage designer in the first place?

PW: *Since I was a child I have loved the theatre, and I have always scribbled a bit and messed around with paints and model theatres, and all that. It seemed the obvious course that I should eventually make this all into a career.*

PW: What you really mean to say is that you thought it would all be great fun and that you were being damned clever to mix the thing you liked to do with a job that would bring in a nice lot of money. Well the one thing you are learning in this grey/black future you now live in is that designing in the theatre is not fun – that's to say if you ever get to designing in the theatre at all. You see, you are just like a thousand other students who have worked hard, listened to lectures on the theory of colour, lighting, costume development and all that. But did anybody ever talk to you about inspiration?

PW: *Of course they did – they were very inspiring teachers ...*

PW: No, I don't mean that kind of inspiration, because any teacher who draws a pay packet should be inspiring, otherwise they are taking money under false pretences. What I mean is did anybody ever try to help you find the possible sources of inspiration? I'm sure they didn't because they were so busy with the history of costume and lighting theories. Nobody told you that the biggest headache in the professional theatre is the post-student who comes in airing views about the theory of light and historical accuracy of costume. But more of this later.

PW: *You are being very unjust. How do you think that anybody can do anything without a sound academic foundation, and that is what these schools give you?*

PW: I never said anything about not having an academic foundation and I never shall, because it is vital. What I am saying is that the person with only an academic foundation is not in any way prepared to go straight into the theatre – or even to approach it as a fully fledged designer.

PW: *What should we do?*

PW: First of all you should go and work in the theatre in any capacity possible – scene-shifter, scene painter, in the wardrobe, as an extra or in any way that anybody will have you. Get to know the feel of the theatre, the smell of it, the changing moods of it, its triumphs and tribulations and its blood, sweat and toil. As you are doing this you can also get to grips with yourself as a designer and it has to come from you because from this time on no other person can teach you.

PW: *But how can I get to grips with myself as a designer if I am not designing anything myself?*

PW: First and foremost you can study the work of all those who have made a success of designing. Study, don't copy, and reason why. As it is ballet that interests you, then read and look at the designs of this century's great ballet designers – Bakst, Gontcharova, Bérard, Clavé ...

PW: *But most of those are old. I'm sick of people like you carrying on about them. You really are a bore.*

PW: By that remark alone you have instantly proved to me your future is not rosy. In the first place I emphasised that you should not copy but study them. You remind me of a young and, as he thought, budding young designer who once came to me and said that he did not approve of Benois's designs for *Petrushka*, and that he intended to re-do them in the right way. The language I spat at him could not be printed even in a Frank Norman book. Needless to say he never budded as a designer, though I hear he is not unsuccessful in some other branch of the dance.

This all points to the fact that designing for ballet is something very different to any other form of designing in the theatre. Diaghilev was first responsible for this integration of the painter with ballet's other elements – before that time designing was any old how. I don't mean by this that ballet did not use fine designers and painters, but they were not an integral part of the whole; they were more like decorators. Diaghilev put them on an equal footing with the rest, and what they did was inextricably woven into the whole. To go back to *Petrushka*, of course the impact of this work was produced by the stars – Karsavina, Nijinsky and Bolm – and also by the then revolutionary score of Stravinsky, but a major part of that success was due to Benois, and even to this day I cannot see how what he did could possibly be altered. To alter it would be a crime something akin to painting out the background of *La Gioconda* so as to throw the actual figure more into relief.

PW: *But surely Benois was rather an exception as a designer because he was more involved in the actual creation of certain ballets than most designers have been since?*

PW: Yes, you are perfectly right, and that goes for Bakst also. The point I want to make is that the status of the ballet designer is different from, say, the designer of plays or operas, because the nature of ballet is such that it is possible for the painter to present his work on the level of a canvas hanging in a gallery, or the level of a composer's work in the concert hall. The only difference is that the

James Bailey Alicia Markova in *Giselle*
Music by Adolphe Adam
Choreography by Jean Coralli and Jules
Perrot
Sadler's Wells Ballet, 1946
Photograph by Gordon Anthony
The Theatre Museum, V&A

main subjects of his canvas are moving. As things stand at the moment in the theatre, drama and opera can continually be re-designed and no great harm is done to the work (sometimes, of course, it can ruin them, and sometimes it can enhance them), but a ballet, if it is a work of importance, and if the commissioning of the design has been done with innate taste and a sense of fitness, cannot but lose if this particular limb is altered or severed.

PW: *Yes, I see all that, but aren't you jumping ahead rather?*

PW: Sorry, I am, and it is an unfortunate habit I have developed from editing a magazine, because always one lives several months ahead of time. Let us go back to what I was originally saying about inspiration. It's fine to study costume books and all that, but what is equally important is to develop a style and an approach. Take Bakst, for instance. He designed ballets in all kinds of styles and in all kinds of periods and localities – Oriental harems, nineteenth-century Romantic moonlight, Greek high noon, eighteenth-century splendour. All these he designed and so much more, but there was never any mistaking that it was Bakst who painted them. So first of all you want to develop a sense of form, and this you can acquire by studying the masters who have gone before you. When you think that you have found the master who strikes the chord that falls into any phrase you may have of your own, then study him. Study him and apply his principles to the style and form as you see them in the light of our times. But it must be personal, it must be something which springs up within you and never, never, never a meagre, shallow reflection of somebody else. Better by far to be bad and original than to be a copyist.

PW: *It's very difficult. How can I develop a personal style?*

PW: That is where your art master should come in. Far more important than harping on Hottenroth and Larousse would be if he could spot the pea of genius that may be latent within you and then bring it out; even during those tedious still life or nature studies you should be doing he might be able to discover it.

Listen a moment to Gordon Craig, and a greater inspirer the theatre never knew. He says: 'Keep continually designing such imaginative costumes. For example, make a barbaric costume; and a barbaric costume for a sly man which has nothing about it which can be said to be historical and yet is both sly and barbaric. Now make another design for another barbaric costume, for a man who is bold and tender. Now make a third for one who is ugly and vindictive. It will be an exercise. You will probably make blunders at first, for it is no easy thing to do, but I promise you if you persevere long enough you will be able to do it. Then go further: attempt to design the clothing for a divine figure and for a demonic figure: these, of course, will be studies in individual costumes, but the main strength of this branch of the work lies in the costumes as a mass. It is the mistake of all theatrical producers that they consider the costumes of the mass individually.

PW: *I see all that, but surely Gordon Craig was not talking of ballet? He was considering the straight theatre.*

PW: He was, but just read very carefully what he says again and I think you will find part of the solution for designing *The Sleeping Beauty*. Craig's book was first published in 1911, and the various chapters date back as far as 1905, for they had appeared in his immortal magazine *The Mask*. I don't know whether Bakst ever read what Craig wrote, but it is very likely, as he was deeply respected in Russia; anyhow, most of this he followed out in his ballet designing, and particularly for his 1921 *The Sleeping Princess*. Anyway, it is something for you to get on with also, and if your master has any ability at all he may be able to develop you from the findings.

If you feel stuck and dreary then get out and about. Learn to use your eyes. Learn to look at everything in the light of the theatre, for the theatre is life, an infinitesimal fragment of it suddenly caught in the beam of a reflecting glass. Look at the houses in a square, look at the sunlight on a wall, look at the formation of a petal or the veining of a leaf, look at summer haze or the cold clear light of winter or the dazzling splendour of autumn. Look at all these things and you will find inspiration all right providing you know how to look. In any event there is plenty for you to get on with until we meet again, but remember that the very basic principle of ballet design can be taught if you are receptive. The application of these principles and the assembly of the finished designer lies absolutely and irrevocably with you.

* * *

PW: Ballet, as I said when we last talked, needs a very different approach to the designing for straight theatre or opera. The principal thing to remember is that it is concerned with movement – violent movement, often with a number of people moving at the same time. Although this is one of the first considerations when you are thinking of both the scenery and the costumes, you should never think of either as separate but as an integral part of the whole conception of design.

PW: *But surely they are separate and need to be understood in entirely different ways?*

PW: They are separate only in certain cases where the settings should be realised with the eye of an architect while the anatomy of costume should be understood with all the know-how of a couturier. But these are rather special cases and we shall talk about them later when we go more deeply into scenery and costume designing. For the moment you must think of them as a whole.

Assuming that you have been commissioned to design a ballet, what do you think should be your first consideration?

PW: *Well I suppose you start scribbling a few rough ideas, work out a few colour schemes and so on?*

PW: Yes, but before that you should sit down and think hard, think very hard, about the shape of the work as is suggested to you by the subject matter and the music, or if there is no subject matter then by the music alone. Before you put pencil or brush to paper, get hold of the score and play it again and again, absorb it until your body and brain reacts to it in the way that you feel is right.

PW: *But there are difficulties, because although a lot of music is on records, a great deal is still only in manuscript.*

PW: That I agree, but on the other hand most choreographers have newly commissioned scores taped, and it should be possible to get

hold of a tape or the manuscript and try to read the piano score or get a pianist to play it for you. I cannot emphasise enough how vitally important it is for anyone designing ballet to know the score well. After that the shape of the ballet and the way of designing it becomes clear.

PW: *What exactly do you mean by the shape of a ballet; surely it can only be the shape dictated by the dimensions of the proscenium arch?*

PW: No, I don't mean that shape at all – ballets have to be designed to fit almost any proscenium arch, because ballet is in the main a nomadic art. It travels about a great deal and has to be seen in theatres and on stages of all shapes and sizes. No, I mean the shape that music conveys. For instance, most music up to the beginning of this century is mainly rounded, but by this I do not mean that you should design sets and costumes in a series of circles. What I do mean is that there should be a certain regularity in your ideas, a blending, a lack of violent discord and no violent angles. Much of the music of this century, after the advent of Stravinsky that is, tends to be more discordant, more spiky, and as a result this allows you to be more spiky also, or more horizontal or vertical.

A rather obvious example of what I mean is to be found in the ballet *Giselle*, which to my way of thinking has an inevitably rounded score. This should be reflected in the design, and was, when it was designed by Alexandre Benois for Diaghilev, Hugh Stevenson for Ballet Rambert and James Bailey for the Royal Ballet. Not long ago, however, the Paris Opéra commissioned a new décor for *Giselle*, and they asked Carzou to do it. Presumably the reason for this commission was because Carzou, a very fine designer indeed, had had an enormous success with his forest scene in Roland Petit's *Le Loup*. And so carried away did somebody seem to be by the arboreal connections in both works that he assumed, wrongly as it turned out, that Carzou would be the obvious choice for the new production. What apparently was never considered was that Adam's score for *Giselle* is essentially flowing and rounded while Dutilleux's score for *Le Loup* definitely is not. Carzou's trademark is that he designs a great deal in vertical lines, and this approach was quite at variance

Natalia Gontcharova *The Firebird*
Music by Igor Stravinsky
Choreography by Michel Fokine
Sadler's Wells Ballet, 1954
Photograph by Houston Rogers
The Theatre Museum, V&A

Diaghilev's original production in 1910 was designed
by Serge Golovine (set and costumes) and Léon Bakst
(costumes) but the best-known production is the
second version (1926) by Gontcharova. The Sadler's
Wells Ballet revived the work in 1954 to commemorate
the 25th anniversary of Diaghilev's death.

with *Giselle*. The result was a series of beautiful designs which had very little to do with the old Romantic ballet.

PW: *But do you really mean to say that you don't believe that anyone other than the pastiche painter should attempt these ballets of another age?*

PW: Not at all. I believe that modern painters can bring a new zest to the old classics provided they have the intelligence to understand the score and also provided that whoever commissions them knows just what he is doing. I often used to think that Tchelitchev, for instance, would have been the ideal designer for *The Sleeping Beauty* as he would have given it a new dimension of magic, and it is a ballet which needs magic. One of the most striking examples of a modern painter being used successfully in a work with a classical score was when Blum commissioned André Derain to design Fokine's *L'Epreuve d'Amour*. His 'Chinoiserie' landscape was painted in a manner completely of our time, yet it exquisitely underlined the Mozart score and the witty eighteenth-century 'Chinoiserie' narrative.

PW: *So far you have only talked about works which have a decided storyline, but how do you feel about the designing of those which are plotless?*

PW: It is in these works that your feeling for the music is most noticeable, and frankly they are the most difficult to design. The Sophie Fedorovitch décor for Ashton's *Symphonic Variations* is a good example of the way in which a plotless ballet should be designed. The 'space' feeling in César Franck's score was admirably reflected in the open and empty lime-green setting and the flow of music was underlined by thin calligraphic lines. It was a visual interpretation of the music.

PW: *Do you think that the person who designs for ballet should be a painter rather than a decorative designer?*

PW: There are really no hard and fast rules in the theatre, because shock and surprise is one of its essential elements, and ballets can be, and have been, successfully designed by all kinds of professional people who were not necessarily painters. But I do believe

emphatically that all ballet designing should be done with a painter's eye, and I think that all designing in the theatre must be done with at least the basic knowledge of the painter's art. Painting is, after all, the greatest of the graphic arts, and only a painter can stand shoulder to shoulder with the work of a great choreographer or a great composer. A painter understands tone values, textures, composition, balance of colour and all those things that are usually rather outside the province of the decorator. A painter reacts to his subject in the way that a composer reacts to music.

PW: *Do you therefore think it is more important for the would-be designer to learn how to be an easel painter rather than to learn all about costumes, lighting theories and architecture?*

PW: It's not more important, but it's as important. After all, most questions connected with the history of costume and architecture can be mugged-up any time when needed, but the art of the painter takes years and years to master – sometimes a whole lifetime. So learn to paint and learn its theory, and then this can be applied to

Jean Rosenthal Anthony Dowell and Antoinette Sibley in *Afternoon of a Faun*
Music by Claude Debussy
Choreography by Jerome Robbins
Photograph by Leslie E. Spatt
Originally created for the New York City Ballet in 1953, and first performed by the Royal Ballet in 1971. Jean Rosenthal also lit this production.

your designing in the theatre. How to create the visual image of a ballet is important – the rest can be filled in later.

PW: *To get back to the idea of music determining the shape of a ballet, do you think that there is any truth in the theories held by some people that certain music symbolises certain colours?*

PW: Colour is something very complex. I do believe there to be a truth in these theories, but I also feel they cannot necessarily be applied to ballet designing, because colour is so often dictated by immediate taste in fashion and trend.

PW: *How can you say that? Surely colours remain the same regardless of changing trends?*

PW: Of course colours remain the same – blue is always blue, green is always green, and so on. What changes is public reaction to colour, and unfortunately a basic untruth about designing for ballet is that the designer can afford to completely ignore colour trends. For instance, in the late 1920s Oliver Messel discovered white, and what he did for the operetta *Helen* sparked-off vast acres of colourless canvas from all kinds of designers who jumped on the 'white' bandwagon. But woe betide anyone today who uses white in this manner, unless the subject really calls for it, as it did in, say, Jean Rosenthal's setting for Robbins's *Afternoon of a Faun*, which was a wonder. But although the general use of white is not so acceptable today, white is still white. If you pay much heed to symbolism then white stands for purity, but I doubt if anyone today would be much impressed by this obvious use of symbolic colour – it has to be far more subtle than that. Where your symbolism comes in is in the relationship of one colour to another, and this is where you have to be very sure what your choreographer's intentions are.

PW: *After studying the score and determining the shape, would you also think it a good idea to postpone designing until it is possible to see the choreography in rehearsal?*

PW: This is, of course, the ideal way of going about it, but it is not always easy, as sets have to be built and costumes made long before the choreographer has finished his creating. Sometimes this is not finished until the actual day of the first performance or, as in one well-known instance, until the audience was actually coming into the theatre. But you must work closely with the choreographer all the time and you should not be getting any preconceived ideas of what you want to do until you have thoroughly absorbed his ideas. Although the shape of your designing must be determined by the music, a choreographer may possibly want to put an entirely contrapuntal idea on to that music, as happened, for instance, in the case of the Petit/Cocteau *Le Jeune Homme et la Mort*. In this work, a harsh and modern Romantic idea was used against the rounded and swelling flow of Bach's C Minor Passacaglia. This strange juxtaposition of a violent idea with a classical score is a dangerous practice, and can only be anything other than disaster when all persons concerned are geniuses in their own way, which in this particular case they were. The idea came from Jean Cocteau, who inspired both the choreographer, Petit, and the designer, Wakhevitch.

Back to more usual practice, and the first thing to get from the choreographer is the story, so that you know exactly where the dramatic moments are and who will be dancing with whom.

PW: *Surely that is the obvious thing to find out?*

PW: You would think so, but it would astound you to know that quite often famous designers overlook this until they suddenly see everyone together at the first dress rehearsal – then they often get a nasty shock. So try to get a rough ground plan from the choreographer so that you know where every dancer is in relation to other dancers – this is vital to you when you start planning the colour.

PW: *I know the score and I have a pretty clear idea of the choreographer's intentions; am I now in a position to start?*

PW: Yes, at last you are. You can start working on roughs like crazy. Don't be too detailed to begin with, just let your brush or pencil move about. Let ideas flow freely. Go out and get inspiration in all kinds of places, no matter how unlikely they might appear to be. After having done hundreds of rough ideas and thrown most of them into the waste-paper basket, you may suddenly find one that satisfies you.

Sophie Fedorovitch
Symphonic Variations
Music by César Franck
Choreography by
Frederick Ashton
Sadler's Wells Ballet, 1946
Photograph of Royal Ballet
revival by Leslie E. Spatt

Make a larger rough drawing of the set and cut out and paint some paper shapes, painting them in the colours you think may be what you want for your costumes. Place these bits of paper on your rough set design and move them around according to what the choreographer has told you. It is at this point that you will start to make a lot of changes – altering colours, heightening or lowering tones and possibly scrapping the whole idea and starting again.

It may seem a rather elementary way of going about things, but it is the best way when designing ballet, for remember that ballet is inevitably violent movement. In designing for plays or operas it is possible to plan a number of pictorial effects because of their more static nature. In ballet you may plan something very splendid and in a second it will be broken up with dancers all over the stage in different places, causing the whole balance of colour to go completely haywire. That is why, at this early stage, you must move your colour ideas around so that at all times your plan is true to the ballet, to the choreography and to yourself.

Remember that you are one third of a triumvirate and an integral part of a whole. You are there to play your part in the complex art of ballet – you are not there to dominate it. So forget all those startling and doubtless highly original ideas which will stun the audience and completely obscure the dancers and what they are dancing. But more of this when we talk again about costumes and settings separately. At the moment you have only crystallised your rough ideas and you know which way you are going.

Draped Life | Peter Farley

In a large light airy room, high above Southampton Row, a group of young men and women are, from time to time, peering with intense concentration at one of their fellows. The subject of their fascination is a medieval nobleman elegantly attired in a simple, perfectly cut, tight-fitting cote-hardie.[1] It is the year 1931, and the observers are students at the Central School of Arts and Crafts engaged in a life-drawing class under the watchful eyes of their drawing tutor, Mr Farleigh, and their costume tutor, Miss Cochrane.

The clothes worn by the model had been designed and made the previous year by a student named Tanya Moiseiwitsch,[2] and were part of a stock of historical costumes for the stage created by former students of Miss Cochrane's costume course. This drawing session was a specialised class aimed at students engaged in the study of all forms of clothing design including historical costumes, dress design, and according to the prospectus, 'treatment of material for stage purposes and fashion drawing', and was modestly entitled 'Draped Life'. As Tanya Moiseiwitsch recalls, 'the drapery wasn't really just hanging in folds, it consisted of costumes that previous students had made and the models climbed into those and stood for hours it seemed.'[3]

The medieval costume with its simplicity of line would have appealed to Jeannetta Cochrane's sense of clarity of design. She admired the designs of Charles Ricketts[4] for their simplicity, and believed that historical accuracy could be achieved without becoming over-decorative. Peter Williams, also her student in the early 1930s, shared her admiration of Ricketts, and felt that her ideas about design were a natural reaction to the flamboyance of decoration in the early years of the century – 'the hangover really, after a kind of Edwardian over-elaboration'.

The simplicity which Miss Cochrane advocated was very much in keeping with the philosophy of the school's first principal William R. Lethaby, who had founded the original school in 1896 and was responsible for the building of the new Southampton Row school in 1907. Lethaby, a friend and follower of William Morris, the Victorian artist-designer and father of the Arts and Crafts Movement, stated that 'as the building will be associated with a school of design, that it should be plain, reasonable and well built, with as little of common place so-called ornament as possible'.[6] Lethaby had also been very emphatic about the kind of instructors the school should employ: 'In the Technical Art classes the effort must be made by the Technical Education Board to get actual producers to teach in the schools' and that 'instruction is useless unless it is given by actual craftsmen producers who actually live by their work'.[7]

Jeannetta Cochrane was the embodiment of the ideal Central School of Arts and Crafts instructor. While head of the costume department, she continued her own professional practice as a costumier from Sheridan House, her premises in Bedford Square. She designed the costumes for many theatre productions, including plays at the London Pavilion for Anthony Ellis, for Ellen Terry, and for John Gielgud's productions of *Hamlet* at the Theatre Royal Haymarket (1944), and *The Relapse* at the Phoenix Theatre (1948). Her most memorable designs, again for Gielgud, were those for his long-running and highly successful revival of Congreve's *Love for Love* (1943), with settings by Rex Whistler,[8] also at the Phoenix Theatre.[9] She was later to work as head designer for the firms of Liberty and Heal.

Peter Williams described Jeannetta Cochrane as, 'a very dynamic lady with her white mane of hair, always looking as though a permanent gale was blowing it about'.[10] She was a specialist in period costume and had an eye for historical accuracy. Being one of the only scholarly specialists in the field, the subject being very poorly documented at the time, she shared the 'excitement of her researches' in a 'spontaneous and open-handed' way,[11] encouraging her students to focus on 'the silhouette, the mood and movement'[12] of the costume to create the feeling of the period.

During the 1930s, when Peter Williams and Tanya Moiseiwitsch were students, the school was under the guidance of its third Principal, P. H. Jowett, and was considered, 'until the Bauhaus, to be the most progressive art school in Europe'.[13] None of the staff were full-time teachers as it was considered important that time was allowed for them to pursue their own professions as designers and craftsmen. Miss Cochrane only gave one or two lectures a week on the subject of costume design. The students specialising in design for the theatre were employed for the rest of the week with drawing, research into historical dress, period pattern-cutting and making costumes – the subject of set design was not taught at the school until 1937. In Jeannetta Cochrane's absence the students were taught by Ruth Keating, who was later to introduce scenic design to the course, and Nora Waugh, Miss Cochrane's assistant, whose books about costume, illustrated by Margaret Woodward, were to become, and are still to this day, the bibles of period pattern cutting.[14]

In the second year of their three-year course, the students concentrated on one major project, that of designing and making a single period costume, complete with accessories, to be exhibited as a demonstration of the skills they had acquired while at the school. In order to decide the type and period of costume each student was to make, Miss Cochrane always started with the character and personality of the individual who was going to wear the finished garment. The students were required to choose someone from the school, normally one of their fellow students, decide which period of history their physiognomy suggested, and create a costume for that person.

Tanya Moiseiwitsch describes the atmosphere of the studio and the struggle of making her medieval costume as follows: 'I think I must have been crazy, I picked two of the teachers, Margaret Watts, and John Gower-Parks. Most people chose fellow students, and that would have been much cleverer – I wouldn't have had so many "nervous breakdowns". The first nervous breakdown I had, which made Miss Cochrane roar with laughter, was that I didn't know that you had to pre-shrink felt. I decided to do a *Richard II* outfit – because I was mad about John Gielgud – and I didn't pre-shrink it, but I did shrink it when I pressed it for the first fitting and I accused Mr Parks of having put on weight! He assured me that he hadn't! When Parks was first being fitted, it didn't fit, it didn't fit anywhere, it hung on him. Miss Keating went past and said rather sharply, "What's that meant to be?", and Mr Parks pursed his lips and said, "It's meant to be a tight-fitting cote-hardie".'[15] We found a slimmer person.

To understand the historical period and intended appearance of the completed costumes, the students spent one day a week researching at the Victoria and Albert Museum where they attended lectures on art and architecture by Bannister Fletcher, and lectures on costume by the distinguished costume historian James Laver. Great emphasis was placed on drawing, especially life-drawing which, through Lethaby, followed William Morris's dictum: 'Everybody ought to be taught to draw, just as much as everybody ought to be taught to read and write.'[16]

A crucial part of the itinerary was Miss Cochrane's lectures which offered 'a profound insight into the historical period under discussion',[17] not only to students specialising in theatre costume, but also to those from dress design, textiles and any others who needed to know about historical dress. However, the subject matter did tend towards the theatrical, her main interest, and was 'spiced with anecdotes about the celebrities she had known such as Sickert, Augustus John, H. G. Wells, Max Beerbohm, and Winston Churchill, as well as the great theatrical faces of more than half a century. Thus, for example, she would bring to life personalities of the times of Richard III by comparing them with such figures as Sir Seymour Hicks and Mrs Patrick Campbell!'[18]

Charles Ricketts Costume design for *Salome*
Play by Oscar Wilde. A replica of one of the lost
costumes designed for the Shockicku Company,
Japan, 1919.
Peter Farley

At the end of each lecture the students could ask questions. Tanya Moiseiwitsch would always put her hand up as she was very interested in the technical aspects of costume. She never received a direct answer because Miss Cochrane never thought it was worth explaining any technical process which could be looked-up in a book. She would say in her charming and witty way, 'Go down to the library and ask Mr Goldie (the Librarian) to find you such and such a book. It will all be in that book, you can read it and learn what it says, and if you still can't do it, I'll try and explain . . . but it really is most awfully boring.'[19]

Self-initiation, self-reliance, observation and resourcefulness were the corner stones of Jeannetta Cochrane's teaching. Lethaby would have approved; he once summed up his thoughts on art education with the words 'Educate, suggest and encourage',[20] believing that looking at the work and listening to the methods of one's mentors was all very well as an ideal but could be 'all bad as an imposed tyranny'.[21]

Once a year the public was invited to view the work of the novice costume designers at a showing which Miss Cochrane dubbed 'The Episodes'. To present this event (there was no stage or performance space at the time) one of the studios was cleared and the students were dressed in the costumes that had been designed and made by their colleagues. Tanya Moiseiwitsch was fitted in a medieval gown because, to her surprise, Miss Cochrane thought she looked medieval. She describes the scene: 'People came in from outside, we just walked on and swanked a lot – the teachers had a good old giggle. The characters didn't speak. There may have been soft music being played on a wind-up gramophone. . . then we put the costumes on stands for people to walk around and look at.'[22]

It was important to Jeannetta Cochrane that the students' costumes should be shown moving on the bodies for which they were designed. Just as she was aware that the design process did not begin with an imaginary character, neither did it end with a two-dimensional design on paper. She started and finished with a live body in motion, encouraging her students to create theatrical characters out of thorough research, artistic skills and

Jeannetta Cochrane
Costumes for
Love for Love
Play by William
Congreve
Produced by John
Gielgud, Phoenix
Theatre, 1943
Set designed by
Rex Whistler
Photograph by Cecil
Beaton
The Beaton Archive,
Sotheby's

Motley *The Haunted Ballroom*
Music by Geoffrey Toye
Choreography by Ninette de Valois
Sadler's Wells Ballet, Sadler's Wells, London, 1934
The Theatre Museum, V&A
In the 1930s as today, it was the custom for theatre design students to be given external placements. Tanya Moiseiwitsch, while still a student, worked with Motley and painted the sets for *The Haunted Ballroom.*

craftsmanship. In 'The Episodes' the costumes could be seen in motion but her dream was that the students should really see their creations in their proper context – that of a theatrical performance.

It had long been Miss Cochrane's theory that there should be a theatre attached to the school with design studios, costume-cutting rooms, a scenic workshop and all the equipment necessary for a completely practical theatre design course. As Peter Williams wrote, 'a place where her beloved students could work with professional artists'.[23] She had talked to Williams about the possibility when he was her student before World War Two. Many years later, in the mid-1950s, perhaps due to her inspirational vision and infectious enthusiasm, she finally managed to catch the imagination of the London County Council Education Committee and a team of young architects was provided to begin the process of turning her dream into a reality. Pegeret Anthony, formerly a student and later a tutor on the course for over forty years, remembers the long and detailed discussions between the architects and Miss Cochrane.[24] Always in tune with the latest developments in design, she collaborated with the architects envisioning a structure which would incorporate the most up-to-date building methods and a simplicity of line of which Lethaby would have approved.

The theatre was to be located next to the school on the corner of Southampton Row and Theobalds Road. The bulk of the theatre was to be separated from the main school building by a narrow alleyway but umbilically joined to its giant parent by a covered corridor connecting a suite of new theatre design studios above the theatre to the art school at first-floor level. The exterior was to be constructed of metal with glass and brick curtain walls in the modern style. The interior was also to be modern and functional with an auditorium which would seat about two hundred and fifty people and a small balcony with seating for approximately another twenty. The stage was to be located behind a proscenium arch and there would be dressing rooms and a scenic workshop incorporated within the building. The new theatre design studios were to be above the auditorium and access to the upper levels of the stage was possible through these rooms. At last Miss Cochrane's students would have direct access to a theatre of their own in which to experiment and experience the whole process of theatre design from conception through to a performance before a live audience.

Sadly, Jeannetta Cochrane never saw the completed theatre for which she had worked so long and hard. She died, quite suddenly, in the spring of 1957. She had been ill with cancer for some time, but in true Cochrane style had continued to work without telling anyone of her illness. In 1964, the theatre was eventually opened, and bears her name to this day. The significance of Miss Cochrane's teaching is evident in the work of her students, who included, besides Tanya Moiseiwitsch, Peter Williams and Pegeret Anthony, many other outstanding designers for the stage. Beginning, early in the century, with 'draped life' and two lectures a week on the history of costume, she witnessed the realisation of a fully equipped department of theatre design, complete with its own fully staffed professional theatre.

In the dark auditorium of The Cochrane Theatre, a group of young men and women are peering with intense concentration at the stage. They become aware of a glimmer of light, which, slowly growing in intensity, forms a soft pool on the stage floor. Into this pool steps a dancer. The year is 1996, the observers are third-year BA Honours Theatre Design degree students at Central Saint Martins College of Art and Design engaged in a lighting rehearsal of The Peter Williams Design for Dance Project under the watchful eyes of their tutors – the two Peters, Tim, Norman, David, Sue and Matthew.[25] Gone are the titles and surnames; the lighting board is computerised; one student has a ring in her nose – I do not think, for a moment, that Miss Cochrane would disapprove.

The Lethaby Galleries at Central Saint Martins
College of Art and Design during *The Designers:
Pushing the Boundaries – Advancing the Dance*
exhibition, November 1995

Ralph Koltai *Cul-de-Sac*
Music by Christopher Whelan
Choreography by Norman Morrice
Ballet Rambert, 1964
Photograph by Ralph Koltai

Norman Morrice and Marie Rambert
Photograph by Anthony Crickmay
The Theatre Museum, V&A

RAMBERT COMPANY IN CRISIS ✳ STOP ✳ PLEASE COME BACK AND DISCUSS ✳ STOP

These were the words with which Norman Morrice, long-time choreographer and dancer with Ballet Rambert, was summoned back from Israel in 1966. He had gone there to think – to think about leaving the Company – a company which, in his opinion, had lost its identity. Ballet Rambert had been started by Marie Rambert in 1926 as a company for choreographers. New works were being created most of the time. By 1966, it had become a touring company. It made long tours of the provinces presenting traditional classical ballets that the theatre managers insisted upon, such as pocket versions of *La Sylphide, Giselle, Swan Lake* Act II and eventually, its own versions of *Don Quixote* and *Coppélia*. The finances of Ballet Rambert had reached crisis point. It was expensive to tour with the size of company needed

for all the big ballets, and touring ninety per cent of the year left no time to make new work. In addition, The Arts Council of Great Britain had recently set up its first Opera and Ballet inquiry, headed by Lord Goodman and advised by Peter Williams, which had discovered that all the touring companies were presenting virtually the same classical repertoire. The whole operation had to be reorganised.

Norman Morrice came back from Israel and met with Madame Rambert and David Ellis, who at that time was Acting Director, and suggested that the company should return to its original philosophy of being 'an instrument for choreographers, not a company that is reliant for its success on what exists for its existence'.[1] Morrice also discussed the problem with his friend and colleague, the designer Ralph Koltai. Koltai had collaborated with Morrice on many works for Ballet Rambert and was now in charge of the Department of Theatre Design at the Central School of Art and Design. Pre-empting the Dance and Opera Report, Norman Morrice went to the Arts Council with Rambert's new plan. He remembers that the committee seemed rather shocked by the proposals and that Lord Goodman thought the company was 'asking rather a lot'. Morrice answered, 'Well, if you want a future?'[2] The plan was agreed.

The aspirations of the reformed Rambert Company were expounded, at the time, in an interview with Marie Rambert and Norman Morrice by Peter Williams in the magazine *Dance and Dancers*:

Peter Williams: *There is much talk about the 'new' Ballet Rambert and this makes it sound like some kind of phoenix. How 'new' in fact is the company we shall see in November ?*

Marie Rambert: It is not all that new, but it is new in comparison with the company of the past few years.

PW: *How did you arrive at the shape and size?*

MR: We decided on a smaller company, without corps, but with soloist standards and spending a lot of time producing new work, because for so long we have only been doing one new ballet a year, which is insufficient in a company like ours, where there are creative elements.

PW: *This is obviously of prime importance but what are you going to do about the past?*

MR: I don't think I have got to do anything about it – the past is past.

PW: *But you have in the past created in your company what amount to the classics of the British repertory and you are the only British company who can keep these works going. In all this onslaught of new works, surely you are not going to let all these works go by the board – all the early Ashtons, Tudors, Howards, Gores and so on?*

MR: God forbid! They are going to be the basis of the new programmes.

PW: *It seems as though you have a pretty big repertory for the first season.*

MR: Well, from the old repertory we are reviving three Tudors – *Dark Elegies*, *Jardin aux Lilas*, and *Judgement of Paris*, a MacMillan – *Laiderette*, and other things that we feel to be right. Of the new works, we have two from Pierre Lacotte and of course we have a work by the Dutch choreographer, Rudi van Dantzig, as well as a first work by John Chesworth.

PW: *Do you have a distinct policy towards the type of modern repertory you will have?*

Norman Morrice: I think we will have to judge from the individual choreographer.

PW: *It would seem a bit difficult when a company is still in a state of formation taking on styles as different as say, Van Dantzig and Lacotte, as well as the existing repertory.*

NM: No, I don't think it is difficult, because always with Ballet Rambert there are dancers capable of an astonishing variety of work. We are at the same time developing our classical technique and really being able to study it, and also taking classes in the Graham technique.

PW: *The Ballet Rambert has always seemed to have a Romantic image, not necessarily in a nineteenth century way, because you have twentieth century romanticism also, but . . .*

MR: The word 'Romantic' is neither here nor there. We did the Romantic classics because the size of our Company allowed us to do so. We don't want to create an image for a start, an image is something that must grow. But I don't think those things matter. It doesn't matter if we become fashionable after the first season, or if we have mud thrown at us, for we say what is deepest in our heart.

PW: *There seems to be a return to programmes of shorter ballets and these are again being appreciated alongside the great* Swan Lake *domination. This of course is only the case when the shorter ballets are really good. The public is intelligent today and no longer fooled by indifferent work.*

NM: I hope our old-new policy will create for people the interest in shorter works.

MR: A work of art doesn't depend on its length or its dimension. But the fact remains that young choreographers can only try their force on shorter works. For a young choreographer to produce a long work on a contemporary subject is a terribly difficult technical achievement.

PW: *The thing that is desperately vital is to develop choreographers, otherwise everything dies.*

MR: I absolutely agree, and because this is so we must allow people to do a short ballet of ten minutes or a quarter of an hour.

NM: We hope at some point in the future to add a club to our work. We hope to be able to give 'experimental evenings'. We wish to invite novice choreographers to try out their first works and also established choreographers who want to do something outrageous. It is essential to do all this within a company. The trouble with various workshop groups in the past has been that dancers come from all over the place, try to rehearse in odd rooms and halls, then arrive one Sunday in a theatre to face the cream of the ballet audience plus all the critics. It is too much to ask the novice to face up to this, the atmosphere is so wrong, they are not really allowed to make their mistakes.

PW: *The greatest luxury in the world is to be allowed to make mistakes.*

NM: I know that from very bitter experience. After all, a choreographer is very fortunate if every fifth ballet is good. The marvellous thing is to have a director who is brave enough to allow one to make the mistakes, because only from mistakes do you learn, but I don't think those mistakes must always be foisted on the public.

MR: And while we are talking about luxuries I must say something about the Arts Council who have allowed us a luxury for the first time in our lives.

NM: We are being given proper time to prepare, time to work on ourselves, time to work with others. This is very important because once we are touring week after week with a repertory it becomes impossible to experiment.

PW: *How do you find the two schools – classical and contemporary – react on each other?*

NM: One of the things that has impressed me seeing the two techniques being taught side by side, is that the newer one is making the dancers rediscover the one that has been a habit for so many years.

PW: *Is it not that in some ways you are going back to the beginning, because with the Graham technique you move upwards from the earth in the natural way of growth whether it be flora, fauna, or dance?*

NM: Yes, this is true and it is astonishing that the two teachers – Eileen Ward and Anna Price – end up saying the same things to the dancers: things that we have perhaps already heard, endlessly repeated over the years by Madame Rambert, without our being truly aware of them. Essentially, this all amounts to a new awareness of ourselves and of our work. The patterns of habit are broken, there is a new excitement in our purpose. We are beginning to grow again – upwards and outwards into the future.[3]

To set up the new venture, the Arts Council had allowed six months; three months to wind down the old company and three months to start the new one. From a retinue numbering thirty-six to forty dancers, Morrice took John Chesworth, Jonathan Taylor and about six or seven other dancers from the original company to form the heart of the 'phoenix' which would eventually comprise twelve soloist dancer-choreographers. Part of Rambert's new objective was a dramatic change in touring policy. Instead of touring ninety per cent of the time, the company would now only travel about ten per cent of the time, the rest of the year being devoted to the creation and performance of new works. The Mercury Theatre premises in Notting Hill had become a rehearsal and administrative headquarters convenient for a touring company but no longer a suitable venue for a resident performing company. What was needed was a central London theatre base where works could be both created and performed.

The answer came in the person of Ralph Koltai, who invited the company to make their home at the recently built Jeannetta Cochrane Theatre in Southampton Row. Koltai had succeeded Jeannetta Cochrane and Michael Tranmer, the previous year, as the third Head of Theatre Design at the Central School of Art and Design. The Jeannetta Cochrane Theatre, at that time solely the province of the Theatre Design Department, was his to use for whatever educational purposes he deemed suitable. The reality of having an innovative dance company actually on the premises was obviously advantageous for his design students. Moreover, the new choreographers could work together with the novice designers, shaping new works and transforming The Jeannetta Cochrane Theatre into what Peter Williams was later to describe as 'a stage of creation'.[4]

Ballet Rambert opened its first season at The Jeannetta Cochrane Theatre six months after the decision had been made. One company was disbanded, another was created. Three new choreographers, Lacotte, Chesworth and Van Dantzig, working with three young designers, Baylis, Corre and Van Schayk respectively, made their débuts with the reformed company, producing four new ballets during the autumn of 1966. Concurrent with the development of choreography from within the company, Norman Morrice also brought choreographers from outside. From America, where he had been inspired by the contemporary dance of, among others, Martha Graham and Merce Cunningham, he brought Glen Tetley to mount the first works of 1967. Of the new pieces, *Pierrot Lunaire*, originally created for the Glen Tetley Company in New York in 1962, and designed by Rouben Ter-Arutunian, was destined to become one of the cardinal works of the Rambert repertoire. Norman Morrice recalls the company's reaction to the design as 'a bit of scaffolding stuck in the middle of the stage. We never thought a piece of scaffolding, linked together with bolts could be a set. This became everything – Pierrot's house, his prison – it was wonderful!'[5] The effect on the company of bringing artists from other cultures was to extend the experience of all, preventing the work from becoming too self-referential.

The company's residency at The Jeannetta Cochrane Theatre also led to major technical innovations in the sphere of dance. Prior to that time, lighting for ballet consisted of two general states of illumination, as Norman Morrice humorously recalls, 'blue for drama or sadness and pink for happy'.[6] Koltai and Morrice realised that a specialised lighting rig, created exclusively for the needs of dance, should be designed. This was done by John B. Read and was the first of its kind in this country. Koltai recalled that because of this, 'one came to acknowledge that lighting was another element in creating a complete design'.[7] For years, dance had suffered from the variable quality of flooring on which it was expected to perform; also, the floors had nothing to do with the designs they

Nadine Baylis Costume design for *Ziggurat*
Music by Karlheinz Stockhausen
Choreography by Glen Tetley
Ballet Rambert, 1967
The artist

supported. Koltai solved the problem by discovering what was then called 'Marley Flooring' – it could be obtained in many shades and could be rolled-up and then unrolled, enabling it to be used even when the company was on tour. This innovation was the forerunner of today's vinyl dance floor, which is now used by most dance companies throughout the world.

In February 1967, the General Administrator of Ballet Rambert made the following announcement: 'I have pleasure in advising you that between Tuesday 14 March and Saturday 18 March 1967, inclusive, The Mercury Theatre Trust, in association with the Arts Council of Great Britain, is presenting a series of "Workshop" ballets in conjunction with the Theatre Department of the Central School of Art and Design, to be danced by a group of Rambert dancers, under the name of

Nadine Baylis Costumes for *That Is the Show*
Music by Luciano Berio
Choreography by Norman Morrice
Ballet Rambert, The Jeannetta Cochrane Theatre, London, 1971
Norman Morrice

Ralph Koltai *Conflicts*
Music by Ernest Bloch
Choreography by Norman Morrice
Ballet Rambert, 1962

Photograph by Anthony Crickmay
The Theatre Museum, V&A
The photographs used as projections
were taken by the designer.

Ralph Koltai Set for *Two Brothers*
Music by Ernst von Dohnányi
Choreography by Norman Morrice
Ballet Rambert, 1958. Photograph by Ralph Koltai

Ralph Koltai Set for *Hazaña*
Music by Carlos Surinach
Choreography by Norman Morrice
Ballet Rambert, 1959. Photograph by Ralph Koltai

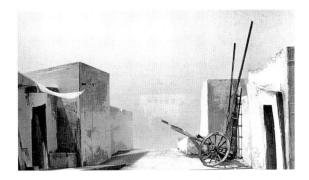

Ralph Koltai *A Place in the Desert*
Music by Carlos Surinach
Choreography by Norman Morrice
Ballet Rambert, 1961. Photograph by Ralph Koltai

Collaborations One.'[8] He went on to say: 'These performances
are in accordance with the artistic policy of Ballet Rambert and
are intended to provide a means whereby novice choreographers, designers and musicians are given the opportunity
to use their talents in a practical field.'[9]

Ralph Koltai, with funds from the Central School of Art and
Design and the Greater London Council, was able to provide a
budget of £100 for each of the new collaborations. The student
designers not only designed but also made all the scenery and
costumes themselves and were responsible for the design of the
lighting.

According to Norman Morrice, *Collaborations One*
introduced a whole new concept of design, lighting and
costume. He remembers: 'A lot of the pieces were initiated by
design. . . The danger has always been the habit of creating a
ballet and then having it "decorated". These pieces began, most
of the time, from scratch, and consequently the designer became
an equal in the process of creating a piece. . . What was being
liberated, from our point of view, was a new content, and a very

exciting one where you never quite knew where the initiation of the idea came from. It could come from the designer, it could come from the choreographer, sometimes it evolved from the dancers.'[10] Apart from anything else, this first *Collaborations* programme set off a whole chain of workshop programmes from several other British ballet companies: the Royal Ballet, Festival Ballet, Western Theatre Ballet and the London Contemporary Dance Group.

Five new pieces, choreographed by David Toguri, Amanda Knott, John Chesworth, Robert North and Teresa Early, designed by John Napier, Philip Jordan, John Chesworth, Tina Lipp and Elaine Garrard respectively, were performed in front of an audience which included several dance critics. Because of the emphasis on design as well as dance, the critics made some interesting comments on the subject. One in particular, Alexander Bland, ballet critic of the *Observer* newspaper, wrote: 'Not only was the claustrophobic atmosphere of the normal ambience broken – the audience was nearer to New York or Liverpool than to St Petersburg, and the chance to wander over during the interval into an excellently presented exhibition in the art school, opened up refreshing visual standards. You could also feel, blowing across the stage, the creative breeze which blows through any good art school, mysteriously floating towards us the ideas which, whether we like them now or not, are going to dominate our taste over the next decade. In the pot-bound world of British ballet, where modernity often masquerades as an arabesque in hipster jeans or one more scraping of the neo-classical barrel, this is a real sign of spring.'[11]

Most of the critics concurred with this view, although Peter Williams in *Dance and Dancers* did point out that 'One of the worrying aspects in most of these programmes is that the young creators tend to be obscure, and this obscurity often leads to the feeling that there is a certain pretentiousness about them.' Nevertheless, he went on to comment that 'Nobody expects wonders, nobody really expects works that can take their place in the existing repertories of firmly established companies, when they happen it is rare and almost miraculous.'[12]

Notwithstanding, two of the works did achieve the 'miraculous' and found their way into Ballet Rambert's repertoire. John Napier and David Toguri's *Inochi*, a work with no sound, projecting as its theme the cycle of life and the loss of innocence in gaining experience – the tree of life suggested by vast serpentine coils surrounding the stage and painted in colours representing segments of the life cycle – and John Chesworth's *Tic-Tack*, an hilarious piece of choreography and design about marriage, based on a Tom Ungerer cartoon.

Nevertheless, Williams was a firm supporter of the idea and wrote, 'What *Collaborations One* has done has been to give various creative artists an opportunity to air their talents, to make their mistakes, to try things out; then perhaps the mistakes may be ironed out in *Collaborations Two, Three, Four, Five . . .*'[13]

There were to be three more *Collaborations* between Ballet Rambert and the Theatre Design Course at the Central School of Art and Design, in 1968, 1976 and 1977. There were also two programmes entitled *Dance for New Dimensions* in 1972 and 1973 designed by former Theatre Design students. Several works subsequently entered the Rambert repertoire. Besides John Napier, the project gave early opportunities to work with choreographers to designers who were later to become well known, such as Maria Bjørnson, Sue Blane, Terry Parsons and, among others from arts schools that later joined the project, Derek Jarman.

During 1967, Ballet Rambert had taken an enormous risk by its reformation and renaissance. It had alienated an audience who had become accustomed to following the *Swan Lakes* and *Coppélias*. However, the company found a new audience comprising students and young people from all over the country. They no longer toured the traditional venues, but found a new vitality on the stages of the many university campuses. An innovative company had been reborn with a new identity and perception of design, choreography and dance – a vision of British contemporary dance on the creative stage of The Jeannetta Cochrane Theatre.

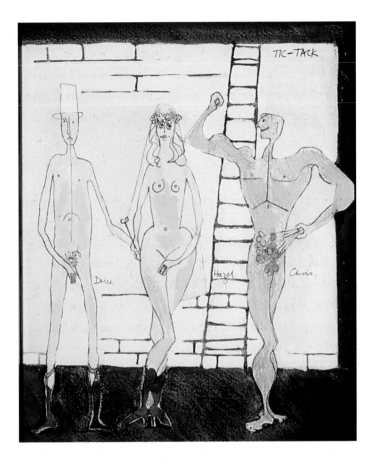

Rouben Ter-Arutunian Christopher Bruce in *Pierrot Lunaire*
Music by Arnold Schoenberg
Choreography by Glen Tetley
Ballet Rambert, 1967
Photograph by Anthony Crickmay
The Theatre Museum, V&A

John Chesworth Costumes for *Tic-Tack*
Music by Fritz Kreisler and Sergei Rachmaninoff
Choreography by John Chesworth
Collaborations One, The Jeannetta Cochrane Theatre,
London, 1967
This piece subsequently entered the Ballet Rambert
repertoire.

Light on the Matter | An Interview with John B. Read by Peter Williams

Dance and Dancers, Vol.21, No.2, February 1971, pp.17–21.

Peter Williams: *How did you first become interested in lighting in the theatre?*

John B. Read: When I was still at school, at about the age of sixteen, I became interested in drama and took drama and literature as a first subject. I found that the technical aspect of the work had a certain excitement, particularly lighting. Gradually the literary side was pushed into the background and I started lighting in a small, amateur way. By the time I was seventeen I decided that I was going to be a lighting designer.

PW: *Where was this very advanced school that allowed you to do this kind of thing?*

JBR: It's a small independent school in Essex, where there are 150 pupils and where the arts and drama play a very forceful part in the curriculum. We were encouraged to do this kind of work even in preference to the sciences. At that time it was very rare for schools to be like this but today, with modern teaching methods, many more schools encourage the use of drama and dance and modern movement. I think that today there is far more scope for students to do this kind of work.

PW: *Had you read many books on lighting or on pioneers in the field of stage lighting such as Adolphe Appia?*

JBR: No, at that time I had very little literary knowledge, and I am afraid that as a schoolboy I read very little. I was much more interested in practical things, such as making radio sets and playing about with tape-recorders. I very rarely went to the theatre or to the ballet.

PW: *When you did go to the theatre or ballet, were you dissatisfied with what you saw, particularly with regard to the lighting?*

BR: Not at an early stage, because I had very little idea about it, so that anything visual in this way was an excitement. I was most intrigued to know how it was done and I would rush round backstage to try and find out, but at this period I wasn't very critical of what had been achieved. I had a certain fixation for switchboards, backstage and all the equipment.

PW: *Were you ever taught about lighting or given any practical knowledge?*

JBR: Not at that time in terms of lighting but certainly with regard to acting. I used to act a bit in a small way, and I had voice lessons and all that side of the work. But on the technical side there were very few people who had the resources, equipment or the time and patience. I had to find out everything on my own and made it my business to find out how it all worked. But I was fortunate in that friends of my father were connected with Marconi in research and development. Through them I managed to get hold of some equipment which they lent me. In this way I was able to experiment on my own.

PW: *Did you have a model theatre in which you could experiment?*

JBR: No, but we had an old barn which had electricity connected to it. Not a very big space, about twelve feet square, but it had roof timbers from which we used to suspend lights on pieces of string and other makeshift arrangements. So I was able to experiment in that way. We never got to giving actual performances, it was all experiment for our own sake.

PW: *What was the first production you actually lit in the theatre?*

JBR: From school I went to drama school, and at the age of seventeen I lit my first production, in London at the Scala Theatre, which was *Spring 1600*. That was a particularly complicated set by Peter Krumins, then in charge of the scenic department of the school I was at. He designed a setting on four levels. In I went headfirst at the Scala Theatre, working with four electricians who were of an average age between fifty and sixty. That was my headlong leap into lighting.

PW: *Did you find that the old professional electricians rather resented you?*

JBR: Oh yes, they did. To them I was a toffee-nosed young boy who knew nothing about anything, but I managed to get over all that by bribing them with ounces of tobacco and various other little gifts. Gradually they began to warm and to realise that there was something in me, and that it was worth letting me have a go although they didn't actually agree with what I was doing. I was attempting to use spotlights where they would have preferred I use floats and battens. Even at the age of seventeen, I could see that the particular set that we had, and indeed the whole production, required spotlighting as opposed to general flood-lighting. After that particular production I went back to college and continued studies in drama and lighting. I ran the two side by side, lighting as much as I could wherever I could, in and out of college. I did one or two productions with Peter Jackson, who was also a student at the same time; these we did in the college theatre and they were quite exciting. Apart from these, I didn't do anything of real note until I had left college, and I didn't take up lighting as such until I had completed National Service. By then I decided I was going to be a lighting designer in spite of everybody warning me against it and saying that I would never make a living at it. None of this deterred me, and I felt that the best thing to do was to get a job as an electrician where I would be in close contact with people lighting the stage, and actually using the equipment as opposed to becoming a stage manager. I couldn't get a job as an electrician but I managed to get a job as an assistant stage manager at the Mermaid Theatre on the original production of *Treasure Island*. I only got that because I had had an acting training as well, so that I was able to ASM and understudy. From that, when a vacancy occurred, I managed to switch sides, and that was the start of it.

PW: *The Mermaid* [not the current theatre on the same site in London] *is a rather interesting theatre to light.*

JBR: Yes. It gives one a great challenge because of that end stage, and it has a particularly difficult ceiling structure which means that it is hard to get lights in at the right angle to the actor. It also needs a very different technique from lighting a straight proscenium stage. But I found it quite fascinating, and I think the whole building is a splendid place.

PW: *After this initial work at the Mermaid where did you go?*

JBR: I was fortunate enough to be invited to go to Chichester, with the opening of the Festival there, as a switchboard operator. There of course I met Sir Laurence Olivier and John Dexter, and from Chichester I went to the National Theatre as an electrician. But while I had been at Chichester, John Dexter invited me to light *The Royal Hunt of the Sun*, which was to go on at the next Festival. That was my biggest step forward yet, because it meant that for the first time I was working on a large production in a fairly large theatre with a lot of equipment – and working with people who demand a very high standard. It was a quite frightening experience – in at the deep end.

PW: *It was a production that relied so much on lighting. Without good lighting it might never have achieved the success it did.*

JBR: The whole of the first act was totally visual, the second act was virtually an argument which depended less on light, but the first act set the whole thing up and set the mood. On that large stage, with the only scenery being that great sun backing, one was virtually lighting an open stage with just actors, so that the whole thing was in terms of light. It required a technique that was similar to lighting a modern ballet.

PW: *Yes, that first act is full of movement, almost a ballet, and this might well have helped you when you later came to light dancers in ballets.*

JBR: Yes, it did. The thing that John Dexter kept saying to me the whole time was 'You must pull the actors away from the set, you must etch them in light. We must see them, we must see their form, we must see their eyes. You must pull them away all the time. It has to have a dramatic content.' This did in fact help me later to understand how to treat and light a dancer and how to use the light to enhance the visual picture.

PW: *When was the first time that you actually lit dancers?*

JBR: I think it must have been in 1967. I was working with Robert Ornbow and Ralph Koltai on a National Theatre production of *As You Like It* and Ralph happened to mention that he was working with Ballet Rambert and also with Nadine Baylis. I had worked with Nadine before on a small opera, so I suggested that I might come along and see what was happening. Ballet Rambert were then looking for a lighting designer, so Ralph and Nadine pushed me forward to reorganise the whole of the company's lighting department.

PW: *What kind of problems did you have to face?*

JBR: It was difficult in that the company already had an existing repertory that had to be lit. Coming in as an outsider, I found it difficult to use entirely the same lighting lay-out as they had used before, so I had to use something that would cope with the existing works and with the new works – with all the demands that Glen Tetley made. Gently one had to reorganise the whole set-up to cope with it; it was a slow thing and I did it gradually. The two Tetley works – *Freefall* and *Ziggurat* – I lit on 'specials' to start with, but later on, as I lit more ballets, these became part of the general system. I programmed the whole thing so that in time we could gradually change the system over. It also meant new thinking and a new approach since previously a lot of work had been lit in what could be termed 'the old style' with very soft colours and the light very much in the background, being no real help to the choreographer or the designer. Because of my particular training and sense of drama, I wanted to break through this and to be a part of the choreography and a part of the design. I wondered, in the beginning, how the

dancers would feel about this, having been beautifully lit from the front before; then I come along and light them very harshly, top light and side light and really pulling the figures away from everything else. Fortunately for me they accepted it utterly and completely, in fact became very excited about the new sort of stimulus that lighting made for their work. Of course it all worked very much with the new style choreography, with Morrice and Tetley working together to produce this new format, and the lighting became a part of that.

PW: *It would seem that Balanchine and Robbins originally worked in a very similar way with Jean Rosenthal.*

JBR: This is very probably so, but unfortunately I never saw the New York City Ballet when Rosenthal was working with them: that is a part of my experience sadly lacking. I have in fact re-lit a couple of Jean Rosenthal ballets that have been performed in this country, and I have found her use of units, lanterns and colour quite fascinating. Obviously she had been working on those lines for many years.

PW: *What John Dexter said to you about lighting actors obviously seems to apply equally to dancers, but are there any other things you look for or try to achieve when you are lighting ballets?*

JBR: I think it is vitally important for the lighting designer to understand the choreographer completely and the way he works. I spend a lot of time sifting through the various comments that a choreographer will make. What is important is to lock on to the style of the particular choreographer you are working for at the moment. They are a race of people who sometimes find it difficult to communicate just how they are working. Often when I see a work in rehearsal it's not even finished.

PW: *You attend as many rehearsals as you can?*

JBR: It is absolutely essential for me to see at least two run-throughs. I like to have a preliminary chat with the choreographer to start with and also with the designer. If it's an unknown choreographer or designer I have to spend a great deal more time with them so as to get on the same wavelength. Then I like to see one rehearsal and one run-through, during which time I take down

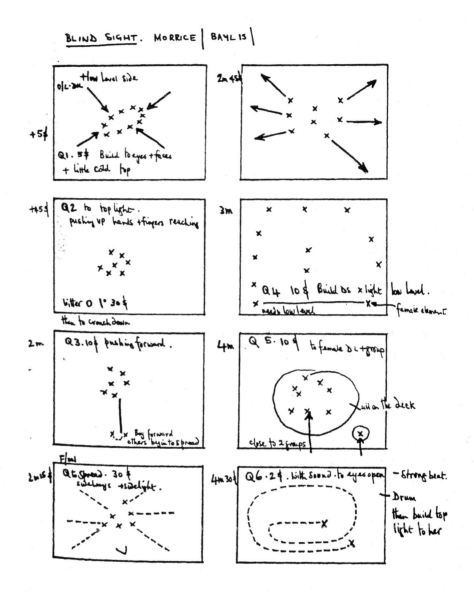

John B. Read Notation for Lighting

At early run-throughs, John B. Read will do his own form of notation of the movement and position of dancers so that he can design and start to plot the lighting. Above is a plan for the first five minutes of Norman Morrice's *Blind Sight* – the crosses represent the dancers, the figures outside the squares show the number of minutes from the beginning.

all the moves, all the choreography, and write down anything that springs to mind that will help me.

PW: *How do you take them down? Have you got a personal form of notation or something?*

JBR: Yes, I go to the rehearsal armed with a foolscap pad covered with small mimic diagrams of the set. I then draw little pictures, writing down every single move that each and every dancer makes. It all sounds rather impossible but with speed and experience it can be done. After this I have a mental picture of the ballet stored up, and I can refer back to it.

After I have seen the first run-through and got all the moves down I go away and think about it; when I have had time to get my thoughts together I hope that I will see the general shape coming to life. After that I need to see a second run-through when I take the notes along, and it is at this run-through that I start to design the lighting and to fully interpret the work. I pencil in all the various points where I think we need to change light, atmosphere, mood, intention. When I've got all that together I go back to the choreographer and talk through the ballet from beginning to end making sure that I have got the correct interpretation. We discuss various points about how he sees this or that and what section should be stronger than another, or clarifying some point that was not very clear. Then I give him a précis version of what I intend to do, so that he is forewarned before we actually come to lighting in the theatre.

PW: *Are you influenced by music when you light?*

JBR: Very much so. A modern choreographer will take a piece of music and interweave his ideas with that, so he gets all this from the music and I will use this as an interpretation of what he's doing.

PW: *You don't have any of these theories, which were expounded a lot at one time, about certain music being related to certain colours?*

JBR: No, I never use that approach. To me the choreographer is more important than the music and I get everything from him. I think that relating colour to music is a particularly clinical method of

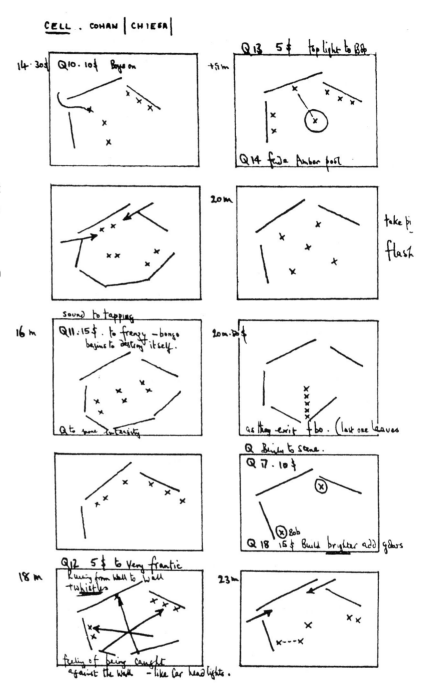

John B. Read Part of layout for Robert Cohan's *Cell*
After Read has notated the works in this way he will then go into a very detailed cue synopsis giving the number of the cue, the speed of the change and the time of the cue from the beginning of the work. In addition there will be action details for each cue showing what the dancers are doing and how the light has to hit them or build or spread.

lighting and not really a very honest one. It's the choreographer's business to interpret the music in the way he wants; it's my business to get whatever he is after.

PW: *Aren't there moments such as, for instance, when the music swells that the lighting swells also?*

JBR: This of course happens instinctively as one feels it emotionally, but you will probably find that the dance also expands and progresses at the same moment so it all happens together.

PW: *What do you feel about lighting painted sets?*

JBR: I much prefer to light a three-dimensional set, such as the kind of thing that Nadine Baylis comes up with, as this has a greater sense of reality for me. I don't object to lighting painted canvas; in fact it is far more difficult to pull a three-dimensional picture from it since the canvas eats up so much light and distracts from the dancers. I think that if any setting needs so much lighting that it detracts from the dancers then it is wrong; but if a two-dimensional setting can sit quietly in the background and doesn't require a lot of lighting or equipment, then obviously it can work. If you have to spend an enormous amount of time sorting the set out before you can start lighting the dancers, then it becomes a particularly difficult problem and probably not very rewarding to anyone in the end.

PW: *How about lighting ballets in the round?*

JBR: The nearest I got to that was lighting Netherlands Dance Theatre's *Mutations* in the Circus Theatre at The Hague. The stage projected something like 30 feet into the auditorium, with a ramp coming out a further 50 feet. That had similar problems to lighting in the round, in so far as the equipment in that particular theatre was in all the wrong places for the ballet – but even more so at Sadler's Wells, where it was almost impossible to light that production well. But the round could be very interesting for ballet. I would love to see a company take, say, the Assembly Hall for the Edinburgh Festival. This building has enormous possibilities; it is virtually in the round and you could get the stage within the auditorium and the dancers so near to the audience. From a lighting point of view it would offer a great excitement.

PW: *Have you got any ideas about how you want to go on, or any theories you want to develop?*

JBR: I think that for at least the next two years I would like to consolidate the work I have done so far in modern ballet in this country. I would like to light a full-length modern ballet, and then I would like to go on and light some classical work, because up to now I have lit no classical ballets and I am sure that I could learn a lot from it.

You see I work as a lighting designer for Richard Pilbrow's Theatre Projects company, but I am allowed to light whatever work I care to. We have a very loose system whereby we can all specialise in the types of work we want to do. For instance I specialise in ballet, Robert Ornbow and Bob Bryan specialise in opera. But we interchange, work with each other, swap ideas and talk to each other about our various problems. Perhaps if one of us isn't busy we will go and watch what another designer is doing, and in this way one can learn and progress and find out how everybody else works.

PW: *Have you a greater interest in ballet or dance theatre than in any other branch of the theatre?*

JBR: It's really fifty-fifty; I much enjoy lighting straight drama, particularly plays by Chekhov and Ibsen, as they demand a strong mood and atmosphere. But I am greatly interested in lighting ballet, I find it a great stimulus and I so enjoy the way our modern companies are working; the discipline and the seriousness of their intention is so good. With very little money they seem to perform masterpieces. It seems to me that in this country it is only the modern companies, such as Ballet Rambert and London Contemporary Dance Theatre, who don't spend money frivolously. They have to count every penny and they make sure that they get the best standards in dance, in choreography and, I hope, in lighting.

Design for Dance: The Story So Far . . . | Peter Farley

In 1989, Pamela Howard, then Director of the Theatre Design course at Central Saint Martins College of Art and Design, decided to develop a new project for the third year BA Hons undergraduates which would enable the students to address the unique design requirements which come into play when designing for dance. Although the Design for Dance project, as it was titled, would be the natural successor to the *Collaborations* projects between Ballet Rambert and the Theatre Design Course begun in the mid-1960s, it would differ in that it would involve all the students of the third year, rather than just those who expressed a specific interest in dance. This would ensure that each novice designer would gain design experience in at least three areas of theatre, namely, drama, opera and, now, dance. In order to implement her plan, Pamela Howard decided it was necessary to enlist the services of a theatre designer who was experienced in both dance design and teaching, and would be able to structure and define the needs of such a project. Peter Docherty, a designer of over fifty ballet and dance productions worldwide and already a part-time lecturer on the course, was her unequivocal choice.

A feasibility study was prepared citing the success of the 1960s' *Collaborations* projects as 'evidence from the past as a guide for the future', which could bring 'a new impetus and vitality to the Theatre Design Course and the College'.[1] Peter Docherty and Pamela Howard recognised that unlike designs for plays and operas which are based upon a text or a libretto, a new work of dance, having no conventional text, or at best an outline narrative, could not be offered to the students as a purely studio-based project. With dance, although the movement could be notated, specialist knowledge was required to understand and visualise it. It was, therefore, important that the students be brought into direct contact with the living, breathing physicality of dance and experience the language of movement at first hand.

With this in mind, Peter Docherty approached Norman Morrice, an ardent promoter of new choreography and design. He had organised the *Collaborations* projects with Ralph Koltai at The Jeannetta Cochrane Theatre in the 1960s and 1970s, and was now Director of Choreographic Studies at The Royal Ballet School. Until then the main focus of Norman Morrice's choreographic classes at The Royal Ballet School had been to encourage interested ballet students to create about ten or so short pieces of new choreography, danced in practice clothes, to be entered for the school's annual 'Ursula Moreton Choreographic Prize'. Morrice suggested that this was the area where the student choreographers and designers could come together. This agreed, Peter Docherty and Norman Morrice discussed the problem of finding a common starting point for the project which would both stimulate and inspire the designers and choreographers alike, and, at the same time, allow them the freedom to explore their ideas.

As both groups of students were training to be visual artists in their own fields, Peter Docherty suggested that the point of departure could be the work of yet another visual artist working in a different medium such as painting, and went on to propose that the students should visit an exhibition of Paul Klee's work which was, at the time, on show at the Tate Gallery. Being a non-representational painter, Klee was open to wide interpretation; also, the use of a common theme, coupled with the Tate Gallery as a meeting place, would enable the students to get to know one another and discuss their impressions of Klee's work on neutral ground. At the same time, perhaps to revive the course's connection with Ballet Rambert, Peter Docherty had discussed the new project with Richard Alston,

Design for Dance
Composite picture of five pieces by young choreographers taught by Norman Morrice at the Royal Ballet School.

Clockwise from top left:
Stephen Yull *Me, Myself and I Alone*
Choreography by Jamie Thompson
Royal Ballet School
The Cochrane Theatre, 1995

Hayley Cotton *Portrait*
Choreography by Christopher Hampson
English National Ballet Company
The Cochrane Theatre, 1994

Bruce French *Sing the Body*
Choreography by Vanessa Fenton
Royal Ballet School
The Cochrane Theatre, 1995

Jason Southgate *Four and Six*
Choreography by Daniel Jones
English National Ballet School
The Cochrane Theatre, 1994

Saffron Webb *Ladies Only*
Choreography by Nicole Ransley-Smith
Royal Ballet School
The Cochrane Theatre, 1994

choreographer and then Director of the renamed Rambert Dance Company. Alston suggested that he could involve the theatre design students in two pieces of choreography on which he was currently working: the first using a Mozart piano sonata which he was actually choreographing at the time; the second, *Image, Reflection and Shadow*, with music by Peter Maxwell Davies, an imaginary project for the future. Pamela Howard submitted the proposal to the Linbury Trust, brainchild of Sir John and Lady Sainsbury and well known for its support of educational theatre projects. The trust agreed to provide a seeding grant. This grant, together with support from the Theatre Design Trust, a charitable organisation set up to enhance the existing academic funding of the Theatre Design course, enabled the project to proceed.

The project work began with eighteen young designers spending two weeks with Sue Ayers, the theatre designer and fine-artist – drawing dancers and making costume shapes with paper and other simple materials in environments to suit. They were given free access to the Royal Ballet School and Rambert Dance to observe classes and rehearsals. Students spent a further week in The Jeannetta Cochrane Theatre with Norman Morrice lecturing on the 'History of Dance' and with Anna Meadmore, a dancer and choreographer who was part of the Teachers' Training course at The Royal Ballet School, taking class and learning and performing pieces from the Royal Ballet repertoire. At the end of the week they attended a choreographic master class with Norman Morrice. They then choreographed and performed their own pieces to an audience of their fellow students. Meanwhile, another choreographer had come forward, offering one more piece in need of a designer. With separate funding from the Linbury Trust, the choreographer and educationalist Christopher Bannerman had launched a project aimed at introducing secondary school children to dance. This was one of a series of arts events organised as the swansong of the Inner London Education Authority, and was to be performed during The London Contemporary Dance Theatre's season at Sadler's Wells Theatre in November that year.

After their initial three weeks in The Jeannetta Cochrane Theatre, Peter Docherty divided the young designers into three groups. Group 'A', numbering nine students, worked with Norman Morrice at the Royal Ballet School where both designers and choreographers collaborated on new pieces. Group 'B', a total of seven students, worked with Richard Alston on *Image, Reflection and Shadow* by Sir Peter Maxwell Davies and on the Mozart piano sonata K331. Group 'C' consisted of two designers who collaborated with Christopher Bannerman on *The Climbing Frame*.

Norman Morrice, in his appraisal of The Royal Ballet School's participation in the 1989 Design for Dance project made the following observations:

> From the choreographers' and dancers' point of view the project was a totally new experience, a new collaborative challenge and an invaluable learning process. Unfortunately, due to the Royal Ballet's call upon the services of several of the students, both choreographers and dancers, only one piece reached completion and the others had to be considered as 'works in progress' when time ran out. However, as a pilot scheme, the project produced much that was valuable, stimulating and creative and although a 'showing' of designed dance works would not be realised in practical terms, it is hoped that such a dream will not be impossible at some future date.[2]

Students from The Royal Ballet School were asked to document their experience of working, for the first time, with a group of designers. Matthew Hart, a student at The Royal Ballet School at the time, later to become a professional dancer and choreographer wrote:

What particularly stimulated me about this project was the research which the designer, the dancers and myself undertook into the work of Klee. We found common characters linking several of his pictures and it was fun to try and translate these characters into our own visual terms. Dancers do not usually have the opportunity to express their reactions to other art forms and I feel the venture was very successful.[3]

Richard Alston also filed a report pointing out that only one of the young designers had chosen to work with the Mozart piece. He found that surprising as there was the opportunity to observe the live rehearsals. Most of the group chose the Peter Maxwell Davies piece which had not yet been choreographed, possibly, as Peter Docherty recollects, because 'it was much more abstract and open-ended'.[4] In his assessment of the project Alston went on to evaluate the work of each of the seven designers in turn, his general observation being that 'the spontaneity of response shown in initial sketches and graphic work needed a chance to let fly in the model'.

The issue that Alston raised is the perennial problem faced by all artists when translating initial sketches into a finished piece of work. The transition is all the more difficult when the process involves a change from two dimensions into three. In the case of the theatre designer, the initial ideas and sketches usually evolve into a set of finished costume drawings and a three-dimensional scale model of the setting. This is where the energy, spontaneity and special personality of the ideas can easily become lost. As the brain switches from creative to practical mode, the concentration on 'making the piece work' can cause an increasing loss of visual energy and personality. This is especially difficult for the novice (and sometimes even the professional) dance designer when confronted with not only the interpretation of his or her own artistic intentions, but also the practical reality of bodies moving through the setting wearing costumes which have to acknowledge the physical needs of the dance.

Objective feedback from those taking part in the project not only contained valuable pointers to improve teaching methods for future projects in this specialist area, but also began to clarify and examine, for the first time, the role of the dance designer from the internal perspective of all the actual practitioners involved.

Although Christopher Bannerman's *The Climbing Frame* was the only performed work from the 1989 project, the students did have the opportunity to show their Design for Dance work at a three-day exhibition in the Bridge Gallery at Central Saint Martins College of Art and Design on 18, 19 and 20 January 1990. Some of the designs shown were described as 'still in progress', and it was hoped that it would 'stimulate the possibility of future collaborations'.[5]

Future collaborations were indeed a possibility and, encouraged by the success of the 1989 pilot, a further project was planned for the following year. The project was to be co-ordinated by Norman Morrice and Peter Docherty, and would include, in addition to students from The Royal Ballet School, those from The London Contemporary Dance School, thus offering the design students experience of both classical and contemporary dance. With further funding from the Linbury Trust, a total of eighteen young designers were linked with six student choreographers from The Royal Ballet School and twelve from The London Contemporary Dance School.

Besides the tutors engaged to oversee the project as a whole, Peter Docherty, using the money from the Linbury Trust, was able to engage a wide range of other leading dance professionals to talk to the students on subjects ranging from choreography and design to scenic construction and costume interpretation; they included Val Bourne, Tom Jobe, Bob Lockyer, Ronald Hynd, Michael Corder, Clement Crisp, Matthew Hamilton, Janice Pullen, John Macfarlane, Kim Brandstrup, William Tuckett, Derek Jarman, Robert Cohan, Stuart Hopps, Wizzy Shawyer, Lloyd Newson and Andrew Logan.

In the week of 26 November there was a lighting workshop

Ian Spurling Set for *Seven Deadly Sins*
Music by Kurt Weill
Choreography by Kenneth MacMillan
Western Theatre Ballet, 1961
The Theatre Museum, V&A

Ian Spurling was closely involved with the
Peter Williams Design for Dance Project
until his death in 1996.

Installation by Matthew Hamilton on the work of
Robert Cohan in the original set for *Cell*, designed by
Norberto Chiesa. The set was lent by London
Contemporary Dance Trust, and the installation
appeared in the exhibition *The Designers: Pushing the
Boundaries – Advancing the Dance*, The Lethaby
Galleries, November 1995

with John B. Read in The Jeannetta Cochrane Theatre. This was the first time lighting had been introduced into the project, extending the visual and dramatic vocabulary of both sets of young artists. Over the six-week project the designers and choreographers created a total of eighteen new pieces of dance and design which culminated in a run-through of the work in progress on the afternoon of Saturday 1 December 1990 on the stage of The Jeannetta Cochrane Theatre.

In his appraisal, written in his capacity of project co-ordinator with Peter Docherty, Norman Morrice wrote:

> The visible results are, of course, still only an indication of what could finally be possible, and inevitably appear as rather separate issues, the designer ending up with a model and costume designs on paper, and the choreographer with the dance piece, hopefully recorded on video-tape; a workshop week when as many of the elements as possible, including 'light', still could only provide an indication of possibilities, some exciting in their potential success, others valuable in their honourable failure. . . At present only the tutors, who are in constant contact with the students through the working processes, can truly assess the immediate growth in knowledge and experience as the collaborations develop.[6]

The 1991 Design for Dance project was again in collaboration with The Royal Ballet School and The London Contemporary Dance School and followed very much the same timetable as the previous year. The students were asked to meet at the Tate Gallery; this time each was to select a painting from the permanent collection of pictures and return with a postcard depicting their choice. Some designers and choreographers had already formed pairs from their meeting at the Tate, the others were matched if they had chosen the same painting or paintings with a common theme. Sadly, the pieces could not be performed at The Jeannetta Cochrane Theatre as the building was in the process of being remodelled at the time. However, Chistopher Bannerman came to the rescue by arranging for The London Contemporary Dance School pieces to be performed at Middlesex University. The Royal Ballet School pieces were shown, in practice clothes, at the annual Ursula Moreton prize-giving. The work of the designers was exhibited alongside on the same evening.

In 1992 the first performances of the Design for Dance project were staged at the newly remodelled and renamed Cochrane Theatre. That year's performances were, once again, designed in collaboration with The London Contemporary Dance School and The Royal Ballet School. John B. Read returned as lighting consultant and created a custom lighting rig designed specially for the project. The pieces were performed in front of an audience consisting of fellow students, professionals from the dance world, tutors from the institutions involved and included the Head of College, Margaret Buck, and John McKenzie, Rector of The London Institute.

The following year, the project produced eleven designed pieces from The Royal Ballet School performed on 19 February, and fourteen from The London Contemporary Dance School, performed on two consecutive evenings, seven pieces each night, on 25 and 26 February 1993. Although there were twenty-three design students involved in the project, one student's work, although visually exciting, proved highly impractical for dance. This left twenty-two designers creating twenty-five pieces, some students designing more than one piece. A member of the audience in 1993 was the seventy-nine-year-old Peter Williams, a student of the legendary Jeannetta Cochrane at the Central School of Arts and Crafts in the early 1930s and, by that time, a grand old man of the dance. He had been to see the Design for Dance performances the previous year and had returned at the invitation of his friend and protégé Peter Docherty.

Over the past two years, Docherty had been toying with the

idea of naming the project after Peter Williams because of Williams's long-standing and highly respected career as a dance designer, teacher, writer, critic and promoter, coupled with his design training at the college before World War Two. Williams had agreed to this request and it was decided that the project should be renamed 'The Peter Williams Design for Dance Project'. The dedication was to take place at an exhibition of twentieth-century dance designs mounted in his honour in May 1993 and opened by John Drummond, Director of the Henry Wood Promenade Concerts, former Controller of BBC Radio Three and himself an expert on dance. Many distinguished figures from the world of dance attended the opening. The exhibition was entitled *From Diaghilev to the Pet Shop Boys* and an introduction to the exhibition by Marina Henderson (with whom I curated the exhibition) precedes a selection of reproductions of costume and set designs to be found later in this book.

On entering The Lethaby Galleries, the visitor was immediately confronted by a pair of three-metre-high costumes, designed by Pablo Picasso for Jean Cocteau's *Parade* (1917). To the left towered the costume for 'The Manager from New York' and to the right, 'The Manager in Evening Dress'. Between the two costumes, in a glass case, was the 'Helmet for Death' designed by E. McKnight Kauffer for Ninette de Valois's 1937 ballet *Checkmate*. The main body of the exhibition consisted mostly of two-dimensional work, generously loaned not only by private and public collections but also by the designers themselves. Visitors returning towards the entrance were temporarily halted by a sign bearing the words 'The Peter Williams Design for Dance Project' under which were large colour photographs of the 1993 student project at The Cochrane Theatre, the celebration of past work itself an occasion to look to the future. The public profile of the newly named project had been considerably heightened by the attention focused on the exhibition and it was hoped that its enhanced status might attract the outside funding which the project desperately needed.

By this time the project had settled into a regular timetable which was tailored to fit the varied curricula of all the institutions involved. Initial meetings between student choreographers and designers usually took place during December of the year prior to the performances so that ideas could be formulated over the Christmas recess, allowing enough time during the following term for the designers to make their costumes and their set pieces with the help of the course's technicians. The students worked on their dance pieces for a total of twelve weeks plus the holidays and the performances were scheduled to be shown at The Cochrane Theatre over a four-week period at the end of the spring term.

For the 1994 season, The English National Ballet School and Company joined the project. Peter Docherty and myself co-ordinated and tutored the overall project for Central Saint Martins, Norman Morrice for The Royal Ballet School, Karen Greenhough for The London Contemporary Dance School and Lynn Wallis for The English National Ballet School and Company. That year, there were two new developments in the working process of the project. The first, that student composers were commissioned to create original music for four of The Royal Ballet School pieces, thus extending the collaborative team to three artists for each of these works. The second was a change in the method of collaboration with The London Contemporary Dance School. Previously, the design students had worked on pieces which the choreographers had already started. Although, with the addition of a designer, the development of the choreography did adjust to include the ideas of the extra collaborator, the pieces were, of necessity, choreographically led. During an initial meeting with Karen Greenhough, who had joined the project for the first time, it was decided that a series of experimental workshops would be employed with those students working with The London Contemporary Dance School, which would try to create new work with both designer and choreographer starting from the same point, namely, from shared ideas developed in the workshops. This method produced eight works for the 1994 season and has been developed and used by Karen Greenhough and myself for all subsequent projects.

That year, the students had access to a small range of specialists to help them develop their designs, including Ian Spurling, a distinguished designer with immense practical knowledge of dance costume. Master classes were given on lighting by John B. Read and on design by Yolanda Sonnabend and Richard Hudson. For all the 1994 performances the theatre was full to capacity, including members of the press, some of whom wrote about the experience. Nicholas Dromgoole, dance critic of the *Sunday Telegraph*, wrote that he had been 'watching a development that is admirable as a project and exciting in performance' and went on to say that it was 'fun to see what the latest influences are, and also to try and spot the talents who may one day rock the dance world'.[7] Sue Merrett, who had been following the year's work from the beginning, devoted three pages of photographs and text to the project in the *Dancing Times*, evaluating each piece within the true context of the project – that of student workshop performances of works in progress.

Inspired by the success of The Peter Williams Design for Dance Project and the 1993 exhibition, *From Diaghilev to the Pet Shop Boys*, Central Saint Martins College of Art and Design, with funding from The London Institute, decided to initiate the Design for Performance Research Project to explore the theory and practice of theatre design. This would generate a body of scenographic knowledge arising from specific themes which had not been drawn together, or published before. The research programme was conceived as a staged development over a number of years. The first area of investigation was to be specifically concerned with the scenography of dance.

In 1995, The Peter Williams Design for Dance Project became directly linked with the newly established Design for Performance Research Project for the first time. Dermot Hayes had succeeded Pamela Howard as head of the Theatre Design Course, and Peter Docherty was appointed as Research Project Director, complementing his teaching duties as Third Year Tutor and Senior Lecturer in Theatre Design. This facilitated the forging of a close link between the third-year undergraduate course and further research into scenographic theory. The collaborators for the 1995 season were The Royal Ballet School, The London Contemporary Dance School, and a newcomer to the project, Central School of Ballet, under the guidance of Cecilia Darker. In order to give the students more than one chance to see their work on stage in front of an audience, and due to public demand, it was decided that there would be two public performances of each programme for the 1995 season. In addition to the new works shown at The Cochrane Theatre, four design students worked on collaborations which were performed elsewhere. One young designer created a design for Ballet Central, the touring company of the Central School of Ballet; three others collaborated with three professional choreographers, Lynn Seymour, Gale Taphouse and Matthew Hart, to create three new pieces of dance with specially composed music by students of the Yehudi Menuhin School. These works were made to celebrate the 75th anniversary of the Surrey branch of the Royal Academy of Dancing and were performed at a gala evening at the New Victoria Theatre, Woking.

In all other respects the 1995 Peter Williams Design for Dance Project followed the pattern set the previous year with the added benefit of its link with the Design for Performance Research Project and the back-up which its staff provided. At the end of the term, over a period of two days, Norman Morrice and Professor Peter Snow, the distinguished painter, designer for dance, and, at that time, head of the Department of Theatre Design at the Slade School of Fine Art, jointly assessed the design students' work. The performances and the students' assessments were carefully documented by Dr Tim White, the Design for Performance Research Project Research Assistant, and myself, now a PhD Researcher into design for dance, assisted by Malcolm Stewart, the Project Secretary, using video and audio recordings; so, too, were all workshops with choreographers and dancers, and seminars by visiting practitioners, and these would eventually become an important component of the Design for Performance archive. During this period the project acquired two patrons, Dame Beryl Grey and Lionel Bart, long-standing supporters of the project. A 'Design for Dance' committee was in the process of being formed to help raise the extra funds needed to enhance the overall production budget. The Dowager Lady Cottesloe agreed to chair this sub-committee of the Theatre Design Trust.

In November 1995, The Design for Performance Research Project staged a further exhibition of dance design in The Lethaby Galleries entitled *The Designers: Pushing the Boundaries – Advancing the Dance.* Complementary to the 1993 *From Diaghilev to the Pet Shop Boys* exhibition, part of the rationale of the sequel exhibition was to examine the work of several pivotal and revolutionary dance scenographers and their successors who, in collaboration with four major twentieth-century choreographers, Robert Cohan, Peter Darrell, Sir Kenneth MacMillan and Norman Morrice (all four having been artistic directors of prestigious dance companies) had truly extended the boundaries of their art, advancing the dance.

The 1995 exhibition included set models, costumes and photographs as well as two-dimensional work and was essentially a demonstration of collaboration, the kind of collaboration that The Peter Williams Design for Dance Project was trying to encourage between the students. Accompanying the exhibition was an illustrated catalogue, published by Central Saint Martins, that included essays by members of the research project. As Sir Peter Wright concluded in his introduction for the catalogue, referring to the designers and choreographers represented in the exhibition: 'Finally, it is of course the great understanding of exchange of ideas that has existed between them and their choreographers that has often led to the creation of great work and enabled boundaries to be pushed back and new advances made in this very challenging area of stage design.'[8]

Peter Docherty Elaine McDonald and Graham Bart in *Mary, Queen of Scots*
Music by John McCabe
Choreography by Peter Darrell
Scottish Ballet, 1976
Photograph by Anthony Crickmay
The Theatre Museum, V&A

The Research Project is planning to study a number of productions in detail. For *Mary, Queen of Scots* it has collected photographs of the designs for sets and costumes, production photographs, a performance videotape, Benesh notation, John B. Read's lighting plans and an interview with Elaine McDonald, the original Mary. A similar study is being made of *George and the Dragon*, one of the results of which is the interview reproduced elsewhere in this book.

In 1996, twenty-three new pieces of dance and design were created and performed during the Peter Williams Design for Dance Project. Four dance schools took part in the project, each producing a total of five or six works of six to ten minutes in duration. Each programme received two performances, both in front of a capacity audience at The Cochrane Theatre. The Royal Ballet School, Central School of Ballet and The London Contemporary Dance School were joined by Susie Cooper and her students from The College of The Royal Academy of

Dancing. Prior to the performances and during the intervals the audience were invited to see an exhibition of pages from the sketchbooks of the young designers taking part, and a video presentation of the 1995 programme produced by The Design for Performance Research Project. A further dimension was added to the 1996 project by the creation of four pieces of dance and design for video. These works were produced in collaboration with students from the Laban Centre for Movement and Dance, Matthew Hamilton and Sue Nash from Dance Unlimited, and students of Fine Art Film and Video at Central Saint Martins College of Art and Design.

To the outsider, the main thrust of The Peter Williams Design for Dance Project would appear to culminate solely in the annual performances at The Cochrane Theatre. Although the organisers realised that the actual performances necessarily form an important focus for the students, the project has always been much more concerned with collaboration, experimentation and the exploration of ideas. As the late Sir Kenneth MacMillan, former director and principal choreographer of the Royal Ballet, said, 'Always remember that choreography is as much about ideas as it is about steps.' He then went on to say, 'And never underestimate the value of the designers' contribution; their ideas and visual sense can be vitally important.'[9]

In this unique situation, where experimentation and risk are possible and positively encouraged, the practical experience gained by student choreographers, designers, composers and dancers in realising their aims on stage cannot be underestimated. Norman Morrice once said, when referring to the performances, that some were 'exciting in their potential success, others valuable in their honourable failure',[10] reaffirming the belief that whether a piece of work is 'successful' or not in performance, has no bearing on the knowledge gained from the experience.

The role of the design tutor during this process has best been described by Peter Docherty, when talking to the students after the 1994 project, as similar to that of a lifeguard at a swimming pool. 'If you are going to sink and drown you need somebody else to come and do something about it, but only then, because you have to go through the process – and this is primarily a learning process. . . It would seem to be a great pity if one [as a design tutor] became too '"hands-on" in this exercise.'[11] The role of the tutor and technician has, therefore, been that of 'facilitator', providing a wealth of creative experience and technical knowledge that enable the young collaborators to transform their ideas into reality.

Over the years, it has become apparent that The Peter Williams Design for Dance Project, by working with a variety of dance schools in different ways, has highlighted various divergent methods of collaboration. The number and specialisations of the collaborators, the juncture at which each associate joins the production, the dynamics of the group and how the contributors actually communicate – how much is verbal, how much is visual and how much is informed by demonstration – are all areas of artistic creation that warrant further investigation. So far, over one hundred pieces of new dance with original design and choreography, and sometimes specially composed music, have been performed as part of The Peter Williams Design for Dance Project at The Cochrane Theatre, creating a bridge between disciplines which seldom meet early enough to experience the vital 'growing pain' learning period that leads to maturity.

The last words are best left to the eloquence of Norman Morrice:

> New horizons are opened when the designer learns about a dancing body and the choreographer learns about colour, light, materials and the volume of stage-space through another's eyes. Finally it is the meeting of minds that may produce the next creative surge that takes art onwards – such collaborations are an investment for the future and probably therein lies their greatest value.[12]

Designing the Space: Devising the Dance |
An Interview with Peter Docherty and Matthew Hamilton by Tim White about
George and the Dragon

Tim White: *How did you meet?*

Peter Docherty: It was in 1990 at the Dance Attic in Putney where we got to know each other, through William Louther, an American dancer/choreographer who was with Graham, Ailey, and then at The Place with London Contemporary Dance Theatre. I'd worked with Louther, bumped into him one day and he was working at Dance Attic in Putney. They had this one big studio where they did experimental dance pieces to invited audiences. Matthew was doing some things there and I started to work with him on a piece.

TW: *How far advanced was* George and the Dragon *when the two of you came together?*

Matthew Hamilton: I'd had a few thoughts. I wasn't doing *George and the Dragon,* I was doing some other idea and the composer, who was heavily into all kinds of fairy tales and mythology saw what I was doing and said what you're doing is a modern-day George and the Dragon – even the structure's the same. He brought the book in and I read it and realised it was exactly the same or at least I decided it was exactly the same. So that was as far as it had got really. I had this vague idea – well two ideas – one my own and one George and the Dragon. I had this dilemma as I'd only ever worked on my own ideas – I had never taken on board a whole story from somewhere else. So I had to throw my ideas out of the window and attach my thoughts to a piece that was already written, which was quite uncomfortable for the first time although it's fine now. That's what we had – a few thoughts and George and the Dragon.

PD: I think what you were talking about was heroic acts. Who was a hero? What was an heroic act? I can remember that.

MH: That's right – that's what the piece was going to be about and what were the consequences of someone's heroic act? They would be a hero but would anyone suffer, would there be fallout from someone's determination to pursue an heroic act? Was it for themselves and so on . . . and that's where *George and the Dragon* came in.

PD: Again, what happened with *George and the Dragon*, that seemed to have happened before, is that after a heroic act the hero is acclaimed and then destroyed, killed or mutilated. There was a thought about water that was quite early on, because I remember this drawing you showed me of this tank of water that was the length of the space.

MH: So often these ideas come up and they don't mean anything until later. You have no idea why you're spending days taking photographs of water, drawing, looking through a box watching people swim – you have no idea why you're doing it. You know it means something so you just do it.

TW: *How did you start working together on the piece?*

PD: Well we saw each other virtually daily because by then I had got a space in the same building as a studio so I was going there on a daily basis to work. We talked a lot about it. The thing that was new for me as a designer was (a) that there wasn't a score – I'd worked before without a score but it was on commissioned pieces, but generally the music had always been an important departure point for me as a designer working either on an opera or on a dance because there are very few commissioned scores – and (b) the co-operative way of working with the dancers, as I'd always worked in a

Peter Docherty Performance space at the
Dance Attic, *George and the Dragon*
Music by Marcus Beale
Choreography by Matthew Hamilton
Dance Unlimited, Dance Attic, London, 1990
Photograph by Peter Docherty

very traditional, authoritarian, autocratic way with the artistic director, the choreographer, and the dancers did not become involved in a creative way at such an early stage. That was new because it allowed a wider debate. Also new was that often with other choreographers I'd worked with they'd had almost a structured plan of action before they started, whether they stuck to it or not. You had some thoughts but not a plan – it developed on a daily basis. I was in the building, the rehearsals were taking place in the building. The water was important and what also seemed important was the idea of decay – in *George and the Dragon* the people are under siege. One of the next thoughts – and there was actually a model of this – was to convert the entire space into a swimming pool, a derelict swimming pool. There was an upper seating area and when we thought of the walls and the shape of the space we considered thinking of it as a derelict swimming pool. Then, out of that we had the idea of having some other sort of swimming pool within a swimming pool and that seemed very attractive, one of those temporary swimming pools that you assemble in the garden. The next thing we discussed was where we might put the audience and how they would get there. We decided to put the audience down either side of the space and some of them could choose to have a seat higher up which was the more conventional view. We then thought it was often very boring to go into the space and wait for it to begin so the next thing that happened was that we decided to use a small ante room to the big space in which we got the audience to mass before the performance. The audience would go into the space of the performance when we opened the door very quickly. Without having time to think, they'd have to sit down as the performance was about to begin. Then we had the problem of how to get people onto the upper level – normally you'd have a passageway or go around and up a staircase. We decided to put staircases in the space. We arrived at the situation of having a pool and these two staircases – the way it eventually looked came purely out of being created in the space but the structure of it was debated. We wanted a tower and we wanted judges, gods who controlled and watched, which led us to the higher level and so we used a tower.

MH: The tower, apart from being part of the story in terms of judges and hierarchy, also had a more subtle connotation that I really liked arising from the relationship between the tower and the swimming pool as in the Olympics. The three people sitting on it could be seen as about to be giving marks out of ten. In terms of design I liked the relationship between the tower and the swimming pool right at the other end as if some kind of event was going to happen. The wonderful thing about the audience was that when they came in, the seats were down both sides and up the staircase, and they weren't numbered and the seats downstairs were covered in white sheets which made it look like this thing had been in the room for a couple of hundred years or people had gone away for the summer and covered everything up. So for a while they didn't know where they wanted to sit so they all stood around in the space.

PD: And the performance had started and was going on around them.

MH: And they weren't concerned about getting out of the way – it was a kind of panic – 'if she's there and they're round the swimming pool where shall we sit?' You had wonderful moments where people had cottoned on that there was a swimming pool and that it got very wet and messy and I remember this one woman who came with an umbrella because they wanted to go by the pool and it looked brilliant because she put it up.

PD: A lot of those people who sat in close proximity to the dancers found that very disturbing – you could see they were disturbed and they commented that they found it so close that they could see the dancers perspire and smell their breath. For most people who'd rarely seen dance in a rehearsal situation they suddenly became very aware of the physicality of dance and a lot of people didn't like that at all.

MH: They were very concerned throughout the whole piece – when you're watching people dance flat out for sometimes up to half an hour right in front of your eyes and then they look like they're going to be ill you can see it whereas you can't from the proscenium. There was a wonderful moment with the woman in front of me when I was upstairs watching the show. One of the devices we had was that we built a snorkel in the swimming pool – the princess was drowned – she was ducked and held under for a very long time. Of course what the audience didn't realise was that she attached her mouth to a snorkel that had been built and painted with a hole drilled above the water so she could be three foot under the water and still breathe. We arranged it so that she would give a signal to the guy who pushed her down that she had found the snorkel and that she was okay and then he would remove his hand and leave the pool. She was under there for twenty minutes. After about two minutes this woman in front of me started to shuffle and said 'oh my God, this can't happen' and she started to panic. After about three minutes she got up to save the girl but I stopped her and told her about the snorkel. It was rather brilliant to see this girl just floating at the bottom of the pool.

PD: The other thing that came in quite early was that the whole thing with George as the hero is that he is this prince on a white charger who comes across the event. What was the contemporary equivalent? It became the biker on his motorbike who came across it by accident. There just so happened to be a Harley in the car park that was available as it had been abandoned. It wasn't mobile but we painted it white and used it. So these elements started to build up and then we decided we needed to put something round the swimming pool. The initial thought was that it was the podium at the Olympics when you get the medals. Number One is always slightly above Number Two and then there's Number Three. Out of that this construction went around which then suddenly suggested some form of castle architecture, another scale. Then, once it had started to be built, we started to find ways of using the space. Initially I thought it was going to be more filled in, but suddenly using it , we found people could go round and under and through it and enter up and out of it, like rats.

MH: It was like a rat run. It was brilliant, because dancers everyday would have got to this point in rehearsal trying to find out what this thing was going to be like. We were leaving it completely open – the structure would determine what they were going to do – it was

purely up to that. We never choreographed it. The dancers all went off to a fire station.

PD: Yes, that was another thing we came to. The dragon is fire – who fights fire? – firemen. We went through firemen's suits and all of that.

MH: At one point we had gas masks – which we kept – as well as the rest of the caboodle. The dancers got very excited and went off to Lambeth Fire Station where they do a training course where they put people through holes filled with smoke for two hundred metres and all sorts of things like that. They came back to rehearsals saying 'this is what we're going to do'. They had a field day – people learnt how to scurry through little holes and up and round very quickly.

PD: At one point they were going to wear firemen's uniform which we got hold of, but they found it was too restrictive. The next thing we dealt with was the idea of the princess – what was a princess and who was a princess and what would she be? How do you present a princess besieged? She was aware of her destiny yet unruffled by it; it is that extraordinary thing of knowing what is going to happen eventually. If one looks at a very barbaric world that we always had, people have always been aware of their destiny. I remember seeing on the television this extraordinary image of people in Beirut in the middle of the bombing and the mayhem, sitting around having cocktails by the swimming pool as if it wasn't happening – well that was the princess. We put her in a white swimming costume – it was simple, she could actually swim in it – and it had to be the most wonderful swimming costume. The next thing we considered was how do we do the idea of rubble, demolition, destruction? I had this wizzy idea to ring up a demolition company and order a demolished building which is basically what we did. We then had to decide how to deal with this construction and it became the idea – when we went back to the original tale of George and the Dragon, which was in the Middle East – that it was some Moorish tiling. I didn't quite know what to do, so I started to paint this back wall and it had something to do with water and the centre – I just wanted to get something on it, on the Sunday, because it was driving me mad being there unpainted. That actually remained and became quite a key point. There was a line from that which came down into the rubble and we decided to continue this line straight through the floor to the other end and then that was the link, the umbilical cord to the tower which then had started to change and develop and start to be used. It had started to become the dragon by the introduction of these poles. So then we started to paint the floor. There was never at any point any drawing or model where we could say 'this is the design for the space now let's get it executed'; it all developed with conversation backwards and forwards, backwards and forwards. Then these people, we had to think of a way of dressing them and undressing them because we had already come to the conclusion that they should end up naked — as vulnerable as possible.

TW: *Who were these people?*

PD: Well, they started off as the firemen because the firemen would fight the dragon and George would come and save them.

MH: Then they ended up as the Dragon i.e. it's the Dragon within, because the Dragon in *George and the Dragon* is within the people in the city. That's how the tower came to be the Dragon as well in visual form i.e. it's three firemen's poles. It looks like a Dragon — a huge tower with blood all around the bottom of it and on top would sit the judges, the biggest dragons of all, the hierarchy who were basically allowing this event to take place. They allow the hero to do the work — the work that they can't achieve — and when it's achieved get rid of the hero and claim it for themselves; and therefore the dragon just gets bigger i.e. it becomes a tower and their position is elevated the whole time. That's how that tower started to work really. These people became the dragon and eventually work against the princess. They look for the easiest option — kill the knight that's closest to you, the path of least resistance, which is the princess so therefore kill the princess. They became the dragon.

PD: At the beginning when they were still firemen we put them in white dungarees as petrol pump men with regular white working dungarees. And they had the gas masks and some sort of helmet, something on their heads. We then started this process of shedding

them so they would take something off. By this time the thing that they were fighting was going to become them so they should become red. They went into these red all-overs, although they weren't actually all-overs but knitted woollen cotton garments. Later on they were going to take them off and they did have some form of swimming costume at one point, or shorts or something . . .

MH: The girls had green swimming costumes and the boys had shorts. The colours again tied them into the tower — the green was the same green as that on the tower, the red was the same red so that you could always link them in.

TW: *Did you have this colour scheme at the beginning or, again, was it something that evolved?*

PD: It evolved as we went along, we were simply there painting the space as a canvas. We were making the installation, the space with the performers, with the painting, doing it. The use of the room and the space, placing of the audience, placing of the performers, evolved together so we were all doing it. Dancers were painting and we were all doing all sorts of things — we just made the space.

MH: We were constantly exploring ideas. For instance, you've got this red paint on the floor which may not have been there on the Saturday, so when the dancers come in on a Monday it's been worked on over Sunday and they, all in their red, want to be part of it. They'll say, 'if we touch the bottom of the poles that links us to the top of the tower, also to the floor, what if we then slip away along the red' — because they're all people involved in art and painting. If I just have my red arm in the red and my left hand on the blue and the princess is at the other end of the blue line, the other end of the studio, that means I've got her, so she has to jump off the blue line. It was that way of thinking the whole time from everybody. If she's sat on the blue line and I touch it and she's fifty metres away I've got her by the head or I can do this to her or do that to her and if I put my hand on the red pole. . . there's this constant working and you never know where you're going. You can't have choreographic ideas until you walk into the studio.

PD: But there was choreography and it was rehearsed. There was preparation, but the piece really evolved and was made in the space and moved in the space. Even the most major thing – which was the rubble – if it hadn't have been so simple we might have thought about it and not ended up with it because there were dilemmas with it. The fact was you could ring up and get it delivered the next day and the man on the phone said 'you can't choose what sort of building, you'll have to have whatever has been knocked down and is on the back of the lorry'. It arrived instantly. And then we brought in Rick Fisher. We'd talked to Rick and he was in and out all the time throughout the process because he was busy doing this, that and the other. Everything took place in that room over the two weeks.

TW: *Did you find it threatening to have dancers make suggestions in what previously had been your exclusive domain, or did you find the mutual give and take liberating?*

PD: I think all of that! I felt all of those things. At times I felt 'it's not really their job' but it did work and I think I had more problems on the other piece we did together [*More about Angels,* 1991] because I had a much more specific idea about that. We didn't have the luxury in the next piece of having the space for the same amount of time, of going in and out of it and doing it at the weekend or whatever. The luxury, or really the necessity of the creation was that we had the space for this much time. And we also didn't take into consideration any other sort of use – we were not going to think of it as something that might go on tour but we would do the piece of work we wanted to do in *this* space, with *these* performers, with *this* score. If it needed to go elsewhere then we would solve that when it arose but we weren't going to restrict ourselves by making something that was a packaged, tourable piece of theatre.

Peter Docherty Kyrie Hardiman as The Princess in the Pool, *George and the Dragon*
Choreography by Matthew Hamilton
Dance Unlimited, Dance Attic, London, 1990
Photograph by Dance Unlimited

On Scenography | Pamela Howard

Edgar in *King Lear* says, sadly, 'I nothing am' (II.3). Scenographers are now optimistically saying 'We Something Are.' Over the past fifty years scenography has been the common term for describing theatre design throughout Europe and particularly the Eastern European countries. A theatre designer is often understood to be someone who designs theatres. Scenography describes the visual side of theatre-making, deriving from the Greek 'scenografia' – literally the writing of the stage space, implying the integration of the designer with the director in the creation of the work on the stage. A scenographer is not doing either sets or costumes but is usually creating a total unified vision as well as initiating ideas. Today, many scenographers are questioning the traditional hierarchy of theatre structure, convinced that the visual artist and the director can come together as theatre makers. Conceivably, scenographers could suggest plays, choose directors to collaborate with; a whole project may be inspired by a new-found space. It is very important to use scenography as a more accurate way of describing the role of the visual artist in the theatre, no longer being a servant but rather a leader, a creator or an initiator and a collaborator – 'We Something Are.'

Scenography is not vision against text. In Shakespeare the text is absolutely the starting point. Scenography enables metaphors and resonances of the text to be expressed visually. Fundamentally it demands an understanding of the power of the performer and the power of the text in the space and the unification of the performer in the space with the text. Scenography is more than decorating a background or being a servant to the production. The totality of the experience does not preclude but enhances the use of text. There is a difference between text-based theatre and literary or narrative theatre, where often the theatre experience consists of two people on stage talking to each other in a room. A room can be designed, nicely or not; that's all it is. It can be a wonderful play but that's all it is. A Shakespearean text is quite different, for its demands are both linear and narrative, with many-layered lateral strands. However simple the visual solution, it has to mesh with this complex web.

Scenography is not about design swamping the play. It is about using the power of the vision to unlock the play. It is fantastically interesting to transform the theatre space so that when the spectator goes into this space they see something that possibly might be ordinary and familiar, yet it might seem that they never saw it before. If there was an actor on stage who was so beautifully lit and so perfectly placed that a spectator might say 'oh, so that's a man, well I never saw a man before', that would be a major achievement. The scenographer strives to increase and enhance the perception of the spectator. It is not necessary to be told what to do by the director or, more importantly, to play the old-fashioned game of guessing what the director has got in his or her head – and usually it was his – in the hope that enough tries and enough variations would eventually hit the mark. Scenographers are capable of reading a text in exactly the same way as directors. Scenographers work on redefining and understanding the nature of theatre, which is much more than the submersion of the text in a colour or a decoration. It considers the spectator, the space, the text and indeed the context in which the performance occurs.

This scenographic expression on the stage cannot define where direction ends and design starts; the experience of the spectator is to 'see with their eyes what they're not hearing with their ears' (Gordon Craig). The Chekhov productions of Peter Stein demonstrate the complete integration of the text with the visual world of the play so that it is impossible to know who thought of putting a tree here, a bench there, and suddenly it hardly seems to matter. If director and artist can both create towards the same end it is irrelevant who does it, although there are clearly defined areas of responsibility. The scenographer's vision and artistry are the inspiration and focus for interpretative artists/craftsmen whose métier is working with hands, working with colour, working with texture and so on. Even the most conceptual artist must lead that team of interpreters and it is essential to inspire them and carry them through, otherwise the scenographic vision will never get on the stage. In the same way a director has to be able to work with an actor and work with voice and interpretation of text. This is the director's equivalent of a scenographer working with a costume interpreter or scene painter. It is the raw material of the production. The director must know how to get the very best from that actor – how to capitalise on the actor's physical, mental and vocal potential – that is the director's work. These two strands eventually come together in the theatre production and the director and the scenographer are able to work in the stage space, 'painting pictures with people' (Caspar Neher, 1921). The director is crafting the actors to be able to come to the point of integration with the vision that is also crafting an interpretation. This leads to a fusion of these disciplines in the 'sceno-grafia', the creation/drawing/writing of the stage space.

There are directors who feel nervous about engaging with the work of designers/scenographers, often because there is not a good common vocabulary to talk about design. It is often difficult for those who work with and write about design to find the right words. Scenographers use words like 'horizontal', 'vertical', 'plane', 'dynamic', 'diagonal', 'the power of the space'. Directors talk about things like 'house', 'street', 'chair'. These important elements are described in very different ways. If there is no dialogue it becomes no more than a kind of 'shopping', the director saying 'I want...', the designer effectively saying 'would you like it delivered now?', instead of each person freely challenging the other with 'how about this?', 'couldn't we try this?', creating a combative intellectual debate about the work.

Scenography is not about doing 'backgrounds' but creating a series of images that in their totality enhance the understanding of the context of the play, the story of the play and the experience for the spectator of participating in the event. This is both very simple and fantastically complicated to achieve. Scenographers may start to create a series of images springing from work on the text, searching for a key which may not be at scene one but somewhere in the middle, or the images may start from associations of colour, or line or form that seem only to have a loose association with the text, but come to be valued as an intuitive response to the piece.

One of the reasons for the term 'scenography' becoming widely used is that it has long been established as an accurate description of the theatre design profession. Theatre design has a long-established international organisation – OISTAT – 'Organisation Internationale des Scénographiers, Techniciens et Architectes Théâtrales', whose headquarters have been in Prague since the beginning in 1948 under the auspices of UNESCO. There are now OISTAT centres in forty-two countries. OISTAT holds regular national and international meetings, with special commissions looking at Scenography, Architecture, Publications, Theory and History and, most importantly, Education. OISTAT was particularly important in facilitating meetings and exchanges of theatre professionals during times when travel between Eastern and Western Europe was not so easy. It gave British artists the opportunity to see some of the most vibrant and lively theatre in former Eastern European countries, and to bring these ideas back home. The theatre often speaks without words and, as in Poland in the 1960s and 1970s, there was the development of the allusive, surrealistic theatre – Mikiewicz, Wsypianski and other writers – and artists, such as Josef Sjáná at his theatre in Nova Huta and, later, Kantor, who from his small cellar in Kraków influenced world theatre. These were painters who used the whole expression of the context of their lives in theatre. We learned that theatre isn't just decoration, it is a really powerful force – it really matters what you do. That is the difference between 'decoration' where something was put behind actors and they did their bit in front of it, and scenography, speaking in an unspoken way to the eyes what the ears were not allowed to hear. I think that distinction is seminal in my own work.

I come from a pretty mixed background and so the concept of Europe and other countries has always been in my life. After I was a student at The Slade, I created an opportunity for myself to go to France. I worked at the Théâtre Nationale Populaire, where Roger Planchon was the Director, as a *stagière*, which is a learning placement, and continued an association over a period of ten years. Being at the TNP taught me nearly everything I know. I was able to travel a lot from there and discovered that there was a great fraternity of theatre people – Strehler, Stein, Planchon, Chéreau – an area in which I was rather junior but nevertheless involved. At the same time I started to volunteer my services with the International Theatre Institute and then OISTAT. I had the opportunity, as a result of one of the very first travel bursaries from the Arts Council of Great Britain, to go to Poland to do a survey on children's theatre. This was the early Sixties and the first time that I had been in an East European country. It was also the first time I realised that I could say 'I am a scenographer' and actually be led to the front of a queue! Being a scenographer had status! Cultural exchange became so much part of my life, and still is, which is why it is logical that I am working on the MA Scenography project because I am able to use a lifetime of contacts. I'm happy that the London Centre at Central Saint Martins College of Art and Design is a place where everybody comes. You can be here for a week and meet people from all over the world in this room.

On Scenofest

I think that making theatre is a celebration. Being so underpaid and overworked, if one can't have a bit of fun with it there's no point in doing it. Scenofest is an annual festival of scenography, normally held in a different centre each year. Scenofest becomes a verb – 'where are you scenofesting next year?' people will ask one another – and is a celebration. I am the Artistic Director of an international course where young scenographers give up a year of their professional lives and come to join in this search for what scenography is all about. We create this international forum of scenography and take a week when absolutely everybody comes together and looks at what is going on in the world, what we do ourselves and also things that we don't know. Scenofest is an opportunity for whoever is organising it to bring to the notice of young professionals and practising people in whatever country it is held the importance of scenographers, and I think this is vital. I started by paraphrasing Shakespeare – 'We Something Are' – and this is a lot to do with Scenofest, to do with saying 'we are scenographers' and we can organise arts festivals and there are enough interesting things going on to have a programme for a week and more. The theme of Scenofest '96 is the *mise en scène* and we've called it 'The Re-presentation of Drama'. In particular, we are looking at how we re-present drama in our times. The Scenofest '96 lecture, entitled 'Visualising Shakespeare', will be given by Professor Dennis Kennedy from Trinity College, Dublin, who has just written a wonderful book on this subject. He is going to be talking about multiculturalism in Shakespeare and showing slides of the work of Ninagawa, Mnouchkine, Brook, Stein, Zadek and so on and generally giving an overview of visualising Shakespeare in a multicultural sense over the past fifty years with particular emphasis on contemporary work. Professor Kennedy's lecture symbolises in a sense what Scenofest is all about.

Pamela Howard *War Music*
Music by Gary Kettle
Choreography by William Louther
Directed by Toby Robertson
Text by Christopher Logue, based on Homer's
The Iliad
Old Vic, London, 1977
The artist

War Music was born of a collaboration between Christopher Logue, the poet and writer, Toby Robertson, who was at the time the director of Prospect Theatre, the choreographer William Louther, and myself. Timothy West was the narrator. The text was Christopher Logue's rewriting of Homer's *Iliad* as a sort of poetic dance/drama. Toby, to his eternal credit, got together this team and included an extraordinary rock musician called Gary Kettle who was a percussionist and had a rock band.

We were all put together and when Toby suddenly had to go away we were left to fight it out. I think I became a prime mover in it because someone had to make sense of this thing we had been contracted to do at the Old Vic and then on tour. Bill Louther and myself started to work out how it could be done. I had the idea of Gary Kettle not just being a musician but representing the gods and having him on stage. He was in a scaffolding cradle that hung permanently right at the top of the stage. This caused the governors of the Old Vic at the time enormous grief as all the people sitting in the gods paying £1 a seat got the best view. They considered this to be undemocratic as those paying £15 in the stalls didn't get as good a view! When Toby did come back the piece was fairly developed and ready for the last rehearsals. That was really my first experience of working collaboratively with a writer, a choreographer, and performers, because we had them there and that

was what we had to work with. I worked very closely with Bill. He did a lot of workshops and I was in there all the time, drawing what he was getting the performers to do and then building ideas for the scenes around what was happening in those workshops in the Old Vic rehearsal room day after day after day. I was trying to take little bits of the text and work out how you would build the Trojan Wall just with people and so on. Most of the actors were only partially covered by a shield and helmet, which helped the budget quite a lot! It wasn't a narrative story, but small moments – 'Achilles puts on his armour', 'the death of Patroclus', etc. Christopher Logue's text is a poem – he has a wonderfully sharp way of using words – and Gary Kettle's percussive sounds reflected the abrasive quality of the text. (Pamela Howard talking to Tim White, 17 April 1996)

The Director/Designer | An Interview with Philip Prowse by Tim White

Philip Prowse Costumes for
Carmina Burana
Music by Carl Orff
Choreography by David Bintley
Birmingham Royal Ballet,
Birmingham Hippodrome, 1995
The artist

Tim White: *You frequently combine the role of director and designer. How did this come about?*

Philip Prowse: It was in 1972 and I was already working at the Citizens Theatre as the designer there. Because I was part of the management as well, I was able to turn round and say 'I'm going to have a go at directing' – a hideous misuse of power – so I did a production of *The Relapse* by Vanbrugh, which was too ambitious. That rather put me off and I didn't do it again for another year. I directed and designed together about once a year after that and each time I'd think I'd never do it again but ended up having another go and gradually I was a director. Now I think of myself as a director – that was over twenty years ago and somehow I've made that transition. I like the idea of designers becoming directors and my managerial work now at Glasgow is very much to encourage people to do that. The problem for me is that it is difficult to understand the actor's problems. In a way, designers can have a rather insensitive attitude to actors which can be salutary for them. On the other hand, if you take that too far, you lose sympathy with them and you don't understand their fears, which are genuine. Antony McDonald has been up twice to do productions as a director at the Citizens and he's been largely sympathetic with the actors but it's by no means a general rule and needs to be addressed time and time again.

TW: *Given that you exercise control over both the performance and the design, have you been tempted to extend this control further by devising work?*

PP: Not really – only insofar as doing an adaptation of *Anna Karenina*, but that's already a novel. I'm more interested in taking these things that interest me and conveying that interest.

TW: *So you're taking ideas in your head and finding something to challenge or confront them?*

PP: Yes. Suppose you're going to do *Hamlet*; there are these words, these hieroglyphs meaning these sounds which add to up to words that therefore express ideas. What world will these people inhabit to express these ideas, to allow this narrative to go forward? Somewhere there are some connections that I make. What they are, how they come, how they are remembered and how they come out in reality – that's the whole process. I'm not supposing that one is going to invent a whole new world order in order to express this play – I'm going to find something that has already existed and therefore I already know about, though it may be a lot of fractured things all brought together. I think a lot of young designers are very concerned to be original which is really rather a waste of time because they won't be. What can be original is their approach to the existing cultural world – what they extrapolate and what they put together. Their mixture will be extremely original if they allow it to be, but sitting down and thinking that they must make something new is a waste of time.

TW: *Are you aware of yourself carrying out two distinct activities?*

PP: When I was doing *Carmina Burana* for David Bintley it was a long time since I had designed anything for someone I didn't really know and of course he's much younger than me so that was quite alarming. I felt very much on my mettle.

TW: *When you go back to designing now do you feel that you're not giving your all to the work?*

PP: Well, that's the great danger and I only really do it for the ballet now, because that's the one area where my role is absolutely defined – I couldn't choreograph a ballet. My role is to support the choreographer's vision and I can do that but I can't really design

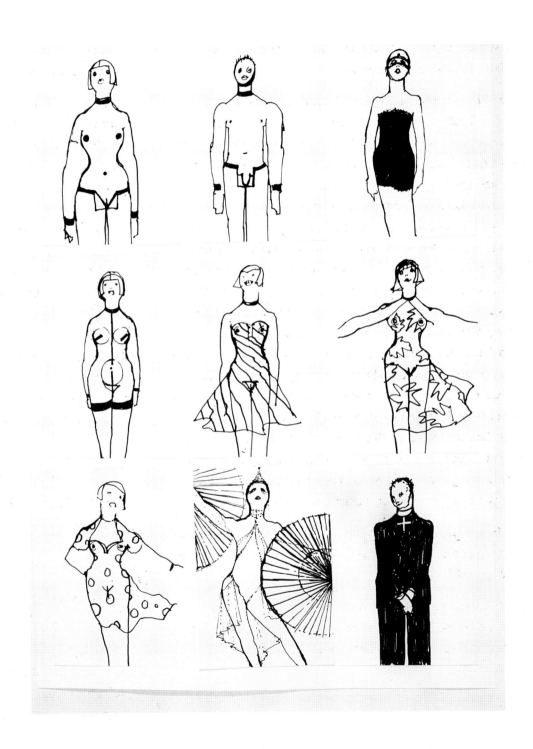

Philip Prowse Costumes for *Carmina Burana*
Music by Carl Orff
Choreography by David Bintley
Birmingham Royal Ballet,
Birmingham Hippodrome, 1995
The artist

opera for other people because all the time I'm thinking 'why don't they get a move on – the solution to this is this' but my solutions are no use to them so it's rather shut me off from designing opera and theatre. There's a marvellous sense of holiday with dance – you do the designs and you try and make it look lovely and then you watch this poor soul wrestling with the technical problems, with the cast and all the rest of it and you can put your feet up in the stalls.

TW: *Do you feel, with hindsight, that you were held back through being a designer and not directing?*

PP: Absolutely – that's why I became a director. It's very liberating if it works for you – a lot of people adore being a designer. I always seem to be a person saying 'don't be a designer, be a director', but I'm not saying that at all. If what you're good at is being a designer then that is what you must be. A good designer is a marvellous thing and a good director needs a good designer.

TW: *Do you think design has a more elevated place in your productions than it might have in those where the designer traditionally is seen as assisting the director?*

PP: The most important thing is the confrontation of the actors, the text – and by that I mean whatever that is, be it opera or narrative – and the audience, within this space that everyone inhabits together. That is the nature of theatre and that is what is important. Design either helps or hinders that; sometimes it helps in the most inspired way, sometimes it hinders in the most hideous and clumsy way and sometimes it's just sort of there. Really, one has to say that if the basic work is working then design isn't really very important. I think that any serious production should be able to do without design. If I've been in rehearsals for about four weeks and the production is about to move onto the stage, I really like to feel that if the theatre burnt down or the costumes or scenery got lost that the show as it is in the rehearsal room on the last run-through could actually be performed. Of course, the people who knew what it was going to look like would miss something but the people who actually saw it would still have an absolutely viable exposition of that piece.

TW: *So, rather like a wedding at which the marquee blows down, the ceremony still goes ahead.*

PP: Yes. The ceremony still means the same.

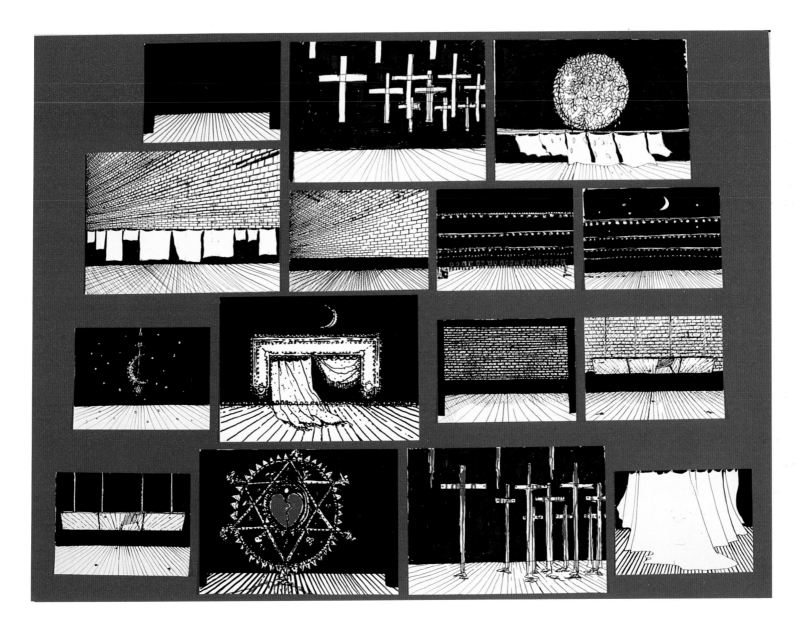

Philip Prowse Storyboard for *Carmina Burana*
Music by Carl Orff
Choreography by David Bintley
Birmingham Royal Ballet,
Birmingham Hippodrome, 1995
The artist

I was telling the story of these three young men leaving a religious order and discovering the outside world. It was like a night journey through a city or from a church in the country through into a city and this city becoming more and more degraded. You ended up in a kind of tarts' area like King's Cross or somewhere like that. Then it moved into a metaphysical/ astrological/spiritual area. The whole thing was to do with the search for love. It ended up in a religious area without ever having achieved an emotional resolution. It is episodic but it's linked by these three young men. It went from a bare stage to a rather pure church to the country then a street with washing out, then a street by itself that turned into a dancehall and then back into a moonlit street. The moon then turned into a nightclub symbol and we go into a café-theatre-nightclub. We go back onto the street which by now is very dingy and a brothel mirror comes in and we see these decayed tarts. From here fortune takes over and a court of love and then back into a church where the pure white has become blood-red. Peter Mumford did the lighting beautifully so you add to this a terrific geometric play of light that describes the space all the time. (Philip Prowse talking to Tim White, 2 May 1996)

II

DESIGNING THE NARRATIVE

David Walker Dame Ninette de Valois with Merle Park and
David Wall photographed on the set of *The Sleeping Beauty*
Music by Pyotr Tchaikovsky
Production by Ninette de Valois after Marius Petipa
Royal Ballet, Royal Opera House, London, 1977
Photograph by Leslie E. Spatt

Nicholas Georgiadis Set model for Act II,
The Sleeping Beauty
Music by Pyotr Tchaikovsky
Choreography and production by
Sir Kenneth MacMillan after Marius Petipa
American Ballet Theatre,
Auditorium Theatre, Chicago, 1987

Nicholas Georgiadis Costume design for Garland
Dancer, Act I, *The Sleeping Beauty*
Music by Pyotr Tchaikovsky
Choreography and production by Rudolf Nureyev after
Marius Petipa
La Scala Ballet, La Scala, Milan, 1966
The artist

Nicholas Georgiadis Costume designs for
Nurse and King, *The Sleeping Beauty*
Music by Pyotr Tchaikovsky
Choreography and production by Sir
Kenneth MacMillan after Marius Petipa
American Ballet Theatre,
Auditorium Theatre, Chicago 1987
The artist

The Challenge of Designing the Tchaikovsky Ballets | Nicholas Georgiadis

It is not the Tchaikovsky ballets that present a problem – the problem is ours. For some reasons that would require a few essays on the history of taste, the visual presentation of nineteenth-century works has become, for the twentieth century, the equivalent of kitsch: it is a situation that cannot be ignored. Various solutions have been proposed, the easiest of which is to attempt a pastiche of nineteenth-century designs, unsatisfactory in the way that every pastiche is unsatisfactory. Another solution is to find a contemporary equivalent of the nineteenth-century design that is at ease with both the supernatural and courtly grandeur; one does this at one's peril. *There is a great danger of creating a contemporary sort of kitsch.* The third option is to ignore the orthography that informs nineteenth-century music and narrative and do something outside of its parameters, such as putting *Giselle* in an insane asylum.

The orthography contains within itself the inevitability of the tutu, because the choreography was conceived for the tutu and this imposes a nineteenth-century view of the works; the tutu was invented to show off the legs and yet at the same time maintain sufficient distance between the ballerina and her partner so as not to suggest impropriety. If one wants to innovate one has to start by thinking of how to replace the tutu. The orthography again requires that one should not dodge the transformations that are to be found throughout the ballets. Part of the designer's responsibility is to find ways of smoothly achieving these transformations, a task simple in theory yet difficult in practice. In the nineteenth century these transformations were done with painted cloths and with 'panoramas'. Even if we possessed the skills and techniques necessary to reproduce these effects, it would be difficult to make the public accept them, and so one has to find other ways. There is also the other difficulty of the new lighting methods – it is evident that to create the illusions that the *trompe l'œil* provides one needs to under-light and that I am afraid is not possible these days when everything tends to be over-lit.

A further challenge to the designer of these ballets is that one has to establish a period. When the main characters that one sees more than anyone else – the ballerina and her partner – have to wear a minimal costume of tutu and tights it is very difficult to make it clear that we are in seventeenth-century France, or eighteenth-century Germany, or medieval Europe. One has to create for the peripheral figures, and by peripheral figures I mean those who don't do much dancing, but are static for much of the time – one has to create costumes that evoke a period, if that is one's intention. If this can be achieved then the transition from the world one has evoked to the tutu and the tights is not shocking to the eye and the mind.

The Sleeping Beauty

Barry Kay Act III, *The Sleeping Beauty*
Music by Pyotr Tchaikovsky
Choreography and production by Kenneth
MacMillan after Marius Petipa
West Berlin State Opera Ballet, 1967
Charles Spencer

Peter Farmer Antoinette Sibley and Anthony Dowell in 'The
Awakening', Act II, *The Sleeping Beauty*
Music by Pyotr Tchaikovsky
Choreography and production by Kenneth MacMillan
The Royal Ballet, Royal Opera House, London, 1973
Photograph by Anthony Crickmay
The Theatre Museum, V&A

· ALHAMBRA ·

The cover of the programme for Diaghilev's production of *The Sleeping Princess* (*The Sleeping Beauty*) at the Alhambra Theatre, 1921. Costume design by Léon Bakst.

Oliver Messel Act III, *The Sleeping Beauty*
Music by Pyotr Tchaikovsky
Choreography by Frederick Ashton and Ninette de
Valois after Marius Petipa
Produced by Konstantin Sergeyev (revised 1952)
Sadler's Wells Ballet, Royal Opera House, London, 1946
By kind permission of Lord Snowdon
The Theatre Museum, V&A

Setting for a *Beauty*: Peter Docherty Discusses His Designs | Sue Merrett

The Dancing Times, Vol.LXXXIV, No.997, October 1993, pp.45, 47.

This extract was published just prior to the première of The Sleeping Beauty *by English National Ballet in Southampton.*

By the time that contracts were drawn up it was September 1992, which left Docherty less than six months to deliver his designs in the following January. On reflection, Docherty felt that his work on *The Sleeping Beauty* began nearly thirty years ago, at around the time that he was studying first at the Central School of Art and Design (where he now teaches), then at the Slade School of Fine Art.

'I was sixteen when I had my first job in the theatre at the Aldwych as a dresser, before being sent to Covent Garden, for my first time of seeing ballet: *La Fille Mal Gardée*. My second was *Beauty*.' In 'his' dressing room he had charge of Ronald Hynd as the Prince, Leslie Edwards as Catalabutte, Ray Powell as Carabosse, and Brian Shaw as the Bluebird. He worked at Covent Garden for the next six years, during the period of Maria Callas's performances as Tosca, the première of MacMillan's *Romeo and Juliet*, and a particular memory – 'One afternoon I was called in to go to Drury Lane for a new young dancer – and that was Rudolf Nureyev.' It was truly an amazing time which included the early visits by the Bolshoi and Kirov companies. As far as *Beauty* was concerned, the first production he saw was the one designed by Oliver Messel for the Royal Ballet; later he worked with Nicholas Georgiadis on two other *Beauties*, and talked with Ronald Hynd about a projected production for Munich.

When the ENB production was mooted, Docherty was in the curious position of it being only the third time of designing for an extant dance work; all the others had been creations even if it had been a reworking of a classic, as in Hynd's *Nutcracker*.

'I started by doing a load of storyboards – how people came on stage, where people were on the stage, just kept going through it, just finding out how the pattern went, the shape, what was needed; and listening to the music. The conception came from that. And I began to think more and more that the clothes were very important. So we started thinking almost in reverse to the usual way. The first priority is light, and it's usually the last we think about; also how the space is used. We are very fortunate to have Paul Pyant to light this, because it is a very important element and he has knowledge from a wide range of theatre work. I don't think he's done a classic before, although he has worked for dance – with Northern Ballet Theatre in particular.'

From his storyboards he had a structure to work to which proved both helpful, and a limit, because he suddenly realised that he had to respect the symmetry, an all-important element with Petipa.

'I always felt the forest was terribly important – dramatically. And the other thing I came back to, and accepted, was that it is a fairy tale. Also, ENB is a national company and scenically it should work everywhere, in all its venues, starting with the Royal Festival Hall which is different from Manchester, which is different from Leeds, etc., etc. We took the limitations of the Festival Hall and used them by not relying on flown scenery or major scene changes, that way we arrived at a composite set, the elements of which can be rearranged.'

One of the other things which became clear was the story-telling aspect of the work. In the Prologue both Hynd and Docherty were anxious that the baby, the young Aurora, was seen and that none of the action should become obscured. 'When the Prologue fairies come on you end up with nineteen or twenty people dancing, taking up the central space, with the Court surrounding. I thought about Balanchine, his lack of scenery, so I thought about a cyclorama background, then arrived at a solution – a series of skies, where all the big dance areas have interest at the sides and above. In the Prologue it's a rather turbulent area – it's a strange act, the Prologue. In Act I there is open blue sky, a summer sky, with a few clouds. Act II is in autumn. In Act III the sky is like a White Night in St Petersburg.

'We also had to make clear the two periods, moving to a hundred years later. Eventually we came to wanting to keep them in the seventeenth and eighteenth centuries, but made it the latter half of seventeenth to the early part of the eighteenth century, which meant that immediately you had a very strong silhouette change. We don't have to be pedantic about dates, likewise about period space, whether it's France, but somehow for me, through the music, there is that element of Russia.'

Colour tones were another important element. 'In the Prologue and Act III there is this Court ensemble, basically walking, promenading, standing, sitting. They become part of the set in colour, texture and tone. So in the seventeenth-century Prologue there is encrusted blue, green and gold, in the eighteenth-century Act III there is light, marble, pale blue with some gold. The Court takes on elements of that too. For the Hunt, though, by the time you have all those dukes, duchesses, etc., in a sense they are the set for that, and the sheer change of colour, texture, tone and shape moving into that century should hold that.'

Another theme was the idea of the rotating seasons. 'The Prologue must be spring or early summer, because Aurora's sixteenth birthday is in the summer, with roses. The Fairies are all an element of nature, coming out of the forest. There are seven including the Lilac Fairy, who brings Wisdom. They ought to be drained of blood, an other-worldly look, possibly even with pale make-up, so there is a lot of silver. The cavaliers and attendants are costumed similarly, looking alike. I didn't want to overdress them, that would clutter the space. I was concerned about clarity, to see the steps, to see the dancing, see the mime, it is crucial to restore that balance. Too often the mime has been

stripped away, but the ballet's balanced so carefully: aria – recitative, so it should be: dance – mime story.

'Carabosse is one of the most fascinating creatures. She is not a witch, she is a wicked old fairy who is on her own, no entourage. The *bosse* must mean humpbacked, twisted, deformed, so I've used that. It means she is turning out to be a combination of a humpbacked beetle and a decaying old rose. I had an interesting conversation with Monica Mason, and she said that there was no moment that Carabosse was not evil, gives in, or softens at all. That is one of the costumes which will have a lead from rehearsal and will develop accordingly. Carabosse flies in and out, and while in the air I felt I wanted the costume to behave differently from when it is on earth, and that's where the rose comes in. A sad tutu – a sad, wet rose; but when flying I hope it will be something strange and hovering.

'Catalabutte is going to lose his hair, a subtle moment. He is very important, in charge of the proceedings of three acts. When Carabosse pulls out the hair, I want patches left behind, so it doesn't become a bald pate – musically it's structured in there. But we're also putting in at the Awakening the touch that the hair has regrown during the enchanted period, and there is a little bit of mime between him and the Queen.

'Act I – there is always a sense of outside/inside with my sets. In this act roses abound, in the garlands, on the arches, up the columns. . . The Christening is a formal occasion, as is Act III, Act I is much more relaxed.

'The King and Queen are not ancient. ENB is a company without older members and therefore it makes more sense to have the characters younger.

'The four princes have become Dukes, four foreign princes in the twentieth century lose their exoticism. These four are a setting for the jewel of Aurora. In the mock Rose Adage in *Rosalinda* [a 1979 work by Hynd, designed by Docherty, based on *Die Fledermaus*], the four men in tails with Rosalinda worked terribly well. So we decided on four Dukes from four corners of France, with vague individual characters, but their colour range is quite similar, and they become a sort of background to

Peter Docherty Act III on stage, *The Sleeping Beauty*
Music by Pyotr Tchaikovsky
Choreography and production by Ronald Hynd after
Marius Petipa
Lighting by Paul Pyant
English National Ballet, Mayflower Theatre,
Southampton, 1993
Photograph by Bill Cooper

Peter Docherty Set model
for Act III, *The Sleeping
Beauty*
Music by Pyotr Tchaikovsky
Choreography and
production by Ronald Hynd
after Marius Petipa
Lighting by Paul Pyant
English National Ballet,
Mayflower Theatre,
Southampton, 1993
The artist

Peter Docherty
Costume for Court Lady, *The Sleeping Beauty*
Music by Pyotr Tchaikovsky
Choreography and production by Ronald Hynd
after Marius Petipa
Lighting by Paul Pyant
English National Ballet, Mayflower Theatre,
Southampton, 1993
The Theatre Museum, V&A

Peter Docherty 'The Spell', Act I, *The Sleeping Beauty*
Music by Pyotr Tchaikovsky
Choreography and production by Ronald Hynd
after Marius Petipa
Lighting by Paul Pyant
English National Ballet, Mayflower Theatre,
Southampton, 1993
Photograph by Bill Cooper

Aurora. A pink tutu? Yes. Why change it? I feel that dance does have to move, to be kept alive, but in this case we are keeping very much to the Petipa tradition and structure as we know it.

'We thought the Dukes should bring gifts to Aurora, but one presents a single rose, which is taken – the other gifts are acknowledged but the rose is taken – so immediately the other three go and pluck a rose and so – into the Rose Adage.

'In the meantime, Carabosse has become part of a group of old women with a spinning wheel (there is a section of music with the treadle in it). Carabosse presents the spindle, and then reveals herself. There is the confrontation, during which one of the Dukes attacks her with his sword, and is killed, sword in hand. The Lilac Fairy signals for Aurora to be taken away and placed behind the sky cloth, a gauze, through which she can be seen. The spell begins. As the Lilac Fairy attendants start to fly up the roses grow up the columns, the existing foliage, which has been there all the time, waiting, begins to descend, and we see through to the sky, the sleeping Aurora, as more foliage comes in, another gauze drops in, and the Lilac Fairy is left within the forest.

'The Hunt begins with the peasants, and there is enough music to set this image of change. We are within the relic of the castle, elements of it are still there, and it is autumn. In comes the entourage, and I've tried to make the Countess rather steely, after all the Prince rejects her. Why? He is a romantic. Again, the Tutor is not old. He is a middle-aged intellectual not a buffoon. The entourage goes, and the Lilac Fairy appears. Aurora will be in quite a different costume, not the one from Act I, because being with all those nymphs . . . well, after all, she is a vision. We talked a lot about the Prince. We wanted a regular man, in regular costume. There is something rather sexy having a man fully dressed with a girl in a tutu; if he is in flowing shirt and tights he becomes a ballet dancer, not a character.

'The Lilac Fairy takes the Prince's hand and they both fly away. We talked endlessly about boats, but fairies can defy gravity, and for her, the fragile fairy, to be able to take this human and fly is rather wonderful. Then, interval.

'At the start of our Act III I've pushed a bit further in time, fairy time, magical space. Snow is falling through the foliage, it is winter. The Lilac Fairy and Prince fly through. The actual panorama is that wonderful music and light. We toyed with all sorts of things. but this is a touring show. People's expectations in the theatre have leapt enormously. *Cats, Phantom of the Opera* – when they tour they are virtually a built-in show, not like us arriving Sunday, opening Monday. Do we want to complicate things with technicalities? So we thought, that score is wonderful, do we want more?

'The by-now skeleton of the Duke with his sword is there, in the sleeping castle, and the Prince takes the sword to kill Carabosse, before climbing up to Aurora. The kiss, and the snow turns to rose petals.

'The entr'acte is a time of preparation, getting the palace back to normal, people with brooms and things, and then the lighting of the chandeliers, which fly up and we go into Act III. The Court arrives and it's into the *divertissements*. We have reduced the number of these, or it's nearly an hour before we get Aurora and the Prince back. We thought we would have them bring wedding gifts: gold and silver for the Gold and Silver *pas de trois*; jet for Puss in Boots and pearls for the White Cat, rubies for Red Riding Hood and emeralds for the Wolf; sapphires for the Bluebird *pas de deux*; and at the end, Aurora and the Prince are the diamonds. It gives it a flow, rather than a series of unconnected *divertissement*s, which makes it so broken up. We see them as members of the Court dressed up, but they are dancers, so it's tutus and tights, and full masks where applicable. And at the end – an apotheosis of fairies.

'Scenically the main emphasis is this huge sky, the inside/outside element will be even more confused now. There will be an emphasis on this marbled effect, great swags of curtains with marbling, echoed in the court costumes too. A sense of period, but a sense of clarity for the dancing.'

Peter Docherty 'The Land of Snow', *The Nutcracker*
Music by Pyotr Tchaikovsky
Choreography by Ronald Hynd, based on the
original ballet by Marius Petipa
London Festival Ballet, Empire Theatre, Liverpool,
1976
Clarissa Dixon-Wright

Philip Prowse 'The Battle', *The Nutcracker*
Music by Pyotr Tchaikovsky
Choreography by Peter Darrell
Scottish Theatre Ballet, 1973
Scottish Ballet

'Darrell first of all wanted to do [*The Nutcracker*] as a one-act ballet and the idea was that one or two years later we would do the whole thing. The first set was scrapped because we were going to open it in York, and the theatre was much too small. I'd designed these massive polystyrene balls like smarties, only they were round. The fireman said we couldn't use them because they were polystyrene. The costumes looked quite pretty – I remember Darrell saying he wanted them all to look like Roses chocolates and they did. Two years later, by which time we had sorted out the fire risk, we did the whole thing in Edinburgh, which was much loved. Peter had some very interesting ideas; Drosselmeyer was a magician with 'entertainers' who arrived to entertain this children's party – I'm not sure they looked too suitable to entertain children. The Snow Queen and the Sugar Plum Fairy became part of Clara's dream at the party. The whole thing was extremely nineteenth-century. It was quite conventional and it had to tour so it was all done on flat cloths with one or two pieces of furniture.' (Philip Prowse talking to Tim White, 2 May 1996)

Nicholas Georgiadis *The Nutcracker*
Music by Pyotr Tchaikovsky
Choreography and production by Rudolf Nureyev
Paris Opéra Ballet, Palais Garnier, Paris, 1986
The artist

Nicholas Georgiadis Stage rehearsal,
'The Land of Snow', *The Nutcracker*
Music by Pyotr Tchaikovsky
Choreography and production by Rudolf Nureyev
Paris Opéra Ballet, Palais Garnier, Paris, 1986
The artist

Nicholas Georgiadis Set model for the Prologue,
The Nutcracker
Music by Pyotr Tchaikovsky
Choreography and production by Rudolf Nureyev
Paris Opéra Ballet, Palais Garnier, Paris, 1986
The artist

John Macfarlane 'The Land of Sweets',
The Nutcracker
Music by Pyotr Tchaikovsky
Choreography by Peter Wright, Lev Ivanov, Vincent Redmon
Birmingham Royal Ballet, Birmingham Hippodrome, 1990
The artist

Yolanda Sonnabend Costumes for the Rats,
The Nutcracker and the Hard Nut
Music by Pyotr Tchaikovsky/Duke Ellington
Choreography by Pilobolus
Ballet du Rhin, Strasbourg, 1993
The artist

Because I'd done *Cinderella* for Lindsay Kemp I met
his agent who also represented Pilobolus and he
arranged a meeting between us. They asked me about
doing *The Nutcracker* and I decided that I wanted
Peter Farley to do it with me, because it was quite
elaborate. Alison Chase of Pilobolus gave us the brief
which was a rich 1930s penthouse Chicago setting
and so the mice were rats. There was a wonderful
bungee dance, with the snowflakes on bungee ropes.
The second half was Duke Ellington's jazz
Nutcracker. The production was full of wonderful
things and we went back to the original story with
lots of magic. It was full of the right sort of
fancifulness, with Tchaikovsky merging into
Ellington in a surreal way.
(Yolanda Sonnabend talking to Tim White,
7 May 1996)

Yolanda Sonnabend Study for Rothbart's Attendants,
Act II, *Swan Lake*
Music by Pyotr Tchaikovsky
Choreography by Marius Petipa and Lev Ivanov with
additional choreography by David Bintley
Produced by Anthony Dowell
The Royal Ballet, Royal Opera House, London, 1986
The artist

Swan Lake

Designing *Swan Lake*
Yolanda Sonnabend

I did *Swan Lake* in the period of Tchaikovsky – Philip Prowse had already done a Gothic/Victorian version – and I felt the piece was very much of its time. Tchaikovsky was a manic-depressive and committed suicide soon after writing the score, so in my mind it is a frantic ballet which accelerates towards suicide. He's in love with death and with poetry, doesn't really care about women and he's gay – you can do it in all sorts of ways, but it had to be a vehicle for the dancers. At the time of Tchaikovsky there was a thing about women as sphinxes and women as birds, captured by people like Klopft, Gilbert and Fabergé. I looked at anything to do with birds and feathers. There was a feather motif all around. Once I'd latched on to that, what you might call a concept, I developed them into constructed or sculpted feathers so that the stage was surrounded by a sculpted feather. I made all the people in the ballroom like bird people because it seemed very much in keeping with this idea. The back of Rothbart was very much based on Klopft's *The Sister*. The two headdresses of the ladies in waiting are absolutely based on Moreau, but overall it was a mixture, there wasn't one source. Tchaikovsky would probably have seen these works and I thought it a perfectly reasonable approach. I noticed that the shapes of women at the time were like swans so the set could have been a hallucinatory image of his mother. There might have been a childhood breakdown and in the gates was an owl embedded in the iron with red eyes, behind which was a swan garden. I wanted to keep these emblems going through it. I didn't think of Gustav Moreau but when I looked at the designs afterwards I realised that was in there. I'm not a great fan of his work but it is rather extraordinary in its way, with those great black cliffs. I did my 'swanscape' with these as side pieces.

I didn't want to do a dull version, not in my terms. Anthony [Dowell] wanted a party and it was his idea to do Act III in fancy dress. I'd never done a tutu before and so I did every possible kind of tutu – I could come to certain things in a fresh way. The swans were my little bit of revolution which no one could deflect me from. They were always going to wear plate tutus and I gave them what's called the 'Maryinsky drop' and they were again like swans. I felt quite close to the piece in a way – I never thought for one minute I wasn't the right person to do it, but one does it at one's peril. You can never really succeed with these masterpieces because you can't do them 'as was', you've got to bring something into it and it's also got to be an evening of entertainment that is dramatic. Things like the dwarves were not my invention but were there in the original production. I wanted to flood the stage but wasn't able to, but they did then – they went in for the most unbelievable theatrical pyrotechnics.

Leslie Hurry Act I, Huntsmen, *Swan Lake*
Music by Pyotr Tchaikovsky
Produced by Konstantin Sergeyev, after Marius Petipa
Sadler's Wells Ballet, New Theatre, London, 1943
(revised 1946)
The Royal Ballet Benevolent Fund

Leslie Hurry Set for Act I, *Swan Lake*
Music by Pyotr Tchaikovsky
Produced by Konstantin Sergeyev, after Marius Petipa
Sadler's Wells Ballet, New Theatre, London, 1943
(revised 1946)
The Royal Ballet Benevolent Fund

Leslie Hurry Act II, Odette, *Swan Lake*
Music by Pyotr Tchaikovsky
Produced by Konstantin Sergeyev,
after Marius Petipa
Sadler's Wells Ballet, New Theatre, London, 1943
(revised 1946)
The Royal Ballet Benevolent Fund

below left:
Leslie Hurry Set for Act III, *Swan Lake*
Music by Pyotr Tchaikovsky
Produced by Konstantin Sergeyev,
after Marius Petipa
Sadler's Wells Ballet, New Theatre, London, 1943
(revised 1946)

below right:
Leslie Hurry Act III, Odile, *Swan Lake*
Music by Pyotr Tchaikovsky
Produced by Konstantin Sergeyev, after Marius Petipa
Sadler's Wells Ballet, New Theatre, London, 1943
(revised 1946)
The Royal Ballet Benevolent Fund

Leslie Hurry Set for Act IV, *Swan Lake*
Music by Pyotr Tchaikovsky
Produced by Konstantin Sergeyev,
after Marius Petipa
Sadler's Wells Ballet, New Theatre, London, 1943
(revised 1946)
The Royal Ballet Benevolent Fund

Carl Toms Costume for Russian Dancer, *Swan Lake*
Music by Pyotr Tchaikovsky
Produced by John Field after Marius Petipa
London Festival Ballet, Coliseum, London 1982
English National Ballet

Nicholas Georgiadis Set model for Act I, *Swan Lake*
Music by Pyotr Tchaikovsky
Choreography and production by Kenneth
MacMillan after Marius Petipa and Lev Ivanov
West Berlin State Opera Ballet, 1969
The artist

Lez Brotherston Costume for the Black Swan, *Swan Lake*
Music by Pyotr Tchaikovsky
Choreography by Dennis Wayne
Northern Ballet Theatre, Grand Theatre, Leeds, 1992
The artist

Lez Brotherston Adam Cooper as the Swan, *Swan Lake*
Music by Pyotr Tchaikovsky
Choreography by Matthew Bourne
Lighting design by Rick Fisher
Adventures in Motion Pictures, Sadler's Wells, 1995
Photograph by Hugo Glendinning

Lighting Swan Lake | An Interview with Rick Fisher by Tim White

Tim White: *You've recently lit* Swan Lake *for Adventures in Motion Pictures. Could you tell me how you approached the work?*

Rick Fisher: *Swan Lake* was created by a young choreographer called Matthew Bourne who has done a lot of work in the theatre, a lot of theatrical dance. He has just done *Oliver!* in the West End. They're putting *Swan Lake* into the West End now and it's interesting that it's a real crossover piece. A lot of people who are interested in dance seem able to accept it but it particularly gets people who don't go to ballet very much at all. The storytelling is very good – they've re-jigged the story along the classical lines but differently. All the swans are men but they're not trying to be women, they're just male swans. It still comes out as being very erotic and full of exciting love, without necessarily being just homoerotic, I think. I'm really proud of the piece and think he's done a very good job. I just approached it like a play, with a little more side light, but then I use a lot of side lighting in my plays anyway. At certain points when we were making it up for the very first time at Sadler's Wells I would sit back and think, 'oh my goodness, this looks like a ballet', and no one was more surprised than me.

I've found that it's very easy to get seduced by nice stage pictures and you just have to make sure that you're harnessing your stage pictures to what's most important, be it the music, be it the dance. Sometimes it should be the stage picture. It's a very difficult thing to do. You just need to have good relationships – I can show things to the choreographer and say 'we could do this now' and he'll go 'wow – that's great' and at other times you think that's too much and it's distracting. At other times you want to be distracted – I like to use shadows a lot in dance because I think it's really important . Sometimes you've got a little dance and you can throw a BIG shadow on the back wall and it looks so exciting! You can do things

with light – you can create more dancers sometimes. In *Swan Lake* there is a point when all the swans come out from under the bed of the prince because he's having a bad dream and it's the simplest thing – it's the oldest trick in the book – but literally we put up a central footlight and all of sudden there's this GIGANTIC person! You enjoy what the dancers are doing but you also enjoy this big shape they're making on the back wall. Everyone goes 'ahh' and you think 'well that's easy'. But that I hope is an indication of when the effect really helps to tell the story because we're in the mind of somebody. The set for *Swan Lake* was largely very white and I was worried when I saw it because there wasn't much room to let light in. It's practically a box with just enough space for the dancers to enter between these big white columns but in the end it's worked quite well and is more flexible than I had imagined.

There's a moment in *Swan Lake* in Act III, a dance usually between the Black Swan and the Prince. In AMP's version the Black Swan is dancing with the Queen and then there's a spin and he ends up in the arms of the Prince. We're now inside the Prince's head – we've been somewhere very pretty. There's dancing and then there's a chord and he ends up with the Prince. It's a snap change with a very dramatic lighting state and a big shadow on one side of the wall and they're allowed to be partly in dark and you *know* you're somewhere different – that's an 'overly smart' cue, but hopefully it works.

TW: *How did you come to be a lighting designer?*

RF: I fell into it by accident, I'm relatively untrained. I was interested in being a stage manager and did general backstage work. One of the things I did was lighting because the shows would come to me – I was working in a venue in South London called the Oval House, that did a lot of performance art work – and they would need help setting up and also need someone to do the lights. They would say 'we need a light there, we need this, we need that' and I would run the shows and learn by doing it. I never really went to school or anything sensible like that – sometimes it still shows, I'm afraid! I did stage managing for a while and got bored with it and when people started to ask me to light shows it was just so much easier than doing everything that I started concentrating on lighting.

TW: *So you didn't come with the expectation of following a script?*

RF: I never had scripts – even as a stage manager I never worked from things that were written down. Usually the types of plays were what you would call performance art – the performers would make a show about various images that had been blocked together – there might be text and often it wasn't written down. The companies were groups like The People Show, who are still going, Hesitate and Demonstrate, and That's Not It, which is a company Jenny Carey and I and Natasha Morgan had together. My cue sheets would be like 'when Jose goes over there bring up this light to this level' and 'when someone breaks the window snap this light on' and I would just be responding visually to what I saw. Most of these companies didn't travel with someone to do the lighting because they couldn't afford to, or else they would have one person who could do it and I would be helping them. Frequently I had a discussion with them about their show and then I'd lock myself in the theatre at night as I had the keys and just run up a ladder, hang a light, run back down the ladder, switch the light on, look at it, have a box of bits of gel that were left over from other shows, hold up the gel and think that was a good colour, run up the ladder, put it in, run back down the ladder, look at it again and think 'oh maybe it's not very good' and run back up the ladder etc. – I did a lot of running up and down ladders. The joy of that was that I didn't have to feel constrained by anyone else, I just had to please myself and I spent as long or as little time on it as I wanted to.

TW: *So as the shows got bigger you must have lost some degree of control – how did you respond to that?*

RF: It happened by accident. I took a job that I thought was a studio

show and it turned out to be the main playhouse, the Liverpool Playhouse, doing *The Seagull* – a real play by a dead author – I accepted thinking it was something else and I got up there to confront this proper theatre – I was terrified, I didn't know what to do. What did you call the place where the lights were hung? How did you turn the headsets on? It was so embarrassing. This was just over ten years ago. I learned quickly how to use the local crew to help me out and somehow re-jig the show to make it look like something good and somehow it didn't look like someone else had lit it – it looked like I had lit it. Slowly but surely that's been the nature of the experience I've had. I don't touch anything anymore, I just point and give notes.

TW: *That's quite a change from running up and down the ladder...*

RF: Yes and you have to articulate clearly what you want and that eventually is a good thing. I always say that most of my work is twenty-five per cent with lights and seventy-five per cent with people – crew and performers. It's important that you're communicating and that it's a team process. When the team breaks down it always shows in the work because it doesn't turn out so well.

TW: *What was your first experience of dance lighting?*

RF: I was first invited to light for The Kosh by Jenny Carey, a designer with whom I'd worked in the theatre a lot but I hadn't really done any dance before. Jenny started to do some shows with The Kosh and tried to rope me in as they didn't really use lighting a lot, because they toured mostly to schools and non-specific venues, where they had to set up in a classroom – just plug it into the wall and hope that it was going to be okay. It became a real challenge working with them on a very limited budget but doing it meant we were completely self-contained. The first piece I did was *A Matter of Chance*, set on a train, and we literally had it down so that we could plug it into the wall as they travelled with their own dimmer board and most of the stuff was low voltage so that it didn't require too much electricity. We had a lot of complicated and stylistic looks and I really was very pleased with it. Again, it was very simple – maybe twenty lamps and there were rarely more than two or three on at one time. The lighting helped to tell the story. We developed a system of lighting so that the physical way the

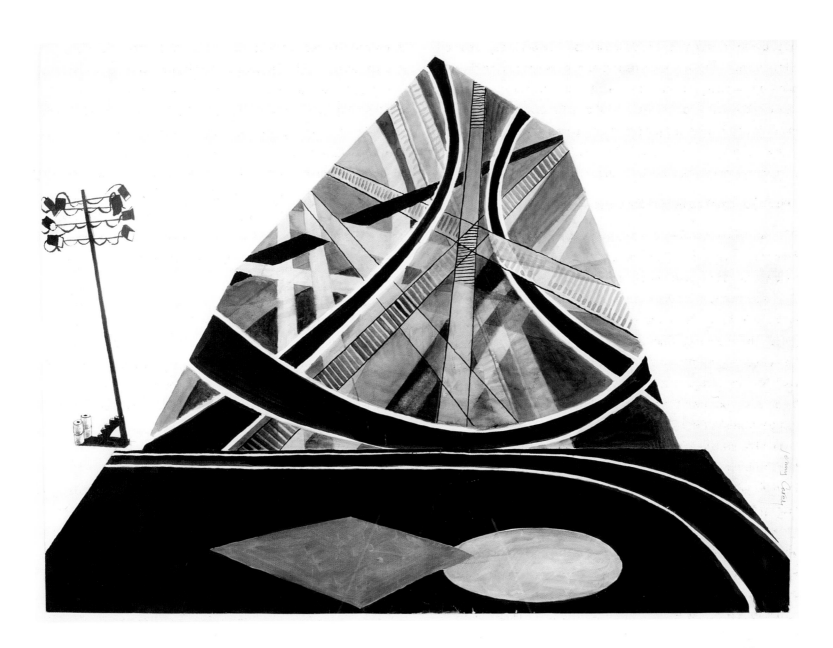

Jennifer Carey Set design for *A Matter of Chance*
Music by Howard Davidson
Choreography by Sian Williams
Directed by Michael Merwitzer
The Kosh, 1990
The artist

lights were hung and what they were was part of the set design and it was really out of my close collaboration with Jenny that we were able to do that.

TW: *Do you recall* George and the Dragon, *a piece you lit that was choreographed by Matthew Hamilton and designed by Peter Docherty?*

RF: I remember that it was interesting to make the water come alive and that we had to do it very simply because we didn't have much equipment or facilities or time. What was good about it was that it was a very good collaboration because we didn't have a lot of things to get in the way, it was just working with people. You can charge things with light, especially with the water that was in the pool that has reflective qualities.

TW: *How do you find lighting for dance?*

RF: In dance you have the traditional sidelights – the shin, the mid and the head that just pick out the body and around that you try to create an atmosphere such as by using a strong colour. But even a clean light shadow on the floor – a lot of times with dance lighting that I've seen they don't refer to the floor very much – sometimes it's nice to have one single shadow of what the dancers are doing on the floor – it just complements, it doesn't distract – whereas if you have five pale shadows then that can be distracting. To do the best dance lighting work, ideally what you'd want to do is of course be with the choreographer, lighting the choreography all the time, in the rehearsal when they're thinking about it. Lighting is still laid over the top at the last minute and that's always destined to be the way unless maybe you're Jennifer Tipton, who is probably the greatest dance lighting designer in terms of new, modern dance.

TW: *How does the scenographer fit into the equation?*

RF: With AMP the sets have been designed and then I'm shown them – 'here, light this' – and that's more common these days and it's partly my fault because I'm too busy, it's partly because it gets to the last minute. It's still sets that inspire me in a way and of course they're there and they're real and you can look at a model and a

drawing of a set often way before the choreography has even been started. You do tend to light then or at least take the cues from that. In dance it's very possible sometimes to light the dancers one way and then choose to light the set in a completely different way – that's okay, but it's not as exciting as when you can combine them all together. I get very excited when I combine both together to tell the story in a way that I think is helpful to the piece but that's not always the case. Although the ideas about the kind of light often are dictated by the set that you've looked at, it's still got to be people first. That's how I've changed over the years – I'm much more interested in lighting people than I used to be. I used to love lighting environments and making them dark or spooky or whatever and I would fight with directors for every single watt of light they wanted to put on stage and try to convince them it was much better that way. People told me I used to light people's shoulders beautifully but never their faces, but I've changed. The challenge is to light people well and let the atmosphere be preserved. The show with which I've had the most success is *An Inspector Calls*, in the West End. There the people are often lit very brightly but I think it still feels that they're in a dark world and that's because of the way that they're lit. I lit them more like they'd be lit in a dance performance traditionally, with sidelight. There is light coming in that's picking them out from the scenery so therefore you treat the scenery in one way, or not treat it as the case may be, and light people like the dancer in space so that you can see perfectly well what they're doing. Somehow the audience still perceives the space but, like television or as in a film, they look at the person and don't question the fact that they can brightly see the actor, so although the actor is rather bright they can still be in a dark world. That's a trick I've learnt to play and it's a lot closer to what you often do in dance where you want to see what the body is doing and what the movement is. The light is not hitting the floor or bits of scenery but just going across the wings and you have a feeling of a dark world with black floor, black background but a brilliantly lit dancer. In *Inspector* I think we could do that very well. Dancers are used to side lighting whereas actors don't like it so much because a lot of the time they end up having a conversation on stage talking to each other like that (side on to audience) so there's a light behind your head. What I tend to do is instead of one light straight across as in dance is to use three – one in front, one direct and one behind so that you can choose the balance that you need. It's curious how often on stage people are blocked in straight lines talking to each other and so I learnt to use three lights to light any position wherever possible.

TW: *You talk about* An Inspector Calls *rather like a film director, being able to zoom and pan around a larger space, using light rather than the limits of the lens to include or exclude . . .*

RF: Absolutely. The lighting should be the camera for the audience, moving in and out. When you think about a play or a dance performance your memory of it has been in close-up even if you've been a long way away. You can picture the whole set but you can also picture a single actor or a single dancer doing something and you remember in a scale much larger than you saw them in, so lighting should help you zoom in and zoom out and with cross-cutting and all that. Obviously, you always have to be aware of the whole picture, which you don't on film or television. There are a lot of things hopefully you notice but sometimes subconsciously. A lot of lighting's information is given subconsciously to an audience and even subconsciously to a lighting designer sometimes.

TW: *So you are providing the lens through which we see the performance and, like a lens it can be rose-coloured or magnify or distort and so on, and that's where the art comes in . . .*

RF: That's right, and it's very much a collaborative art. It's not me coming in and saying this is what I'm going to do on this. It's doing it with the choreographer, with the director, with the designer, with the actor, with the dancer – the way it turns out is often not how I intended it in my mind or on my drawing board or in my conversations. It's a bastard art because the meaning of what you're doing is so subconscious. I can articulate in a way that no one else can but when I try to describe it to somebody they might think totally the opposite from the words I'm using. You just have to come to some consensus and hope that it's the most interesting thing rather than the most boring thing.

TW: *How do you prepare for a project?*

RF: You prepare by having conversations with the director/choreographer, looking at the set and the space it's going to be in. My real work is done in the theatre, always has to be done in the space where the performance is. You can arm yourself with a variety of tools – it's like a painter having a palette ready with lots of different colours of paint. You don't quite know how it's going to end up on the canvas – you might start out putting some white down, then some blue down and then some yellow on top of it and it goes green round the edges. That's very much how a lighting designer works – so you hopefully prepare enough of the bright blobs of paint and react very quickly to it. The lighting has got to be something that organically grows on top of the performance. That's why the technical time is so important. One of the things that has been good about AMP and The Kosh is that the directors and the choreographers have wanted to invest the time in getting the lighting to be part of it, and you keep on refining it and changing it.

TW: *Do you think designers, directors and choreographers are becoming more conversant with the possibilities that the lighting designer can bring to the performance?*

RF: I'd like to hope so. What they often don't really remember is that you need space to let light in. Light doesn't just hit the stage from nowhere – it requires a volume of air space to achieve its desired goal and also it just keeps going until it hits something solid. The penchant of a lot of British designers to put things in boxes with side walls and ceilings may make nice stage pictures but can mean that the light has no way to get out and often no way to get in and that's a challenge. However, the lighting equipment is getting more sophisticated, the control equipment is getting more sophisticated, the kind of gadgets we can get that either move or change colour, meaning that one light can do a lot more than it used to. I think they are becoming more aware – it costs more money and sometimes they're willing to budget a bit more money for the lighting.

We, You, They | Peter Williams

Dance and Dancers, Vol.1, No.1, January 1950, p.2.

This is not just another ballet paper, though it is certain that ballet will feature to no mean extent. Our title – *Dance and Dancers* – is self explanatory. Whenever and wherever Dancers dance we hope to be there. Ballet is not such a large segment of that seductive apple, dance, as many people are apt to think. True ballet is the ultimate form of theatrical dance presentation, but to reach its present revered state it has gone through many refineries and become admixed with the arts of literature and painting until frequently the original mainspring, dance, has been neglected altogether. It is, therefore, equally important to consider many of the less refined phases of this development. Dancing in musical plays, films and television will play a large part in the future of this paper as well as the dancing of all peoples, inspired by man's natural desire to express himself in movement.

There is only one person who can make the dance possible – The Dancer. It is our intention to introduce dancers to you so that by knowing something of their background you will more easily be able to assess their true value.

If this sounds dull reading, there is no need to worry for we have always at our beck and call, those Court jesters – Scandal and Gossip. Whenever we feel that we are becoming ponderous we shall not hesitate to summon them for it is they, after all, who make dancing one of the lively arts.

You too, O patient reader, will be allowed to raise your voice and ride your hobby-horse through our pages. How often have we heard you say that you have messages of vital importance to the world? You have always been so keen on airing your views in the foyer, the Crush Bar and round draughty stage-doors. Now, you can write it all down and we can only hope that our Guardian Angels are in the vicinity.

All these slightly pompous statements are a means of introducing ourselves to you and of trying to explain our 'policy' (that dreary word that always seems to mean something that is never adhered to). We hope to give you what you want and that you will tell us what you want. We should like to make it quite clear that you will never find in our pages anything on Ballroom dancing (*Dancing Times*, please note!); Jolly scribbly drawings (*Ballet and Opera*, please note!); Instructive articles on how to make festive table decorations out of old ballet shoes (*Vogue, House and Gardens*, please note!); Nostalgic Nosegays; Patterns for making practice costumes out of old dusters. In short, we hope to be informative, irreverent and indefatigable.

Jean-Denis Malclès Robert Helpmann, Alexander Grant, Frederick Ashton in *Cinderella*
Music by Serge Prokofiev
Choreography by Frederick Ashton
Sadler's Wells Ballet, Royal Opera House, London, 1948
The front cover of the first copy of *Dance and Dancers*, January 1950.

Cinderella

Designing *Cinderella*
Tim Hatley

Cinderella was the first collaboration Christopher Gable and I had done together and I just did a lot of drawings and he reacted to them. We built up the ideas together – it was quite a joint effort. I think it's quite important that everybody's on the same ship. The music for *Cinderella* was by Philip Feeney, so it was a completely new score and it didn't have any of those problems of being stuck in a time period. It was all new and so it gave the opportunity to do something that wasn't tied in to a specific period or place. It's interesting designing for dance; in a way you're not wanted as a designer because you're getting in the way of the choreography. At the end of the day dancers think 'oh we just want the space', which is fair enough because that is what they do need. I decided to use the space over and above their heads and to block off the maximum dance space and just use things and bring things in within that.

The idea was to create a world in a magic box. What we've got is a blue box with sliding panels all the way round and giving the idea that it's being overgrown by branches and roots. It is the magical world where the story takes place. The various pieces slide up and down and different pieces of set get pushed on or pushed in and revealed. Some of the panels had to be fixed to give the box rigidity but most moved. The corner ones were fixed and the ones with the ladders were fixed. There is a walkway along the top and the ravens, who were in black rubber, slid down the ladders and the doves were also up on the ladders with just the white section of the costume showing as if they were flying. The idea was that you could be in anywhere-land when it was just a closed-down box and then the panels would slide up to reveal Cinderella's fireplace. There were doorways that came in and down and then for the ball other panels came

up and the space became a magical palace. I don't think there's room these days in the theatre or dance to have a blackout, wheel the set around for five minutes and then come back to it – you've got to keep the momentum going. We're so used to seeing visual things fast on TV, video and film – even theatre now – you've got to keep up with that and people don't expect to sit there in darkness for two minutes while you move from the kitchen to the ball. That's why I designed it so that you could move between scenes quickly.

I worked quite closely with Paul Pyant, the lighting designer, on ensuring that the box set didn't compromise the lighting. The scenes where we wanted a lot of side lighting – which is one of the ball scenes, the side panels all flew out and so we actually blasted it with light and then at the end of the ball everyone ran out through there towards the light and the panels slid down to shut them off and then suddenly we were in the woods and Cinderella was left behind. The scene moved around her – she didn't go anywhere. When we wanted sidelights we just opened the panels up, but we worked out we didn't want a lot of side lighting all the time.

We wanted to give a blue blank canvas and then to inject a lot of colour and energy into the costumes so that the characters would really be expressive and so the locations would be indicated – you knew you were at the ballroom because everybody was fit to go to the ball. We spent a lot of energy on costumes. The idea was to make it a fashionable world. The transformation comes from the fact that we had a lot of locations and you've got to move from location to location and I believe you have to do that in a beautiful, simple way.

David Walker Costumes for courtiers, *Cinderella*
Music by Serge Prokofiev
Choreography by Ben Stevenson
English National Ballet, London, 1992
The artist

Tim Hatley Costumes for stepsisters and mother,
Cinderella
Music by Philip Feeney
Choreography by Christopher Gable
Northern Ballet Theatre, 1993
The artist

'The idea with them was to make them sort of cheap
Versace trash sisters who had everything. They had all
the make-up in the world they wanted, all the
jewellery they wanted, they painted their faces and it
all comes from the mother. They almost wanted to
look like their mother.' (Tim Hatley talking to Tim
White, 2 May 1996)

Philip Prowse Costume designs for projected
Scottish Ballet production of *Cinderella* by Peter Darrell
The artist

Tim Hatley Set model for *Cinderella*
Music by Philip Feeney
Choreography by Christopher Gable
Northern Ballet Theatre, 1993
Photograph by Michael Dyer Associates Ltd

Tim Hatley Set model for *Cinderella*
Music by Philip Feeney
Choreography by Christopher Gable
Northern Ballet Theatre, 1993
Photograph by Michael Dyer Associates Ltd

Coppélia

Loudon Sainthill *Coppélia*
Music by Léo Delibes
Choreography by Lev Ivanov and Enrico Cecchetti,
reproduced by Konstantin Sergeyev
Sadler's Wells Theatre Ballet, Sadler's Wells, 1951
Photograph by Denis de Marnay
The Theatre Museum, V&A

Peter Snow Set for Act III, *Coppélia*
Music by Léo Delibes
Production and choreography by Peter Wright after
Marius Petipa and Enrico Cecchetti for Sadler's Wells
Royal Ballet, Royal Shakespeare Theatre,
Stratford-upon-Avon, 1979
The artist

Peter Snow Costume for Swanhilde, *Coppélia*
Music by Léo Delibes
Production and choreography by Peter Wright after
Marius Petipa and Enrico Cecchetti for Sadler's Wells
Royal Ballet, Royal Shakespeare Theatre,
Stratford-upon-Avon, 1979
The artist

Peter Snow Costume for Franz, *Coppélia*
Music by Léo Delibes
Production and choreography by Peter Wright after
Marius Petipa and Enrico Cecchetti for Sadler's Wells
Royal Ballet, Royal Shakespeare Theatre,
Stratford-upon-Avon, 1979
The artist

Richard Bridgland Costume for the Squire, *Coppélia*
Music by Léo Delibes
Production by Kenny Burke after Marius Petipa for
Scottish Ballet, Theatre Royal Glasgow, 1993
The artist

Shakespeare

Leslie Hurry Set design for *Hamlet*
Music by Pyotr Tchaikovsky
Choreography by Robert Helpmann
Sadler's Wells Ballet, New Theatre, London, 1942
John Hurry Armstrong

Barry Kay Set design for *Images of Love*
Music by Peter Tranchell
Choreography by Kenneth MacMillan
The Royal Ballet, Royal Opera House, London, 1964
Noël Goodwin

A suite of nine dances inspired by lines from
Shakespeare on the theme of love.

Nicholas Georgiadis Set model for Scene 2,
The Tempest
Music by Pyotr Tchaikovsky, edited John Lanchbery
Choreography by Rudolf Nureyev
Royal Ballet, Royal Opera House, London, 1982
The artist

Nicholas Georgiadis Costume for Rudolf Nureyev as
Prospero, *The Tempest*
Music by Pyotr Tchaikovsky, edited John Lanchbery
Choreography by Rudolf Nureyev
Royal Ballet, Royal Opera House, London, 1982
The artist

Nicholas Georgiadis
Set model for Prologue,
The Tempest
Music by Pyotr Tchaikovsky, edited John Lanchbery
Choreography by Rudolf Nureyev
Royal Ballet, Royal Opera House, London, 1982
The artist

Nicholas Georgiadis Set model for The Market Place,
Romeo and Juliet
Music by Serge Prokofiev
Choreography by Sir Kenneth MacMillan
Teatro Colón, Buenos Aires
Shown in the exhibition *The Designers: Pushing the
Boundaries – Advancing the Dance*, The Lethaby
Galleries, November 1995
The artist

Nicholas Georgiadis Set model for The Ball,
Romeo and Juliet
Music by Serge Prokofiev
Choreography by Sir Kenneth MacMillan
Teatro Colón, Buenos Aires
Shown in the exhibition *The Designers: Pushing the
Boundaries – Advancing the Dance*, The Lethaby
Galleries, November 1995
The artist

Nicholas Georgiadis Set model for The Balcony,
Romeo and Juliet
Music by Serge Prokofiev
Choreography by Sir Kenneth MacMillan
Teatro Colón, Buenos Aires
The artist

Nicholas Georgiadis Set model for The Tomb,
Romeo and Juliet
Music by Serge Prokofiev
Choreography by Sir Kenneth MacMillan
Teatro Colón, Buenos Aires
The artist

Elisabeth Dalton Costume design for *The Taming of the Shrew*
Music by Domenico Scarlatti
Choreography by John Cranko
Stuttgart Ballet, Stuttgart, 1969
The artist

Peter Farmer Costumes for *The Dream*
Music by Felix Mendelssohn, arranged by John Lanchbery
Choreography by Sir Frederick Ashton
The Royal Ballet Touring Company, New Theatre, Oxford, 1966
The Royal Opera House

Bob Ringwood *Such Sweet Thunder*
Music by Duke Ellington
Choreography by Peter Darrell
Scottish Ballet, Theatre Royal, Glasgow, 1979
Photograph by Bill Cooper

'. . . I never heard
So musical a discord, such sweet thunder'
A Midsummer Night's Dream, Act IV Scene 1, lines 123–4

Robin Don Set model for *Macbeth*
Music by David Earl
Choreography by André Prokovsky
Ballet de Santiago, Teatro Municipal Santiago de
Chile, 1991
The artist

Norberto Chiesa *A Midsummer Night's Dream*
Music by Felix Mendelssohn
Choreography by Robert Cohan
Scottish Ballet, 1993
Photograph by Bill Cooper

Ralph Koltai Set model for Steel Show Drop,
Metropolis
Music by Joe Brooks
Choreography by Tom Jobe

Book and lyrics by Joe Brooks and Dusty Hughes,
based on the film by Fritz Lang
Director Jerome Savory
Piccadilly Theatre, London, 1989
The artist

Ralph Koltai Rebellion of the Workers, *Metropolis*
Music by Joe Brooks
Choreography by Tom Jobe
Book and lyrics by Joe Brooks and Dusty Hughes,
based on the film by Fritz Lang
Director Jerome Savory
Piccadilly Theatre, London, 1989
The artist

Ralph Koltai Machine Room, *Metropolis*
Music by Joe Brooks
Choreography by Tom Jobe
Book and lyrics by Joe Brooks and Dusty Hughes,
based on the film by Fritz Lang
Director Jerome Savory
Piccadilly Theatre, London, 1989
The artist

Ralph Koltai Set model for Machine Room,
Metropolis
Music by Joe Brooks
Choreography by Tom Jobe
Book and lyrics by Joe Brooks and Dusty Hughes,
based on the film by Fritz Lang
Director Jerome Savory
Piccadilly Theatre, London, 1989
The artist

Anthony Powell Costume designs for Miss Norma
Desmond, *Sunset Boulevard*
Music by Andrew Lloyd Webber
Choreography by Maggie Goodwin
Book and lyrics by Don Black and Christopher
Hampton, based on the film by Billy Wilder
Director Trevor Nunn
Set designed by John Napier
Adelphi Theatre, London, 1993
The artist

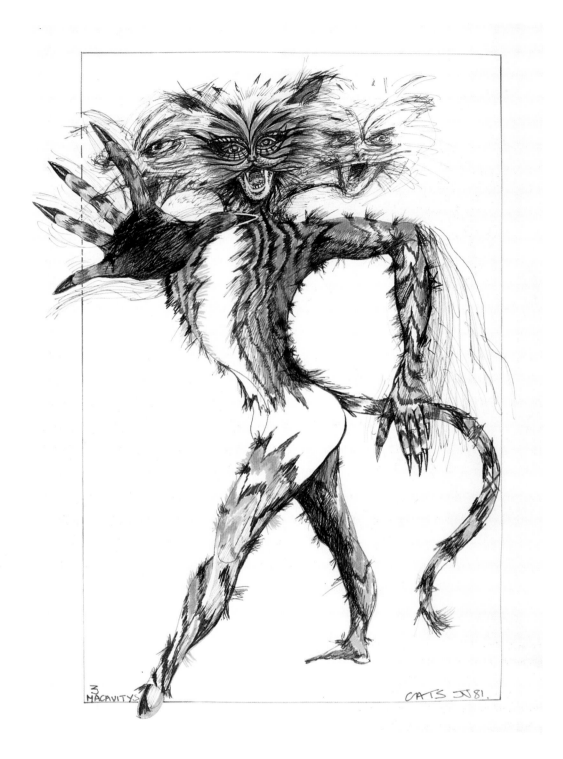

John Napier Costume for Macavity, *Cats*
Music by Andrew Lloyd Webber
Choreography by Gillian Lynne
Based on T.S. Eliot's *Old Possum's Book of Practical Cats*
Additional material by Trevor Nunn and Richard Stilgoe
Director Trevor Nunn
New London Theatre, London, 1981
Private Collection

Maria Bjørnson *Follies*
Music and lyrics by Stephen Sondheim
Choreography by Bob Avian
Director Mike Ockrent
Shaftesbury Theatre, London, 1987
Photograph by Clive Barda

Maria Bjørnson *The Phantom of the Opera*
Music by Andrew Lloyd Webber
Choreography by Gillian Lynne
Book by Richard Stilgoe, lyrics by Charles Hart and
Richard Stilgoe
Director Harold Prince
Her Majesty's Theatre, London, 1986
Photograph by Clive Barda

Ann Curtis Costume designs for *Me and My Girl*
Music by Noel Gay
Choreography by Gillian Gregory
Book and lyrics by Arthur Rose and Douglas Furber,
revised by Stephen Fry
Set designed by Martin Johns
Director Mike Ockrent
Marriot Marquis Theatre, New York, 1986
The artist

Robin Don Costumes for *Song and Dance*
Music by Andrew Lloyd Webber
Choreography by Anthony van Laast
Director John Caird
Palace Theatre, London, 1982
The artist

FROM DIAGHILEV TO THE PET SHOP BOYS

The majority of works illustrated in this publication were gathered together for the 1993 exhibition *From Diaghilev to the Pet Shop Boys* (a list of exhibits can be found after the plates). A remarkable collection of costume and set designs spanning eighty years, it has been the inspiration for this book, which takes an historical and catholic approach to dance design in Parts One and Two, 'Designers on Design 1920–1996'. and 'Designing the Narrative'. The exhibition was conceived by Peter Docherty to increase public awareness of the work of the dance scenographer and to dedicate the student Design for Dance project to Peter Williams. Docherty co-opted Marina Henderson, the theatre design historian, writer and gallery owner, and Peter Farley, designer, teacher and exhibition curator, to devise and mount the exhibition with financial support from the Theatre Design Trust. Marina Henderson's introduction to the exhibition conveys succinctly its intent and is reproduced overleaf

Peter J. Davison *Edward II*
After Christopher Marlowe
Music by John McCabe
Choreography by David Bintley
Costumes by Jasper Conran
Stuttgart Ballet, 1995
Stuttgart Ballet

Introduction | Marina Henderson

The successful design of any ballet or dance piece embodies and reflects its choreography, music, mood and character. And once the production is over, the curtain down, the music stilled, we recollect the event in pictures – the dancers in costume, the action against a setting. Such pictures are created by the designer, whose sketches remain as partial but lasting evidence of the complex collaborative process that only reaches an ephemeral completion in a live performance.

The drawings in *From Diaghilev to the Pet Shop Boys* cover more than ninety years of dance productions. No exhibition could comprehensively document a period which has witnessed the most diverse and dynamic developments in the history of dance. The limitations of time, money and availability further made the selection of designs somewhat arbitrary. Yet they ranged from a traditional re-staging of the very first *ballet blanc*, *La Sylphide*, to the peripatetic experiment of *Waving at the Tide*; from the finished painting of Burra's *Miracle in the Gorbals* front-cloth to Rex Whistler's rapid costumier sketches for *The Rake's Progress*; from Sophie Fedorovitch's minimal *Nocturne* impressions to Picasso's meticulous record for *Tricorne*.

Whether work-a-day sketches or works of art, stage designs can be, at the least, a useful historical document, at the best (as a comparison of Hurry's *Swan Lake* drawings with production photographs readily demonstrates), the most vivid and immediate evocation of the essential spirit of a dance production. Yet the function of the stage designer is frequently overlooked and imperfectly understood. Designers are often asked what do they do with a ballet or dance company. It may be some consolation that Diaghilev was asked the same question. (He replied 'The lighting'.) This exhibition is an important contribution to answering this question and to illustrating the vital role of the designer in dance.

Paul Nash Costume design, wedding dress for Tamara Karsavina as Karissima, *The Truth About Russian Dancers*
Music by Sir Arnold Bax
Choreography by Tamara Karsavina
Ballet-play by J. M. Barrie
Coliseum, London, 1920
© The Paul Nash Trust Courtesy of Department of Prints and Drawings, V&A

Christopher Wood Costumes for *Luna Park*
Music by Lord Berners
Choreography by George Balanchine
Cochran's 1930 Revue, London Pavilion, London, 1930
James Gordon

Christopher Wood Set for *Luna Park*
Music by Lord Berners
Choreography by George Balanchine
Cochran's 1930 Revue, London Pavilion, London, 1930
James Gordon

Duncan Grant Costume for Lydia Lopokova
Believed to be from *The Postman*
Choreography by Nicholas Legat,
Coliseum, London, 1925
© 1978 Estate of Duncan Grant
James Gordon

William Chappell Costumes for *High Yellow*
Music by Spike Hughes
Choreography by Buddy Bradley and Frederick
Ashton
Camargo Society, Savoy Theatre, London, 1932
James Gordon

William Chappell Costume for *Capriol Suite*
Music by Peter Warlock
Choreography by Frederick Ashton
Ballet Rambert, Sadler's Wells, London, 1983
Revival of the 1930 production
Rambert Dance Company Archives

John Armstrong Design for backcloth, *Façade*
Music by William Walton
Choreography by Frederick Ashton
Vic-Wells Ballet, Sadler's Wells, London, 1935
Originally created for the Camargo Society 1931
The Royal Opera House

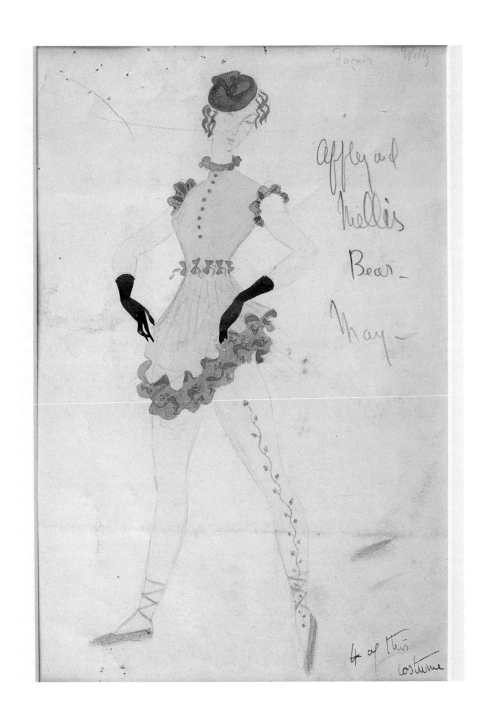

John Armstrong Waltz costume, *Façade*
Music by William Walton
Choreography by Frederick Ashton
Vic-Wells Ballet, Sadler's Wells, London, 1935
Originally created for the Camargo Society, 1931
James Gordon

Rex Whistler *The Rake's Progress*
Music by Gavin Gordon
Choreography by Ninette de Valois
Vic-Wells Ballet, Sadler's Wells, London, 1935
The Theatre Museum, V&A

John Banting *Prometheus*
Music by Ludwig van Beethoven arranged Constant Lambert
Choreography by Ninette de Valois
Vic-Wells Ballet, Sadler's Wells, London, 1936
Photograph by J.W. Debenham
The Theatre Museum, V&A

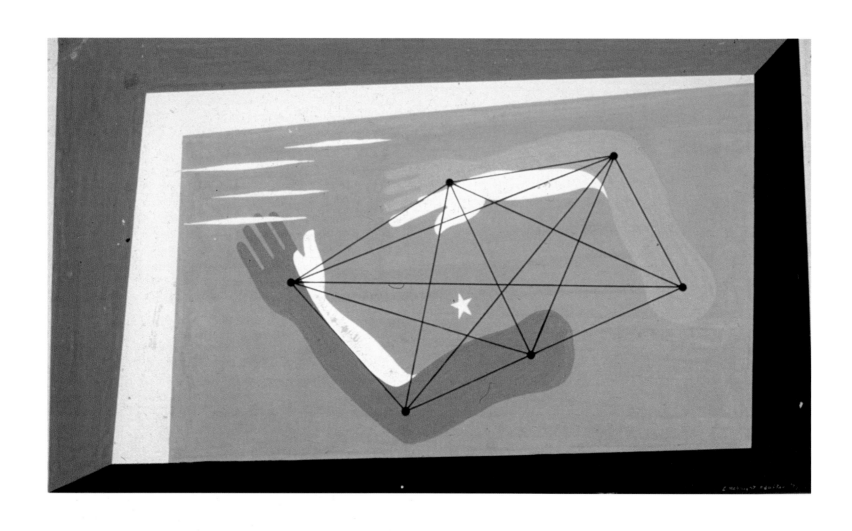

E. McKnight Kauffer Cloth for *Checkmate*
Music by Arthur Bliss
Choreography by Ninette de Valois
Vic-Wells Ballet, Théâtre des Champs-Elysées,
Paris, 1937
The Department of Prints and Drawings, V&A
The original designs were lost in 1940. This is from
E. McKnight Kauffer's 1947 redesign of the work.

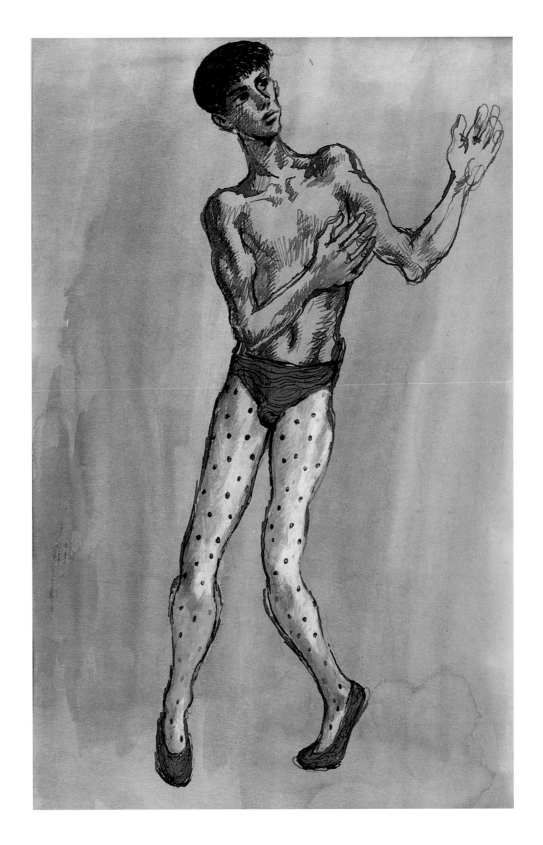

John Minton Costume project for a ballet
James Gordon

Edward Burra Set for *Miracle in the Gorbals*
Music by Arthur Bliss
Choreography by Robert Helpmann
Scenario by Michael Benthall
Sadler's Wells Ballet, Princes Theatre, London, 1944
James Gordon

Edward Burra Frontcloth for *Miracle in the Gorbals*
Music by Arthur Bliss
Choreography by Robert Helpmann
Scenario by Michael Benthall
Sadler's Wells Ballet, Princes Theatre, London, 1944
James Gordon

Jean Hugo Set and costumes for *Les Amours de Jupiter*
Music by Jacques Ibert
Choreography by Roland Petit
Ballet des Champs-Elysées, Paris, 1946
Madame Jean Hugo

Jean Hugo Set and costumes for *Les Amours de Jupiter*
Music by Jacques Ibert
Choreography by Roland Petit
Ballet des Champs-Elysées, Paris, 1946
Madame Jean Hugo

Peter Williams Set for Act II, *Giselle*
Music by Adolphe Adam
Choreography after Marius Petipa
Metropolitan Ballet Company, London, 1947
The artist

Peter Williams Costume for the Polovtsian Chief,
Prince Igor
Music by Alexander Borodin
Choreography by Michel Fokine
Metropolitan Ballet Company, London, 1948
The artist

Leonard Rosoman Backcloth for *Pleasuredrome*
Music by John Lanchbery
Choreography by Rosella Hightower
Metropolitan Ballet Company, Coliseum, Harrow, 1949
Peter Williams

Peter Snow Set for *Variations on a Theme of Purcell*
Music by Benjamin Britten
Choreography by Frederick Ashton
Sadler's Wells Ballet, Royal Opera House, London,
1955
The artist

Cecil Beaton Margot Fonteyn and Rudolf Nureyev in
Marguerite and Armand
Music by Franz Liszt, orchestrated by Humphrey
Searle
Choreography by Sir Frederick Ashton
The Royal Ballet, Royal Opera House, London, 1963
Photograph by Houston Rogers
The Theatre Museum, V&A

Nicholas Georgiadis *Danses Concertantes*
Music by Igor Stravinsky
Choreography by Kenneth MacMillan
Original production, Sadler's Wells Theatre Ballet,
Sadler's Wells, London, 1955
Photograph by Denis de Marnay
The Theatre Museum, V&A

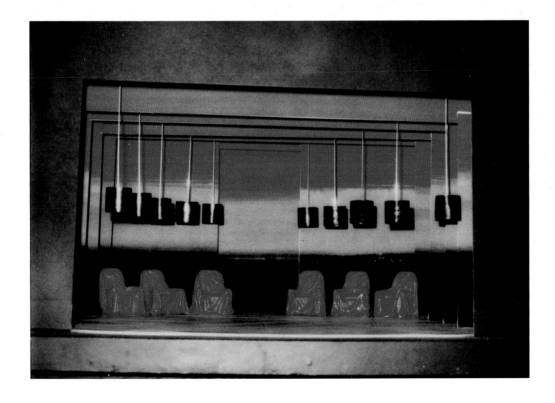

Nicholas Georgiadis Set model for *Danses Concertantes*
Music by Igor Stravinsky
Choreography by Kenneth MacMillan
New design, Sadler's Wells Royal Ballet, 1979
The artist

Lila de Nobili Sets for *Ondine*
Music by Hans Werner Henze
Choreography and scenario by Frederick Ashton
(revised 1959 and 1964)
The Royal Ballet, Royal Opera House, London, 1958
The Royal Opera House

Lila de Nobili Costumes for the corps de ballet,
Ondine
Music by Hans Werner Henze
Choreography and scenario by Frederick Ashton
(revised 1959 and 1964)
The Royal Ballet, Royal Opera House, London, 1958
The Royal Opera House

NOËL COWARD'S "LONDON MORNING"
"Nuns and Schoolchildren".

Norman Mc Dowell 1959.

Norman McDowell Costumes for the Nun and the
Schoolgirl, *London Morning*
Music by Noël Coward
Choreography by Jack Carter
London Festival Ballet, Royal Festival Hall, London, 1959
English National Ballet

Keith Vaughan Costume project for a ballet on the theme of *Francesca da Rimini*
James Gordon

Nicholas Georgiadis *Las Hermanas*
Music by Frank Martin
Choreography by Kenneth MacMillan
Sadler's Wells Ballet, Sadler's Wells, London, 1971
Photograph by Anthony Crickmay
The Theatre Museum, V&A

Derek Jarman *Jazz Calendar*
Music by Richard Rodney Bennett
Choreography by Sir Frederick Ashton
The Royal Ballet, Royal Opera House, London, 1968
Photograph by Anthony Crickmay
The Theatre Museum, V&A

Patrick Procktor Frontcloth, *Cage of God*
Music by Alan Rawsthorne
Choreography by Jack Carter
Western Theatre Ballet, Sadler's Wells, London, 1967
Peter Williams

Barry Kay Costume for a relative, Act III, *Anastasia*
Music by Pyotr Tchaikovsky, Bohuslav Martinů and
Fritz Winckel and Rüdiger Rüfer from Studio
Technical University, West Berlin
Choreography by Kenneth MacMillan
The Royal Ballet, Royal Opera House, London, 1971
The Royal Opera House

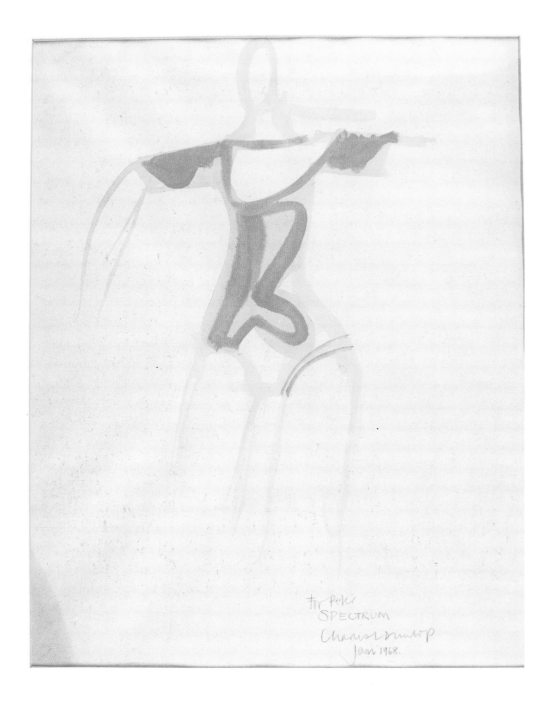

Charles Dunlop Costume design for *Spectrum*
Music by Malcolm Williamson
Choreography by Clover Roope
Western Theatre Ballet, Theatre Royal, Bury St
Edmunds, 1967
Peter Docherty

Yolanda Sonnabend Set for *Requiem*
Music by Gabriel Fauré
Choreography by Kenneth MacMillan
Stuttgart Ballet, Württemberg State Theatre,
Stuttgart, 1976
The artist

David Walker Set for Act II, *La Sylphide*
Music by Herman Løvenskjold
Choreography by Peter Schaufuss after August
Bournonville
West Berlin State Opera Ballet, Berlin, 1982
The artist

David Hockney Set for *Varii Capricci*
Music by William Walton
Choreography by Sir Frederick Ashton
The Royal Ballet, Royal Opera House, London, 1983
The Royal Opera House

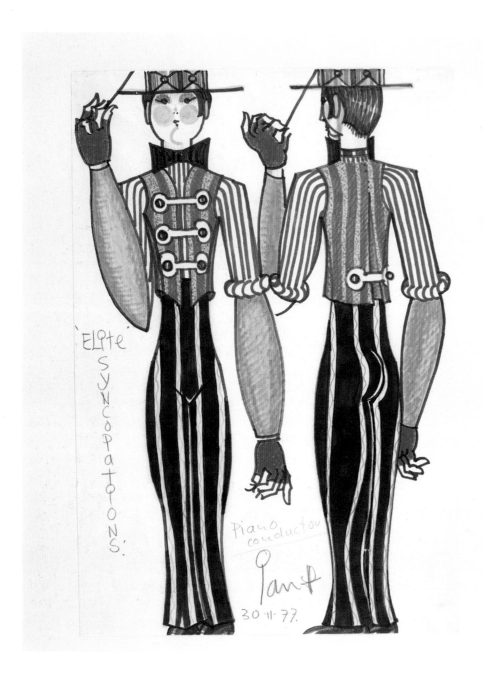

Ian Spurling Costumes for *Elite Syncopations*
Music by Scott Joplin and others
Choreography by Kenneth MacMillan
The Royal Ballet, Royal Opera House, London, 1974
The artist

Terry Bartlett The Swan Cloak from *The Swan of Tuonela*
Music by Jean Sibelius
Choreography by David Bintley
Sadler's Wells Royal Ballet, Sadler's Wells, London, 1982
The artist

Bridget Riley Set for *Colour Moves*
Music by Christopher Bensted
Choreography by Robert North
Ballet Rambert, Kings Theatre, Edinburgh, 1983
1996 © Bridget Riley. Courtesy Karsten Schubert,
London. All rights reserved.
James Gordon

Patrick Caulfield Costumes for *Party Game*
Music by Igor Stravinsky
Choreography by Michael Corder
The Royal Ballet, Royal Opera House, London, 1984
James Gordon

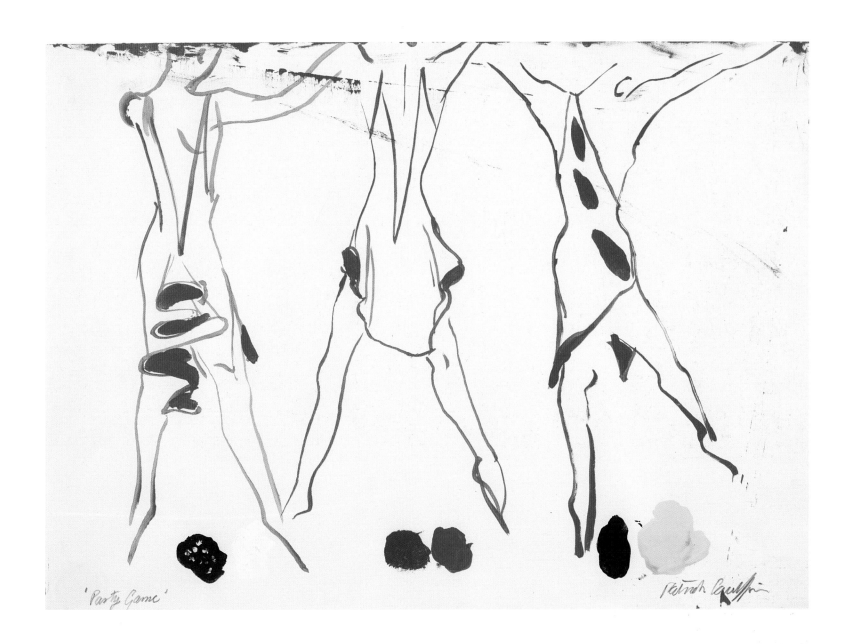

'Party Game'

Richard Hudson Costume for *St Anthony Variations*
Music by Johannes Brahms
Choreography by Michael Corder
Sadler's Wells Royal Ballet, Sadler's Wells, London,
1983
The artist

Mathilde Sandberg Set for *Fleeting Figures*
Music by Josef Suk
Choreography by Derek Deane
The Royal Ballet, Royal Opera House, London, 1984
The artist

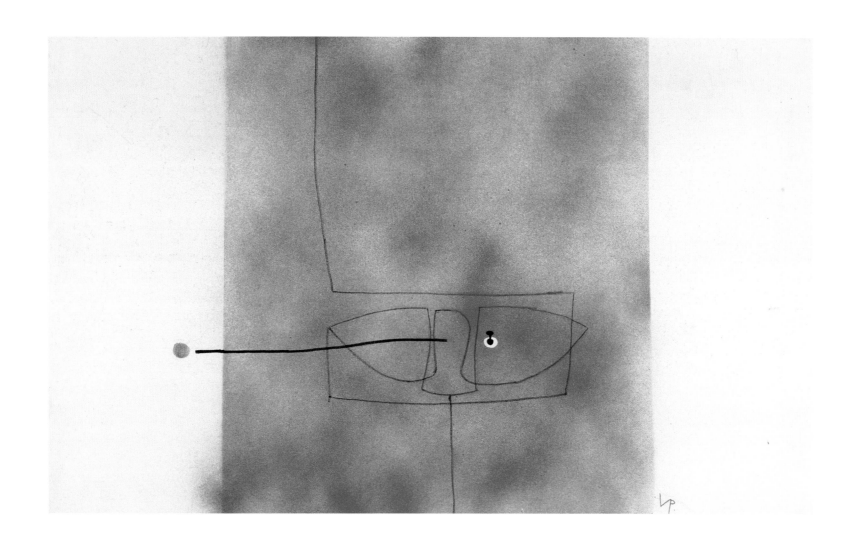

Victor Pasmore Set for *Young Apollo*
Music by Benjamin Britten and Gordon Crosse
Choreography by David Bintley
The Royal Ballet, Royal Opera House, London, 1984
James Gordon

Richard Smith Costumes for *Dangerous Liaisons*
Music by Simon Waters
Choreography by Richard Alston
Ballet Rambert, Gaumont Theatre, Southampton, 1985
Rambert Dance Company Archive

John Hoyland Costumes for *Zanza*
Music by Nigel Osborne
Choreography by Richard Alston
Ballet Rambert, London, 1986
James Gordon

Peter Logan *Red and Blue Crayons*, a dancing sculpture
Norwich Cathedral Cloisters, 1986
Photograph by the artist

David Buckland Set for *Rushes*
Music by Micheal Finnissy
Choreography by Siobhan Davies
Rambert Dance Company, Oxford Playhouse, 1987
Rambert Dance Company Archive

Andrew Logan Costume for Bastet, *Bastet*
Music by Michael Berkeley
Choreography by Lynn Seymour
Sadler's Wells Royal Ballet, Sadler's Wells, London,
1988
The artist

Jennifer Carey Dancers Entrance, *Waving at the Tide*
Music by Howard Davidson
Choreography by Sian Williams
Directed by Michael Merwitzer
The Kosh
Edinburgh, 1989
The artist

Antony McDonald Costume design for *Heaven Ablaze in His Breast*
Music by Judith Weir
Choreography by Ian Spink
Second Stride, 1989
The artist

SBM'90

Stephen Meaha Costume for *Enclosure*
Music by Alban Berg
Choreography by William Tuckett
The Royal Ballet, Royal Opera House, London, 1990
Brendan Thorpe

BACK

"Enclosure" / William Tuckett / Alban Berg / Royal Opera House, Covent Garden / August 1990

Dana Fouras

Paul Andrews Costumes for Romeo and Harlot,
Romeo and Juliet
Music by Serge Prokofiev
Choreography by Sir Kenneth MacMillan
Birmingham Royal Ballet, Birmingham
Hippodrome, 1992
The artist

REFUGEES
I'm NOT SCARED.

2 GIRLS

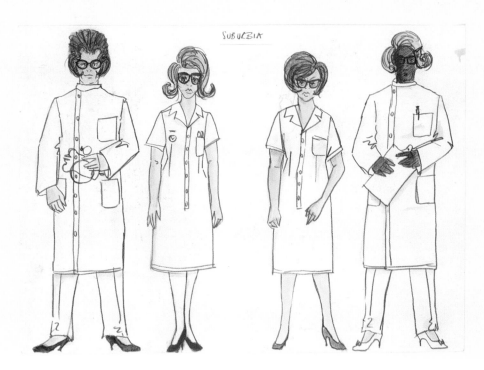

SUBURBIA

David Fielding Costumes for the Pet Shop Boys

1991 tour
The artist

BALLERINA
RUSSIAN ROULETTE

PUMPKIN GIRLS
SURFING SCENE

Dark Horizons.

DESIGN ②

David Yow

Peter Farley Costume for David Yow, *Dark Horizons*
Music by Dmitri Shostakovitch
Choreography by Oliver Hindle
Birmingham Royal Ballet, Birmingham
Hippodrome, 1992
The artist

Jock McFadyen Set for *The Judas Tree*
Music by Brian Elias
Choreography by Sir Kenneth MacMillan
The Royal Ballet, Royal Opera House, London, 1992
James Gordon

Deanna Petherbridge Floorcloth for *Bloodlines*
Music by Bruce Gilbert
Choreography by Ashley Page
The Royal Ballet, Royal Opera House, London, 1992
The Theatre Museum, V&A

Peter Whiteman Set design for Act II, The Forest,
The Snow Princess
Music by various composers
Choreography by Ben Stevenson
Ballet de Santiago, Chile, 1992
The artist

Bernadette Roberts Set and costumes for *Simple Symphony*
Music by Benjamin Britten
Choreography by Matthew Hart
The Royal Ballet School, Royal Opera House,
London, 1993
The artist

Complete List of Works in the Exhibition

Page numbers refer to those works illustrated in this book

1901–10

Léon Bakst Costume for a Slave, *Oedipus at Colonus* (1904)

Alexandre Benois Set for Act I, *Giselle* (1910)

Alexandre Benois Costume for Nijinsky as Albrecht in *Giselle* (1910)

1911–20

Mikhail Larionov Make-up for Kikimora, *Contes Russes* (1917)

Pablo Picasso Costume for The Manager from New York, *Parade* (1917)

Pablo Picasso Costume for The Manager in Evening Dress, *Parade* (1917)

Pablo Picasso Costume for *Le Tricorne* (1919) [production photograph of 1973 restaging, page 22]

Pablo Picasso Costume for *Le Tricorne* (1919)

Pablo Picasso Costume for *Le Tricorne* (1919)

Pablo Picasso Costume for *Le Tricorne* (1919)

Pablo Picasso Costume for *Le Tricorne* (1919)

Pablo Picasso Costume for *Le Tricorne* (1919)

Charles Ricketts Costume for Wilde's *Salome* (1919) [page 36]

Paul Nash Costume design, wedding dress for Tamara Karsavina as Karissima, *The Truth About Russian Dancers* (1920) [page 137]

1921–30

Léon Bakst Costume for La Marquise, *The Sleeping Princess* (1921) [programme cover, page 88]

Charles Ricketts Costume for a Lobster, Maeterlinck's *The Betrothal* (1921)

Léon Bakst Design for the wings, *Le Martyre de Saint-Sébastien* (1922)

Duncan Grant Costume for Lydia Lopokova (*c*.1925) [page 140]

John Banting Costumes for *Pomona* (1930)

Christian Bérard Drawing for projection, *La Nuit* (1930)

William Chappell Costume for *Capriol Suite* (1930) [page 141]

William Chappell Costume for *Capriol Suite* (1930)

Alexandra Exter Project for a revue, from the book *Décors de Théâtre*, Paris (1930)

Alexandra Exter Project for a revue, from the book *Décors de Théâtre*, Paris (1930)

Alexandra Exter Lighting project for dance, from the book *Décors de Théâtre*, Paris (1930)

Alexandra Exter Lighting project for dance, from the book *Décors de Théâtre*, Paris (1930)

Christopher Wood Costumes for *Luna Park* (1930) [page 138]

Christopher Wood Set for *Luna Park* (1930) [page 139]

1931–40

William Chappell Costumes for *High Yellow* (1932) [page 141]

Nadia Benois Costume for Elizabeth Schooling, *The Descent of Hebe* (1933)

Pavel Tchelitchev Costume for *Errante* (1933)

Pavel Tchelitchev Costume for *Errante* (1933)

John Armstrong Design for backcloth, *Façade* (1935) [page 142]

John Armstrong Waltz costume, *Façade* (1935) [page 143]

John Armstrong Working drawing for flats, *Façade* (1935)

John Armstrong Detail of window from backcloth, *Façade* (1940)

Sir Jacob Epstein Curtain, *David* (1935)

Rex Whistler Detail of the frontcloth, *The Rake's Progress* (1935) [production photograph, page 144]

Rex Whistler Costumes for *The Rake's Progress* (1935)

Rex Whistler Costumes for *The Rake's Progress* (1935)

John Banting Costumes for *Prometheus* (1936) [production photograph, page 145]

Christian Bérard Costume for The Beloved, *Symphonie fantastique* (1936)

Sophie Fedorovitch Costume for *Nocturne* (1936)

Sophie Fedorovitch Costume for *Nocturne* (1936)

Sophie Fedorovitch Set for *Nocturne* (1936)

E. McKnight Kauffer Set for *Checkmate* (1937)

E. McKnight Kauffer Cloth for *Checkmate* (1937) [page 146]

E. McKnight Kauffer Costume for Helmet of Death, *Checkmate* (1937)

Natalia Gontcharova Costumes for *Cendrillon* (1938)

1941–50

John Minton Costume project for a ballet (*c*.1940) [page 147]

Chiang Yee Set for *The Birds* (1942)

Maxwell Armfield Costume for Valo as David in *The Phoenix Ceremony* (1943)

Leslie Hurry Set for Act I, *Swan Lake* (1943) [page 102]

Leslie Hurry Huntsmen, Act I, *Swan Lake* (1943) [page 102]

Leslie Hurry Odette, Act II, *Swan Lake* (1943) [page 103]

Leslie Hurry Set for Act III, *Swan Lake* (1943) [page 103]

Leslie Hurry Odile, Act III, *Swan Lake* (1943) [page 103]

Leslie Hurry Set for Act IV, *Swan Lake* (1943) [page 104]

John Piper Set for Scene 2, *The Quest* (1943)

John Piper Costume for Lechery, *The Quest* (1943)

Edward Burra Set for *Miracle in the Gorbals* (1944) [page 148]

Edward Burra Costume for The Suicide, *Miracle in the Gorbals* (1944)

Edward Burra Frontcloth, *Miracle in the Gorbals* (1944) [page 149]

Alexandre Benois Costume for the Neapolitan Dance, *Swan Lake* (1945)

James Bailey Set for Act I, *Giselle* (1946) [production photograph, page 27]

Jean Hugo Set and costumes for *Les Amours de Jupiter* (1946) [page 150]

Jean Hugo Set and costumes for *Les Amours de Jupiter* (1946) [page 151]

Oliver Messel Backdrop and cut cloths, Act II, *The Sleeping Beauty* (1946) [Set design page 89]

Peter Williams Set for Act II, *Giselle* (1947) [page 152]

Peter Williams Costume for the Polovtsian Chief, *Prince Igor* (1948) [page 153]

Peter Williams Preliminary set sketch, *Prince Igor* (1948)

Leonard Rosoman Backcloth for *Pleasuredrome* (1949) [page 154]

Cecil Beaton Set for *Illuminations* (1950)

1951–60

Robert Colquhoun and Robert MacBryde Costume for *Donald of the Burthens* (1951)

Robert Colquhoun and Robert MacBryde Costume for *Donald of the Burthens* (1951)

Nicholas Georgiadis Set for *Danses Concertantes* (1955) [photographs of 1955 and 1979 designs, page 157]

Peter Snow Set for *Variations on a Theme of Purcell* (1955) [page 155]

Mstislav Doboujinski Set for *Coppélia* (1957)

Lila de Nobili Sets for *Ondine* (1958) [page 158]

Lila de Nobili Costumes for the corps de ballet, *Ondine* (1958) [page 159]

Norman McDowell Costumes for the Nun and the Schoolgirl, *London Morning* (1959) [page 160]

1961–70

Keith Vaughan Set project for a ballet on the theme of *Francesca da Rimini* (c.1960s) [page 161]

Ralph Koltai Costumes for *A Place in the Desert* (1961) [production photograph, page 47]

André Levasseur Costume for Margot Fonteyn, *Le Corsaire* pas de deux (1962)

André Levasseur Costume for Rudolf Nureyev, *Le Corsaire* pas de deux (1962)

Nicholas Georgiadis Set for *Las Hermanas* (1963) [production photograph, page 162]

Harry Cordwell Set for *Sweet Dancer* (1964)

Nicholas Georgiadis Set for Act III, Scene 4, *Romeo and Juliet* (1965) [four photographs of redesigned model, pages 120–1]

Nicholas Georgiadis Costume for Benvolio, Act I, *Romeo and Juliet* (1965)

Peter Farmer Costumes for *The Dream* (1967) [page 122]

Peter Farmer Costumes for *The Dream* (1967)

Patrick Procktor Frontcloth, *Cage of God* (1967) [page 164]

Charles Dunlop Costume design for *Spectrum* (1967) [page 166]

Derek Jarman Costume for Monday's Child, *Jazz Calendar* (1968) [production photograph, page 163]

1971–80

Nadine Baylis Costumes for *That Is the Show* (1971) [page 46]

Barry Kay Costume for a relative, Act III, *Anastasia* (1971) [page 165]

Ian Spurling Hats for *Elite Syncopations* (1974)

Ian Spurling Costumes for *Elite Syncopations* (1974) [page 170]

Nicholas Georgiadis Set for the Prologue, *The Sleeping Beauty* (1975)

Peter Docherty 'The Land of Snow', *The Nutcracker* (1976) [page 95]

Yolanda Sonnabend Costume designs for *Requiem* (1976)

Yolanda Sonnabend Set for *Requiem* (1976) [page 167]

Pamela Howard *War Music* (1977) [page 76]

Peter Snow Set, Act III, *Coppélia*. (1978) [page 117]

Peter Snow Costume for *Coppélia* (1978) [page 117]

Peter Snow Costume for Franz, *Coppélia* (1978) [page 117]

1981–90

Norberto Chiesa Costume for Siobhan Davies, *Masque of Separation* (1981)

John Napier Costume for Macavity, *Cats* (1981) [page 129]

Terry Bartlett The Swan Cloak from *The Swan of Tuonela* (1982) [page 171]

Carl Toms Costume for Russian Dancer, *Swan Lake* (1982) [page 104]

David Walker Set for Act II, *La Sylphide* (1982) [page 168]

David Hockney Set for *Varii Capricci* (1983) [page 169]

Richard Hudson Costume for *St Anthony Variations* (1983) [page 174]

Bridget Riley Set for *Colour Moves* (1983) [page 172]

Mathilde Sandberg Two banners which formed the set for *Riccordi* (1983)

Patrick Caulfield Set for *Party Game* (1984) [page 173]

Victor Pasmore Set for *Young Apollo* (1984) [page 176]

Mathilde Sandberg Costume for Leslie Collier, *Fleeting Figures* (1984)

Mathilde Sandberg Set for *Fleeting Figures* (1984) [page 175]

Richard Smith Costume for *Dangerous Liaisons* (1985) [page 177]

Terry Bartlett Costume for The Wolf, *The Snow Queen* (1986)

John Hoyland Costume for *Zanza* (1986) [page 178]

Richard Hudson Costume for the Burnt Fairy, *Mignon* (1986)

Peter Logan *Red and Blue Crayons*, a dancing sculpture (1986) [page 179]

Yolanda Sonnabend Study for Rothbart's attendants, Act II, *Swan Lake* (1986) [page 100]

David Buckland Set for *Rushes* (1987) [page 180]

Andrew Logan Costume for Female Cat Attendants, *Bastet* (1988)

Andrew Logan Costume for Bastet, *Bastet* (1988) [page 181]

Jennifer Carey Dancers Entrance, *Waving at the Tide* (1989) [page 182]

Robin Don Costumes for *Song and Dance* (1989) [page 133]

Antony McDonald Costume design for *Heaven Ablaze in His Breast* (1989) [page 183]

Allen Jones Costumes for *Cinema* (1989)

Jennifer Carey Set design for *A Matter of Chance* (1990) [page 109]

John Macfarlane 'The Land of Sweets', *The Nutcracker* (1990) [page 98]

John Macfarlane Costume for Drosselmeyer's Servant, *The Nutcracker* (1990)

John Macfarlane Design for Drosselmeyer's cloak, *The Nutcracker* (1990)

Stephen Meaha Costume for *Enclosure* (1990) [page 184]

1991–93

David Fielding Costumes for the Pet Shop Boys (1991) [page 186]

David Fielding Costumes for the Pet Shop Boys (1991) [page 187]

Paul Andrews Costumes for Romeo and Harlot, *Romeo and Juliet* (1992) [page 185]

Lez Brotherston Costume for the Black Swan, *Swan Lake* (1992) [page 105]

Lez Brotherston Costume for Rothbart, *Swan Lake* (1992)

Peter Farley Costumes for Joseph Cippola and David Yow, *Dark Horizons* (1992) [costume for David Yow, page 188]

Jock McFadyen Set for *The Judas Tree* (1992) [page 189]

Deanna Petherbridge Floorcloth for *Bloodlines* (1992) [page 190]

David Walker Costumes for Courtiers, *Cinderella* (1992) [page 114]

Peter Whiteman Costume for a Penguin, *The Snow Princess* (1992)

Peter Whiteman Set design for Act II, The Forest, *The Snow Princess* (1992) [page 191]

Richard Bridgland Costume for the Squire, *Coppélia* (1993) [page 117]

Peter Docherty Costume for Court Lady, *The Sleeping Beauty* (1993) [page 93]

Bernadette Roberts Set and costumes for *Simple Symphony* (1993) [page 192]

Yolanda Sonnabend Costumes for the Rats, *The Nutcracker and the Hard Nut* (1993) [page 99]

Yolanda Sonnabend Costume for a Rat, *The Nutcracker and the Hard Nut* (1993)

Theatre Artists Featured in the Book

Selected dance designs by the listed artists follow the biographical information. The choreographer's name appears after the title in each case.

Paul Andrews

Trained at Wimbledon School of Art and Design. During his final degree show, Sir Kenneth MacMillan saw his work and invited him to design the set and costumes for a new production of his ballet *Romeo and Juliet* for the Birmingham Royal Ballet, his first commission for the professional stage. He has designed for musicals and theatre as well as dance, including several productions for Theatre Clwyd and West Yorkshire Playhouse designs which include *West Side Story* and *Mail Order Bride.*

1992 *Romeo and Juliet*, MacMillan, Birmingham Royal Ballet, Birmingham Hippodrome

Maxwell Armfield

Born in Ringwood, Hampshire in 1881, he studied at the Birmingham School of Art and at the Atelier Colarossi in Paris. After travelling through Italy, he returned to England in 1905, holding his first solo exhibition three years later. With his wife, Constance Smedley, he illustrated the *Christian Science Monitor* before sailing to America in 1915. Together the two of them ran Berkeley University's stage design course from 1918 onward. He developed an interest in tempera painting and, on his return to England in the 1920s, worked in this medium, writing *A Manual of Tempera Painting*

in 1930. An interest in architecture, developed in America, led him to design his own house at Ibsley, while his later paintings exhibited an enthusiasm for symbolic and theosophical ideas. Armfield and his wife were responsible for founding The Greenleaf Theatre and wrote plays performed by the group. Shortly before his death, in 1972, the Fine Art Society honoured his work with a 90th birthday exhibition.

1919 *Miriam, Sister of Moses*, Shawn, Ted Shawn and Ruth St Denis, Greek Theatre, University of California

John Armstrong

Born in Hastings in 1893, John Armstrong studied at St John's College, Oxford, and St John's Wood School of Art where his studies were interrupted by the war. In 1928 he held his first one-man show at the Leicester Galleries, London. During the 1930s he worked as a designer for theatre, films and ballet, including the celebrated *Façade*. His film work included Sir Alexander Korda's *Henry VIII*, *Rembrandt* and *The Scarlet Pimpernel*. In World War Two he was an Official War Artist. In 1933 Armstrong became a member of the Unit One movement, exhibiting with the group the following year at the Mayor Gallery. Commissions following the war included the painting *The Storm* for the Festival of Britain (1951) and a mural for the Royal Marsden Hospital at Sutton, Surrey (1961). In 1966 he was elected ARA. He died in London in 1973.

1926 *Riverside Nights* (revue), Lyric Theatre, Hammersmith
1931 *Façade*, Ashton, Camargo Society,

Cambridge Theatre, London
1933 *The Birthday of Oberon*, de Valois, Vic-Wells Ballet, Sadler's Wells, London
1935 *Façade*, Ashton, Vic-Wells Ballet, Sadler's Wells, London, redesigned 1940

James Bailey

Born in 1921, James Bailey's principal design work was for drama, both in Britain and America, rather than dance, though he was the first British designer to be commissioned to design a full-length ballet for La Scala Opera House in Milan. His theatre work includes *Hamlet* for Paul Scofield at Stratford-upon-Avon, *As You Like It* in New York for Katherine Hepburn (for whom he also designed *The Millionairess* in London and New York) and *The Way of the World* for John Gielgud. From 1960 he devoted more time to his paintings, exhibiting in London and abroad including a show at the Casino, Monte Carlo in 1978. He died in 1980.

1946 *Giselle* (revised 1951), after Coralli, produced by Sergeyev, Sadler's Wells Ballet, Royal Opera House, London
1952 *Vision of Marguerite*, Ashton, London Festival Ballet, Stoll Theatre, London
1957 *Casse-Noisette*, Rodrigues after Ivanov, produced by Rodrigues, La Scala, Milan
1960 *Giselle*, Coralli/Perrot, revised Sergeyev with Ashton, produced by Ashton/Karsavina, The Royal Ballet, Metropolitan Opera House, New York
1980 *Giselle*, Coralli/Perrot, revised Sergeyev with Ashton, produced in revised form by Morrice, The Royal Ballet, Covent Garden

Léon Bakst

Born in Grodno, Russia, in 1866, Bakst co-founded the magazine *The World of Art* in 1899, which was published by Diaghilev. Through Diaghilev he worked extensively with the Ballets Russes from 1909 onward. Bakst and Alexandre Benois together provided the visual foundation of Diaghilev's Ballets Russes. He resolutely went his own way with a style that made no concessions to the dislocations of Cubism or the broad strokes of Expressionism, favouring instead grandeur and incorporation of oriental motifs. Besides his work with Diaghilev, Bakst designed *Le Martyre de Saint-Sébastien* for Ida Rubinstein and his scenery was used by Meyerhold in his production of *La Pisanella*. Bakst both devised and designed *Artémis Troublée* in 1922. He died in Paris in 1924.

1901 *Sylvia*, N. Legat and S. Legat, Maryinsky Theatre, St Petersburg (not produced)

1902 *Le Coeur de la Marquise*, Petipa, Hermitage Theatre, St Petersburg

1903 *The Fairy Doll (Die Puppenfee)*, N. Legat and S. Legat, Hermitage Theatre, St Petersburg

1906 *Flight of the Bumblebee*, Fokine after Petipa, St Petersburg

1907 Costume for Kshessinska and torch dancers for *Eunice*, Fokine, Maryinsky Theatre, St Petersburg; costumes with Vera Fokina for *Chopiniana*, Fokine, Maryinsky Theatre, St Petersburg; costume for Pavlova for *The Dying Swan*, Fokine, Maryinsky Theatre, St Petersburg; costumes for Karsavina for *Torch Dance (Danse Assyrienne)*, Fokine, Maryinsky Theatre, St Petersburg

1908 Costumes with Oreste Allegri for *Egyptian Nights*, Fokine, Maryinsky Theatre, St Petersburg; *Bal Poudre*, Fokine, Pavlov Hall, St Petersburg; costumes for *Salome*, Fokine, Maryinsky Theatre, St Petersburg; *Rêverie Romantique, Ballet sur la musique de Chopin* (*Chopiniana* 2nd version), with Vera Fokine, Maryinsky Theatre, St Petersburg; *Dance of the Seven Veils*, Fokine, Theatre of the Conservatoire, St Petersburg

1909 Costumes with Alexandre Benois and others for *Le Festin, Suite de danses*, Petipa, Diaghilev's Ballets Russes, Théâtre du Châtelet, Paris (set by Konstantin Korovin); *Cléopâtre* (version of *Egyptian Nights*), Fokine, Diaghilev's Ballets Russes, Théâtre du Châtelet, Paris

1910 Costume for Pavlova for *Bacchanale*, Fokine, Hall of the Assembly of the Nobility, St Petersburg; costumes for *Dance Siamoise* (later part of *Les Orientales*), Nijinsky, Maryinsky Theatre, St Petersburg; costumes for *Le Carnaval*, Fokine, Diaghilev's Ballets Russes, Pavlov Hall, St Petersburg; *Schéhérazade*, Fokine, Diaghilev's Ballets Russes, Théâtre National de l'Opéra, Paris; costumes with Alexander Golovin for *L'Oiseau de Feu* (*The Firebird*), Fokine, Diaghilev's Ballets Russes, Théâtre National de l'Opéra, Paris; costumes with Konstantin Korovin for *Les Orientales*, Fokine, Théâtre National de l'Opéra, Paris

1911 *Le Spectre de la Rose*, Fokine, Diaghilev's Ballets Russes, Théâtre de Monte Carlo, Monte Carlo; *Narcisse*, Fokine, Diaghilev's Ballets Russes, Théâtre de l'Opéra, Monte Carlo; *Le Martyre de Saint-Sébastien*, Fokine, Ida Rubinstein's Company, Théâtre du Châtelet, Paris; costumes with Boris Anisfeldt for *Sadko*, Fokine, Diaghilev's Ballets Russes, Théâtre du Châtelet, Paris; *La Péri*, Diaghilev's Ballets Russes (not produced)

1912 *Le Dieu Bleu*, Fokine, Diaghilev's Ballets Russes, Théâtre du Châtelet, Paris; costumes for *Thamar*, Fokine, Diaghilev's Ballets Russes, Théâtre du Châtelet, Paris; *Salome*, Fokine, Ida Rubinstein's Company, Théâtre du Châtelet, Paris; *Les Papillons*, Fokine, Maryinsky Theatre, St Petersburg; *Daphnis et Chloë*, Fokine, Diaghilev's Ballets Russes, Théâtre du Châtelet, Paris; *L'Après-midi d'un Faune*, Nijinsky, Diaghilev's Ballets Russes, Théâtre du Châtelet, Paris

1913 *La Pisanelle ou La Mort Parfumée*, Fokine, Ida Rubinstein's Company, Théâtre du Châtelet, Paris; *Oriental Fantasy*, Zajlich, Pavlova's Company, London; *Orpheus* (not produced); *Jeux*, Nijinsky, Diaghilev's Ballets Russes, Théâtre des Champs-Elysées, Paris

1914 Costumes for *La Légende de Joseph*, Fokine, Diaghilev's Ballets Russes, Théâtre de l'Opéra, Paris; (with Doboujinsky); *Midas*, Fokine, Diaghilev's Ballets Russes, Théâtre de l'Opéra, Paris; *Mefistofele* (opera, choreographed by Ambrosing, Royal Opera House, London

1915 New costumes for Firebird and Ivan for *L'Oiseau de Feu*, Fokine, Diaghilev's Ballets Russes; new set and costumes for *Schéhérazade,* Fokine, Diaghilev's Ballets Russes

1916 *The Sleeping Beauty* Act II, Clustine, Anna Pavlova's Company, Paris

1917 *Les Femmes de Bonne Humeur*, Massine, Diaghilev's Ballets Russes, Teatro Costanzi, Rome

1918 Costumes for *La Boutique Fantasque*, Massine, Diaghilev's Ballets Russes (not used, Bakst replaced by Derain)

1919 Costumes for *Aladin ou La Lampe Merveilleuse* (revue), Quinault, Théâtre

Marigny, Paris

1920 *Mecca*, melodrama, choreographed by
Fokine, Century Theatre, New York

1921 *The Sleeping Princess*, Petipa, Ivanov, with
additions by Nijinska, Diaghilev's Ballets
Russes, Alhambra Theatre, London

1922 *Artémis Troublée*, Guerra, Paris Opéra

John Banting

Born in 1902, Banting's art training began with
evening classes while working as a bank clerk.
He then studied for a year in Paris before
returning to clerical work in England. His
career as an artist gained momentum at the end
of the 1920s with his first exhibition in 1929 and
the ballet designs for *Pomona* and *Prometheus*.
The following year he took a studio in Paris and
later exhibited in the International Surrealist
Exhibition in London (1936). His enthusiasm
for art, and his extensive knowledge of the field,
informed both his subsequent positions; art
director for Strand Films and, in 1941, art editor
for the magazine *Our Time*. He moved to
Ireland to work in 1947 and died in 1972.

1930 *Pomona*, Ashton, Camargo Society,
Cambridge Theatre, London

1936 *Prometheus*, de Valois, Vic-Wells Ballet,
Sadler's Wells, London

1937 *Pomona*, Ashton, Vic-Wells Ballet, Sadler's
Wells, London

Terry Bartlett

Having completed a degree in Theatre Design
at Wimbledon School of Art, Terry Bartlett
enrolled on the Fine Art/Theatre Design Higher
Diploma course at the Slade School of Art from
1977 until 1979. During his studies he worked
as a design assistant to Nicholas Georgiadis
(*Mayerling*) before assisting Philip Prowse on a
succession of productions between 1979 and
1980. His first commission as designer was for
David Bintley's *Night Moves*, and his subsequent
work has largely been for the dance in
collaboration with Bintley. Bartlett has designed
a number of theatre productions for the
Citizens' Theatre in Glasgow and taught
Theatre Design in several London colleges. In
1993 Terry Bartlett was one of the guest lecturers
for The Peter Williams Design for Dance
Project at Central Saint Martins College of Art
and Design.

1981 *Night Moves*, Bintley, Sadler's Wells Royal
Ballet, Sadler's Wells, London

1982 *The Swan of Tuonela*, Bintley, Sadler's
Wells Royal Ballet, Sadler's Wells, London

1983 *Choros*, Bintley, Sadler's Wells Royal
Ballet, Sadler's Wells, London; *Consort
Lessons*, Bintley, The Royal Ballet, Royal
Opera House, London

1985 *Carmen* (two-act version), Darrell,
Scottish Ballet; *The Sons of Horus*, Bintley,
The Royal Ballet, Royal Opera House,
London

1986 *The Snow Queen*, Bintley, Sadler's Wells
Royal Ballet, Birmingham Hippodrome

1987 *Allegri Diversi*, Bintley, Sadler's Wells
Royal Ballet, Sadler's Wells, London; *Consort
Lessons*, Bintley, Les Grands Ballets
Canadiens; *Carmen* (one-act version),
Darrell, Scottish Ballet

1988 *The Sons of Horus*, Bintley, San Francisco
Ballet; *Allegri Diversi*, Bintley, Ballett
Bayerische Staatsoper; *The Trial of
Prometheus*, Bintley, The Royal Ballet, Royal
Opera House, London; *The Spirit of Fugue*,
Bintley, The Royal Ballet, Royal Opera
House, London

1990 *The Wanderer Fantasy*, Bintley, San
Francisco Ballet; *Allegri Diversi*, Bintley,
Boston Ballet

Nadine Baylis

Nadine Baylis trained at the Central School of
Art and Design. She has worked with major
dance companies including American Ballet
Theatre, Dance Theatre of Harlem, Canadian
National Ballet, Stuttgart Ballet, Royal Danish
Ballet, Nederlands Dans Theater, Ballet
Rambert, London Festival Ballet and the Royal
Ballet. She has worked with choreographers
such as Glen Tetley, Christopher Bruce and Jirí
Kylián, and designed the costumes for
Raymonda for Rudolf Nureyev. Her other work
includes a production of *Hamlet* at Elsinore and
ice shows for John Curry. Opera commissions
include *L'Incoronazione di Poppea* for Kent
Opera.

1965 *Realms of Choice*, Morrice, Ballet Rambert;
costumes for *Raymonda*, Nureyev after
Petipa, Australian Ballet, Birmingham
Theatre, Birmingham, England

1966 *Time Base*, Chesworth, Ballet Rambert

1967 *Hazard*, Morrice, Ballet Rambert;
Ziggurat, Tetley, Ballet Rambert; *L'Après-midi
d'un Faune*, Nijinsky, Ballet Rambert

1968 *Embrace Tiger and Return to Mountain*,
Tetley, Ballet Rambert; *Them and Us*,
Morrice, Ballet Rambert

1969 *Blind Sight*, Morrice, Ballet Rambert;
Living Space, Bruce, Ballet Rambert; *Pastorale
Variée*, Morrice, Ballet Rambert

1970 *Imaginary Film*, Tetley, Nederlands Dans Theater; *Field Figures*, Tetley, The Royal Ballet, Theatre Royal, Nottingham; set for *Mutations*, Tetley/Van Manen, Nederlands Dans Theater

1971 *Rag Dances*, Tetley, Ballet Rambert; *That Is the Show*, Morrice, Ballet Rambert; *Solo*, Morrice, Ballet Rambert; *Games for Five Players*, Chesworth, Northern Dance Theatre

1972 *Small Parades*, Tetley, Nederlands Dans Theater; *Threshold*, Tetley, Hamburg State Opera; *Dance for New Dimensions* (. . . *for these who die as cattle*), Bruce; *Ladies Ladies*, Morrice; *4 Pieces for 6 Dancers*, Law; *Theme and Variations*, Jones; *Full Circle*, Avrahami; *Stop-Over*, Scoglio; *Sonata for Two*, Taylor; *Pattern for an Escalator*, Chesworth (all Ballet Rambert)

1973 *Gemini*, Tetley, Australian Ballet; *There Was a Time*, Bruce, Ballet Rambert; *Isolde*, Morrice, Ballet Rambert; *Duets*, Bruce, Ballet Rambert

1974 *Sacre du Printemps*, Tetley, Munich State Opera; *Tristan*, Tetley, Paris Opéra; *Unfamiliar Playground*, Bruce, Sadler's Wells Royal Ballet, Sadler's Wells, London; *Project 6354/9116 Mk II*, Chesworth, Ballet Rambert

1975 *Greening*, Tetley, Stuttgart Ballet; *Ancient Voices of Children*, Bruce, Ballet Rambert; *Freefall*, Tetley, Ballet Rambert

1976 *Moveable Garden*, Tetley, Ballet Rambert; *Girl with a Straw Hat*, Bruce, Ballet Rambert; *Promenade*, Bruce, Ballet Rambert; *Black Angels*, Bruce, Ballet Rambert; *Reflections*, North, Ballet Rambert; *Will-o'-the-Wisp* (also known as *Feux Follets*), MacMillan, John Curry Theatre of Skating

1977 *Episode One*, Flier, Ballet Rambert; *Echoes of a Night Sky*, Bruce, Ballet Rambert; *Frames, Pulse and Interruptions*, Flier, Ballet Rambert; *Sleeping Birds* (redesigned), Sugihara, Ballet Rambert

1978 *Praeludium*, Tetley, Ballet Rambert; *Laocoon*, Imre, Ballet Rambert; *Fourfold*, Vardi, Ballet Rambert; *Seven Deadly Sins*, Alston, English National Opera, London Coliseum with Ralph Koltai

1979 *Echoi*, Flier, Ballet Rambert; *The Tempest*, Tetley, Ballet Rambert

1980 *Journey to Avalon*, Moreland, London Festival Ballet

1983 *Murderer Hope of Women*, Tetley, Ballet Rambert

1987 *The Phantasmagoria*, Cohan, Jobe, Bhuller, London Contemporary Dance Theatre; *Paramour*, Lustig, Sadler's Wells Royal Ballet, Birmingham Hippodrome

1988 *The Edge of Silence*, Lustig, Sadler's Wells Royal Ballet, Sadler's Wells, London

1991 *Choreatium*, Massine, Birmingham Royal Ballet, Birmingham Hippodrome (reconstruction and production by Leskova)

1992 *Alice in Wonderland*, Stevenson, Houston Ballet

Sir Cecil Beaton

Born in 1904, educated at Harrow and St John's College, Cambridge (1922–5), Beaton made his name as a photographer. He was employed by *Vogue* in London and New York and held one-man exhibitions at the Cooling Gallery, London in 1927 and 1930. His first work for the stage was with Cochran's revues in the early 1930s. His theatre designs include *Lady Windermere's Fan* (1945), *An Ideal Husband* (1940) and *Quadrille* (1952) for Noël Coward. Opera designs include *Turandot* (1961) and *La Traviata* (1966), though his most widely seen design is that for *My Fair Lady* (1956) which was made into a double Oscar-winning film in 1963. He published several books, including *The Book of Beauty* (1930), a play, *The Gainsborough Girls* (1951) and six volumes of diaries between 1922 and 1980. He was awarded the Legion of Honour (1950), a CBE (1957) and was knighted in 1972. Beaton died in 1980.

1931 *The First Shoot*, Ashton, C.B. Cochran Revue

1936 *Apparitions*, Ashton, Vic-Wells Ballet, Sadler's Wells, London (revised in 1949 and 1952); *Le Pavillon*, Lichine, Ballets Russes de Monte Carlo, Royal Opera House, London

1946 *Les Sirènes*, Ashton, Sadler's Wells Ballet, Royal Opera House, London; *Camille*, Taras, Original Ballet Russe, Metropolitan Opera House, New York; *Les Patineurs*, Ashton, American Ballet Theatre, New York

1949 *Devoirs de Vacances*, Taras, Théâtre des Champs-Elysées, Paris

1950 *Illuminations*, Ashton, New York City Ballet, City Center, New York

1951 *Swan Lake*, Balanchine after Ivanov, New York City Ballet, City Center, New York; *Lady of the Camellias*, Tudor, New York City Ballet, City Center, New York; *Casse-Noisette*, Ivanov, arranged and produced by Ashton, Sadler's Wells Theatre Ballet, Sadler's Wells, London

1952 *Picnic at Tintagel*, Ashton, New York City Ballet, City Center, New York

1955 *Soirée*, Solov, Metropolitan Opera Ballet, Metropolitan Opera House, New York

1963 *Marguerite and Armand*, Ashton, The Royal Ballet, Royal Opera House, London

Alexandre Benois

Born in St Petersburg in 1870, Benois, in his work with Diaghilev's Ballets Russes, extended the role of the stage designer into all areas of production. He had been studying art in Paris some two years before Diaghilev's arrival and his love of ballet and breadth of knowledge clearly influenced the impresario's decision to turn to the stage. One of his many triumphs with the Ballets Russes was *Petrushka*, his design being complemented by Stravinsky's music, Fokine's choreography and Nijinsky's performance. Though best known for his dance designs, Benois was also adept at working for the theatre and opera, and the acclaim for his work with Diaghilev ensured a steady stream of commissions. After a long collaboration with Diaghilev, Benois was appointed principal designer for Ida Rubinstein's company's 1928 season and continued working for various companies until shortly before his death in 1960.

1901 Set for Act I of *Sylvia*, Mérante, Maryinsky Theatre, St Petersburg (not produced)

1907 *Le Pavillon d'Armide*, Fokine, Maryinsky Theatre, St Petersburg (restaged with revised designs by Diaghilev's Ballets Russes in 1909, Paris)

1908 *The Cheated Buyer*, Russian Merchant's Club, St Petersburg

1909 *Les Sylphides* (*Chopiniana*), Fokine, Théâtre du Châtelet, Paris; costumes with Léon Bakst and others for *Le Festin*, Fokine and others, Diaghilev's Ballets Russes, Paris

1910 *Giselle*, Petipa after Coralli, Perrot (staged by Fokine), Diaghilev's Ballets Russes, Théâtre National de l'Opéra, Paris

1911 *Petrushka*, Fokine, Diaghilev's Ballets Russes, Théâtre du Châtelet, Paris

1912 *Les Fêtes* (not produced)

1914 *Le Rossignol* (*Song of the Nightingale*), opera, Romanov, Diaghilev's Ballets Russes, Théâtre National de l'Opéra, Paris

1922 *Aurora's Wedding*, Petipa (additional costumes by Natalia Gontcharova), staged by Nijinska, Diaghilev's Ballets Russes, Théâtre National de l'Opéra, Paris

1924 *Le Médecin Malgré Lui*, opera, choreographed by Nijinska, Théâtre de Monte Carlo, Monte Carlo

1927 *The Sleeping Beauty*, after Petipa, Casino, Paris; *Le Coq d'Or*, opera-ballet, Théâtre Nationale de l'Opéra, Paris

1928 *La Bien-Aimée*, Nijinska, Ida Rubinstein Company, Paris; *Le Baiser de la Fée*, Nijinska, Ida Rubinstein Company, Paris; *Les Noces de l'Amour et de Psyché*, Nijinska, Ida Rubinstein Company, Paris; *Bolero*, Nijinska, Ida Rubinstein Company, Paris; *La Princesse Cygne*, Nijinska, Ida Rubinstein Company, Paris; *David*, Nijinska, Ida Rubinstein Company, Paris

1929 *La Valse*, Nijinska, Ida Rubinstein Company, Monte Carlo; *Les Enchantements d'Alcine*, Massine, Ida Rubinstein Company, Paris

1931 *Amphion*, Massine, Ida Rubinstein Company, Paris

1932 *Le Bourgeois Gentilhomme*, Balanchine, Ballets Russes de Monte Carlo, Monte Carlo

1934 *Semiramis*, Fokine, Ida Rubinstein Company, Paris; *Diane de Poitiers*, Fokine, Ida Rubinstein Company, Paris

1935 *Psyché*, Fokine, Olga Spessivtseva Concert, Paris

1938 *The Nutcracker*, after Ivanov, La Scala, Milan

1940 *Graduation Ball*, Lichine, Original Ballet Russe, Sydney; *The Nutcracker*, Fedorova after Ivanov, Ballets Russes de Monte Carlo, New York; *Les Sylphides*, Fokine, Sadler's Wells Ballet

1945 *Swan Lake*, after Petipa, Ivanov, Ballet Russe de Monte Carlo

1946 *Raymonda*, Danilova, Balanchine after Petipa, Ballet Russe de Monte Carlo, New York

1949 *Le Moulin Enchanté*, Lichine, de Cuevas Grand Ballet de Monte Carlo

1950 *Les Sylphides*, Fokine, La Scala, Milan

1955 *Le Spectre de la Rose*, Fokine, La Scala, Milan

1957 *The Nutcracker*, Ivanov, London Festival Ballet, London; *Graduation Ball*, Lichine, London Festival Ballet, London; *Petrushka*, Fokine, revived Grigoriev/Tchernicheva, The Royal Ballet, Royal Opera House, London

Nadia Benois

Nadia Benois was born near St Petersburg, Russia, in 1896. Her father was an architect and the theatre designer Alexandre Benois was her uncle. She studied art at a private school in St Petersburg. She married Iona Ustinov in 1920 and moved to England where, in 1924, she had her first exhibition of paintings at the Little Gallery in the Adelphi. She died in 1975.

1913 *Invitation to the Dance*, Zajlich, Anna Pavlova Ballet

1935 *The Descent of Hebe*, Tudor, Ballet Rambert

1937 *Dark Elegies*, Tudor, Ballet Rambert; *Suite of Airs*, Tudor, Ballet Rambert

1938 *La Péri*, Staff, Ballet Rambert

1939 *Lady into Fox*, Howard, Ballet Rambert; *The Sleeping Princess*, produced by Sergeyev, after Petipa, Sadler's Wells Ballet, Sadler's Wells, London
1940 *Cap over Mill*, Gore, Ballet Rambert
1970 *Suite No.3*, Balanchine, New York City Ballet

Christian Bérard

Born in 1902, Christian Bérard's stage design is characterised by a numinous quality arising from his involvement with the neo-humanist movement, a short-lived, loose collection of artists concerned to redress what they saw as an over-abundance of intellectual and abstract pursuit, to the detriment of the spiritual. Often with the most simple materials he created the illusion of transforming the everyday, a quality that endeared him to fashion designers who took up his methods during the inter-war years. Although his solitary design for Diaghilev, *Coppélia*, was never produced, Bérard undoubtedly sated the appetites of the Parisian society that had grown accustomed to the impresario's emphasis upon design. He was co-founder, with writer Boris Kochno and choreographer Roland Petit, of the Ballets des Champs-Elysées in 1945. He continued to design for dance until his death in Paris in 1949.

1929 *Coppélia*, after Petipa, Cecchetti, Diaghilev's Ballets Russes (not produced)
1930 *La Nuit*, Lifar, Cochran's 1930 Revue, London and Manchester
1932 *Cotillon*, Balanchine, Ballets Russes de Monte Carlo, Monte Carlo
1933 *Mozartiana*, Balanchine, Les Ballets 1933, Paris

1936 *La Symphonie Fantastique*, Massine, Colonel de Basil's Ballet Russe, London
1937 *Les Elfes*, Fokine, Ballet de Monte Carlo, Monte Carlo
1938 *Seventh Symphony*, Massine, Ballet Russe de Monte Carlo, Monte Carlo
1944 *La Jeune Fille Endormie*, Petit, Salle Pleyel, Paris
1945 *Les Forains*, Petit, Ballets des Champs-Elysées, Paris
1946 Costumes for *La Sylphide*, Gsovsky, Ballets des Champs-Elysées, Paris; costumes for *Le Jeune Homme et la Mort*, Petit, Ballets des Champs-Elysées, Théâtre des Champs-Elysées, Paris
1947 *La Rencontre ou L'Oedipe et le Sphinx*, Lichine, Ballets des Champs-Elysées, Paris
1948 *Clock Symphony*, Massine, Sadler's Wells Ballet, Royal Opera House, London

Maria Bjørnson

Maria Bjørnson trained at Central Saint Martins. After graduating she embarked on a career that embraces theatre, opera, musical and dance design. Among her many opera designs are *Le Nozze di Figaro* (Geneva), *Die Walküre* and *Carmen* for English National Opera and *The Gambler* for Netherlands Opera. Her designs for the 1982 Janacek Cycle for Welsh National Opera won the Prague Biennale. She is perhaps best known for designs for musicals which include *The Phantom of the Opera*, *Aspects of Love* and *Follies*. She has taught on the Theatre Design course at Central Saint Martins College of Art and Design and has for some years been an external examiner at the college.

1973 *Ballet*, untitled, Carroll, *Collaborations 3*,

Ballet Rambert/Central School of Art and Design, with Sue Blane
1986 *The Phantom of the Opera*, directed by Harold Prince, Her Majesty's Theatre, London
1987 *Follies*, Avian, directed by Mike Ockrent, Phoenix Theatre, London
1994 *The Sleeping Beauty*, Petipa, produced by Dowell, The Royal Ballet, Royal Opera House, London

Richard Bridgland

Richard Bridgland was born in Chicago and studied English Literature at Durham University where he designed sets and costumes for more than 20 productions. He then studied theatre design at Central Saint Martins College of Art and Design. He won the Portugal 600 Award for his designs for *The Passion of Marianne*, and worked with Gerald Scarfe on designs for *The Magic Flute* directed by Sir Peter Hall for the Los Angeles Opera. His film credits include the recent *Richard III* starring Sir Ian MacKellen.

1992 *Trance*, Anderson, The Cholmondleys; *Six Pack*, Craft, Ben Craft; *Blue*, Bhuller, Darshan Singh Bhuller; *Biscopis Populi*, Page, London City Ballet
1993 *Coppélia*, Petipa, produced by Burke, Scottish Ballet

Lez Brotherston

Lez Brotherston trained at Central School of Art and Design. On graduating in 1984 he designed the film *Letter to Brezhnev*. He has designed for numerous opera companies including Welsh National Opera (*Hänsel and Gretel*), Scottish Opera (*Pearl Fishers*) and productions for the Hong Kong Arts Festival. His theatre work includes a long association with the Actor's Touring Company, designs for whom include *The Maids* and *No Way Out*. Lez Brotherston has also designed extensively for Greenwich Theatre. Designs for musicals include West Yorkshire Playhouse's *High Society* and *Cabaret* for Sheffield Crucible. Future projects include *Dracula* for Northern Ballet Theatre.

1990 *Strange Meeting*, Pink, Northern Ballet Theatre

1991 *Romeo and Juliet*, Moricone, produced by Gable, Northern Ballet Theatre, Grand Theatre, Blackpool

1992 *Swan Lake*, Wayne, produced by Gable, Northern Ballet Theatre

1992 *A Christmas Carol*, Moricone, produced by Gable, Northern Ballet Theatre

1994 *Highland Fling*, Bourne, Adventures in Motion Pictures

1995 *The Brontës*, Lynne, produced by Gable, Northern Ballet Theatre; *Swan Lake*, Bourne, Adventures in Motion Pictures

David Buckland

David Buckland is both a designer and artist. He studied at the London College of Printing 1967–70, was awarded a fellowship in Creative Photography from 1971–3 with Northern Arts Association and won the Kodak Fellowship for a Photographic Study of Dance in 1978–9. He has worked with numerous dance companies, including the Siobhan Davies Dance Company, Rambert Dance Company and English

National Ballet. He recently designed the opera *The Man with the Wind at his Heels* for English National Opera. His work has been exhibited worldwide and is featured in the collections of many galleries, including the Metropolitan Museum, New York, the Centre Georges Pompidou, Paris, and the National Portrait Gallery, London. Three collections of his work have been published.

1980 *Rainbow Ripples*, Alston, Ballet Rambert

1981 *Free Setting*, Davies, London Contemporary Dance Theatre; *Plain Song*, Davies, Siobhan Davies and Dancers, Theatre Royal, Stratford East; *Standing Waves*, Davies, Siobhan Davies and Dancers, Theatre Royal, Stratford East

1982 *Carnival*, Davies, Second Stride, Art Centre, University of Warwick (with Antony McDonald)

1983 *The Dancing Department*, Davies, LCDT, Apollo Theatre, Oxford

1984 Design and lighting, with Peter Mumford, for *New Galileo*, Davies, LCDT, Grand Theatre, Leeds; *Silent Partners*, Davies, Second Stride, Gardner Centre, Brighton

1985 *Bridge the Distance*, Davies, LCDT, Apollo Theatre, Oxford (frontcloth painted with Peter Morgan)

1986 *The Run to Earth*, Davies, LCDT, Congress Theatre, Eastbourne, with Russell Mills; *and they do*, Davies, LCDT, Sadler's Wells, London

1987 *Rushes*, Davies, Rambert Dance Company, Oxford Playhouse

1988 *Embarque*, Davies, Rambert Dance Company, Royal Northern College of Music, Manchester; *White Man Sleeps*, Davies, Siobhan Davies Company, Riverside Studios, London; *Wyoming*, Davies, Siobhan Davies Company, Riverside Studios, London

1989 *Cover Him with Grass*, Davies, Siobhan Davies Company, Riverside Studios, London (floorcloth by Patrick Jeffs)

1990 *Dancing Ledge*, Davies, English National Ballet, London Coliseum; *Different Trains*, Davies, Siobhan Davies Company, Sadler's Wells, London

1991 *Plainsong*, Davies, Rambert Dance Company; *Antic Heart*, Davies, Siobhan Davies Dance Company, Swindon

1992 *Arctic Heart*, Davies, Siobhan Davies Dance Company

1993 *Wanting to Tell Stories*, Davies, Siobhan Davies Dance Company, Gardner Centre, Brighton (costumes by Antony McDonald)

Edward Burra

Born in South Kensington, London, in 1905, Burra studied art at Chelsea Polytechnic (1921–3) and the Royal College of Art (1923–4). His first one-man show was at the Leicester Galleries in 1929 and he subsequently exhibited with the English Surrealists in 1936 and 1938. His early subject matter included the haunts of popular entertainment – cinemas, dance halls and bars – and his canvas captured the vitality of 1930s Harlem. He was ideally suited to convey the exuberance of Ashton's *Rio Grande* with its evocation of the transient pleasures of sailors on shore leave. His later interest in landscapes was again mirrored in his stage works, particularly in his realisation of Cervantes's and Chaucer's travellers' tales. He was elected an Associate of the Royal Academy in 1963 and was the subject of a retrospective exhibition at the Tate in 1973. Burra died in 1976.

1931 *Rio Grande*, Ashton, Camargo Society,

Savoy Theatre, London

1936 *Barabau*, de Valois, Sadler's Wells Ballet, Sadler's Wells, London

1944 *Miracle in the Gorbals*, Helpmann, Sadler's Wells Ballet, Prince's Theatre, London

1948 *Don Juan*, Ashton, Sadler's Wells Ballet, Royal Opera House, London

1950 *Don Quixote*, de Valois, Sadler's Wells Ballet, Royal Opera House, London

1951 *Canterbury Prologue*, Paltenghi, Ballet Rambert, King's Theatre, Hammersmith

Jennifer Carey

Jennifer Carey studied at Kingston School of Art prior to a diploma course at the Slade School of Fine Art, 1951–4. In 1955 she was awarded a French Government Scholarship and has worked extensively in theatre in addition to dance and opera commissions. During the 1970s she designed *Animal Farm* (National Theatre, directed by Peter Hall), *Dr Faustus* (with Michael Annals, Royal Shakespeare Company, directed by John Barton) and *Bow Down* (National Theatre collaboration between Harrison Birtwistle and Tony Harrison) as well as productions for fringe companies. As co-founder of 'That's Not It Theatre Company' with Natasha Morgan and Rick Fisher, she designed, co-devised and performed in eight productions that toured nationally. Opera designs include *L'Enfant et les Sortilèges* in Rotterdam and Nicholas Hytner's production of *Curlew River*. Her teaching and workshop experience is extensive; she is currently a Lecturer at Central Saint Martins College of Art and Design on the BA Hons Theatre Design course.

1985 *Marked Cards*, Williams, directed by Merwitzer, The Kosh

1986 *Telling Tales*, Williams, directed by Merwitzer, The Kosh; *Peasant on the Run*, Williams, directed by Merwitzer, The Kosh

1987 *The Edge*, Williams, directed by Merwitzer, The Kosh

1989 *Waving at the Tide*, Williams, directed by Merwitzer, The Kosh; *Endangered Species*, Williams, directed by Merwitzer, The Kosh

1990 *A Matter of Chance*, Williams, directed by Merwitzer, The Kosh

Patrick Caulfield

Patrick Caulfield was born in London in 1936 and studied at Chelsea School of Art (1956–9) and at the Royal College of Art where his work was seen within the context of Pop Art. His first one-man exhibition was held at the Robert Fraser Gallery, London in 1965, with further solo shows in New York (1966) and Milan (1967). He taught at Chelsea School of Art from 1963 until 1971 and won the Prix des Jeunes Artistes for graphics in Paris in 1965. A retrospective of his work was held at the Tate Gallery in 1981. Patrick Caulfield was made an Honorary Fellow of the London Institute in 1996.

1984 *Party Game*, Corder, The Royal Ballet, Royal Opera House, London

1995 *Rhapsody*, Ashton, The Royal Ballet, Royal Opera House, London

William Chappell

William Chappell was both a dancer and a designer. Born in Wolverhampton in 1908, he trained at Chelsea School of Art. He first appeared as a dancer with Ida Rubinstein's Company in 1929, a year after his first design commission. He was an early member of Ballet Rambert and also performed with the Camargo Society and the Vic-Wells Ballet. He is perhaps best known for his long association with the work of Frederick Ashton. He designed for a number of ballet companies and latterly directed plays, musicals and revues. In 1979, Chappell was adviser for the Nureyev season and for the Joffrey Ballet. As a writer he produced a biography of Margot Fonteyn and the book *Studies in Ballet*. He died in 1994.

1928 Costumes for *Leda and the Swan*, Ashton, Marie Rambert Dancers, London

1930 *Capriol Suite*, Ashton, Marie Rambert Dancers, London; costumes for *Mars and Venus*, Ashton, Marie Rambert Dancers, London; costumes for *Saudade do Brésil*, Ashton, Marie Rambert Dancers, London; costumes for *Follow Your Saint, The Passionate Pavane* and *Dances on a Scotch Theme*, Ashton, Arts Theatre Club, London

1931 *Cephalus and Procris*, de Valois, Camargo Society, London; *Le Boxing*, Salaman, Ballet Club, London; *La Péri*, Ashton, Ballet Club, London; *Mercury*, Ashton, Ballet Club, London; *The Lady of Shalott*, Ashton, Ballet Club, London; *The Jackdaw and the Pigeons*, de Valois, Old Vic Theatre, London; *Regatta*, Ashton, Vic-Wells Ballet, Old Vic Theatre, London; costumes, after Aubrey Beardsley, for *The Dancer's Reward*, de Valois, Camargo Society, London

1932 Costumes for *High Yellow*, Bradley and Ashton, Camargo Society, London; *Lysistrata*, Tudor, Ballet Club, London; *Foyer de Danse* (after Degas), Ashton, Ballet Club, London; *The Origin of Design*, after Inigo Jones, de Valois, Camargo Society, London; *Narcissus and Echo*, de Valois, Vic-Wells Ballet, Sadler's Wells, London; *An 1805 Impression* (later *Récamier*), Ashton, in *Magic Nights*, Charles B. Cochran Revue, London; (revue, costumes only with Norman Edwards), *Ballyhoo*, Ashton, Ballet Club, London

1933 *Les Rendezvous* (revised 1939), Ashton, Vic-Wells Ballet, Old Vic Theatre, London; *Atalanta of the East*, Tudor, Ballet Club, London; *The Wise and Foolish Virgins*, de Valois, Vic-Wells Ballet, Sadler's Wells, London; *Fête Polonaise*, de Valois, Vic-Wells Ballet, London; costumes for *The Sleeping Princess: Blue Bird pas de deux (The Enchanted Princess)*, Petipa, Vic-Wells Ballet, Sadler's Wells, London; *Pride*, de Valois, Vic-Wells Ballet, Sadler's Wells, London

1934 *Bar aux Folies-Bergère*, after Manet, de Valois, Ballet Rambert, London; costumes for *Paramour*, Tudor, Ballet Rambert, London; *The Jar*, de Valois, Vic-Wells Ballet, Sadler's Wells, London

1935 *Giselle*, after Coralli (staged Sergeyev), Vic-Wells Ballet, London; *Nursery Suite*, de Valois, Vic-Wells Ballet, London

1936 *Passionate Pavane*, Ashton, Ballet Rambert, London; costumes for *The Sleeping Princess*, Act III 'Aurora' *pas de deux*, Petipa, Vic-Wells Ballet, London

1937 *Les Patineurs*, Ashton, Vic-Wells Ballet, Sadler's Wells, London; costume for Joy Newton in *Perpetuum Mobile*, Ashton, Vic-Wells Ballet, London

1938 *The Judgement of Paris*, Ashton, Vic-Wells Ballet, Sadler's Wells, London; *The Tartans*, Staff, Ballet Rambert, London

1940 *Coppélia*, Petipa/Ivanov/Cecchetti, reconstructed by Sergeyev, Vic-Wells Ballet, Sadler's Wells, London (redesigned for Vic-Wells in 1946); *The Seasons*, Staff, London Ballet, London

1941 *Fête Polonaise* (as *Coppélia* Act III), de Valois, Sadler's Wells Ballet; *Bartlemas Dances*, Gore, Oxford University Ballet Club, Oxford; *Amoras*, Inglesby, International Ballet, London; *Swan Lake* Act II, Ivanov (staged Sergeyev), International Ballet, Glasgow; *Pavane pour une Infante Défunte*, Staff, Ballet Rambert, London

1943 Costumes for *Everyman*, Inglesby, International Ballet, London

1947 *Swan Lake*, Petipa, International Ballet, London

1948 *Capriol Suite*, Ashton, Sadler's Wells Theatre Ballet, Sadler's Wells, London; Costumes for 'Peasant' *pas de deux*, *Giselle*, Coralli, Sadler's Wells Theatre Ballet, Sadler's Wells, London

1972 *The Walk to the Paradise Garden*, Ashton, The Royal Ballet, Royal Opera House, London

1979 Costumes for *Salut d'Amour à Margot Fonteyn*, Ashton, The Royal Ballet, Royal Opera House, London

1980 Costumes for *Rhapsody*, Ashton, The Royal Ballet, Royal Opera House, London (set by Ashton)

John Chesworth

Born in Manchester, John Chesworth is best known for his work as a choreographer, dancer and ballet director. Having trained at the Rambert School, he went on to create roles in many of its ground-breaking productions, including Norman Morrice's first work, *Two Brothers* (1958) and Glen Tetley's *Ziggurat* (1967). As a choreographer he created work for Ballet Rambert including *Time Base* (1966) and *Pawn to King 5* (1968), and for other companies. He was Artistic Director of Ballet Rambert in the period 1974–80, which saw the continuation of the *Collaborations* series with Central School of Art and Design. He is an ardent promoter of the International Dance Course for Professional Choreographers and Composers and has been Artistic Director of the National Youth Dance Company since 1984.

1967 *Tic-Tack*, Chesworth, Ballet Rambert/ Central School of Art and Design, the Jeannetta Cochrane Theatre, London

1968 *H*, Chesworth, Ballet Rambert; (with M. Carney) *Pawn to King 5*, Chesworth, Ballet Rambert

Norberto Chiesa

After obtaining a BA in Fine Arts from the Cooper Union School of Art and Architecture in New York in 1964, Norberto Chiesa taught at the Sarah Lawrence College until 1970, offering instruction in Sculpture, Drawing and Printing Techniques, Intermedia and Environmental Design, and working also as Visiting Artist at Skidmore College, New York. He has taught courses in Design for the Stage at the London

Contemporary Dance School where he also designed many works for the London Contemporary Dance Theatre. In particular, his collaboration with Robert Cohan is one of the most enduring partnerships in dance, now into its third decade.

1969 *Cell*, Cohan, London Contemporary Dance Theatre, The Place, London
1972 Set and (with Jane Hoyland), costumes for *People Alone*, Cohan, LCDT, The Place, London; *One Was the Other*, Lapzeson and North, LCDT, The Place, London
1973 *Mass,* Cohan, LCDT, Oxford Playhouse; *People Together*, Cohan, LCDT, The Place, London
1975 *Myth* (renamed *Masque of Separation*), Cohan, LCDT, Shaw Theatre, London
1976 *Khamsin*, Cohan, LCDT, The Playhouse, Leeds; *Nympheas*, Cohan, LCDT, Theatre Royal, York
1977 *Night Watch*, Bergese, Cohan, Davies and North, LCDT, Sadler's Wells, London; *Continuum*, Bergese, LCDT, Eden Court, Inverness; *Forest*, Cohan, LCDT, Sadler's Wells, London
1978 *Dreams with Silences*, North, LCDT, Pavilion Theatre, Bournemouth; *Ice*, Cohan, LCDT, Sadler's Wells, London
1979 *Songs, Lamentations and Praises*, Cohan, LCDT, Jerusalem
1981 *Dances of Love and Death*, Cohan, LCDT, Edinburgh Festival
1982 *Chamber Dances*, Cohan, LCDT, Gaumont Theatre, Southampton
1984 *Agora* (working title *Common Ground*) Cohan, LCDT, Grand Theatre, Leeds; *Skyward (Skylark)*, Cohan, LCDT, Derngate, Northampton
1986 *Ceremony: Slow Dance on a Burial*

Ground, Cohan, LCDT, Congress Theatre, Eastbourne; *Video-Life*, Cohan, LCDT, Rimini, Italy
1993 *Midsummer Night's Dream*, Cohan, Scottish Ballet

Jeannetta Cochrane

Born in 1882, Jeannetta Cochrane founded the Department of Theatre Design at the Central School of Arts and Crafts, and was its guide for more than half a century. She founded Sheridan House, a costume business, designing costumes for many Lord Mayor's Shows and historical pageants. She worked briefly as an assistant to Paul Poiret in Paris before designing plays at the London Pavilion for Anthony Ellis, for Ellen Terry, and also at the Abbey Theatre, Dublin. During World War Two she worked with John Gielgud on his *Hamlet* at the Theatre Royal Haymarket, *Cradle Song* at the Apollo Theatre and, perhaps most memorably, *Love for Love* and *The Relapse* at the Phoenix Theatre. She combined her teaching with design for the firms of Liberty and Heal. She died in 1957 and The Cochrane Theatre, London, is named after her.

Robert Colquhoun and Robert MacBryde

Robert Colquhoun was born in 1914 in Kilmarnock, Ayrshire and Robert MacBryde was born Robert MacBride in 1913 in Maybole, Ayrshire. They met while studying at the Glasgow School of Art. During the war they moved to London where they established a studio together at 77 Bedford Gardens,

Campden Hill, and it became a unique meeting place for young artists and writers. They were ejected from their studio in 1947 by the landlord who complained about their 'drunken orgies', and this led gradually to a loss of confidence and an increase in alcoholic consumption. In 1951 they designed the sets and costumes for a new Scottish ballet, *Donald of the Burthens*, choreographed by Massine and starring Beryl Grey and Alexander Grant. They also designed *King Lear* at Stratford two years later starring Michael Redgrave, Marius Goring and Yvonne Mitchell. The distress caused by Colquhoun's death in 1962 resulted in MacBryde leaving the London scene in which the two of them had played so prominent a part, and retiring to Dublin, where he was killed in a car accident in 1966.

1951 *Donald of the Burthens*, Massine, Sadler's Wells Ballet, Royal Opera House, London

Harry Cordwell

Born in 1922, Harry Cordwell's first involvement with dance was as a dancer with the Manchester Ballet Club. He moved to Ballet Rambert in the 1940s and travelled to Australia with the company (1947–9). He designed a number of ballets for Rambert and elsewhere although he moved into designing for films in later life. His film credits include *Women in Love* (1970, directed by Ken Russell) for which he was a set dresser, *Victor/Victoria* (1982, Blake Edwards) as production designer, for which he received an Academy Award nomination, and *Mountains of the Moon* (1990, Bob Rafelson) as set decorator. He died in 1995.

1947 *Plaisance*, Gore, Ballet Rambert, Theatre Royal, Bristol

1949 *Antonia*, Gore, Ballet Rambert, King's Theatre, London

1951 *Fantasm*, Cordwell, Ballet Workshop, Mercury Theatre, London

1953 *The Gentle Poltergeist*, Gore, The Walter Gore Ballet, Prince's Theatre, London

1957 *The Nutcracker*, Gore after Ivanov, Stadsschouwburg, Amsterdam

1964 *Sweet Dancer*, Gore, Ballet Rambert, New Theatre, Oxford

John Craxton

John Craxton was born in St John's Wood, London, in 1922. After being educated at various private schools, he studied at Westminster Art School and the Central School of Art. In 1944 he had his first main London one-man show at the Leicester Galleries. For the latter half of the 1940s he travelled extensively, particularly in Greece. Returning to London in 1951, he designed *Daphnis and Chloë* and then studied life drawing for two months at the Académie Julien, Paris. He continued his travels, making excursions from the two semi-permanent working bases he had established, in London and Xania in Crete. A retrospective of his work, *John Craxton: paintings and drawings 1941–1966*, was held at the Whitechapel Art Gallery in 1967.

1951 *Daphnis and Chloë*, Ashton, Sadler's Wells Ballet, Royal Opera House, London

1966 *Apollo*, Balanchine, The Royal Ballet, Royal Opera House, London

1970 Costumes for *Apollo*, Balanchine, Royal Ballet Touring Company (set by Elisabeth Dalton)

Ann Curtis

Ann Curtis has over three decades of costume design commissions to her name. Her early work included a partnership with John Bury on *The Wars of the Roses* (1963), *The Histories Cycle* and *Macbeth*. She designed set and costumes for the Royal Shakespeare Company's *When Thou Art King* as well as costumes for other plays. Opera work includes *The Magic Flute* for the Royal Opera and *A Night in Venice* for English National Opera. She has worked extensively in Canada, both as a designer for Shakespeare productions at the Stratford Festival and elsewhere and as a Visiting Tutor at the National Theatre School in Montreal. Ann Curtis is a Lecturer in the history of costume at Central Saint Martins College of Art and Design.

1984 Costumes for *Me and My Girl*, musical, choreographed by Gillian Gregory, Leicester Haymarket, Adelphi, London 1985, Marriot Marquis, New York, 1986 (set by Martin Johns)

Elisabeth Dalton

Elisabeth Dalton studied Theatre Design at Wimbledon School of Art and The Slade. After working as an assistant to Nicholas Georgiadis on Nureyev's *Nutcracker*, and *Aida* and *The Trojans* for the Royal Opera, Covent Garden, Elisabeth Dalton has since gone on to design productions worldwide. Her opera designs include a long collaboration with the director John Cox that embraces, among others, *The Merry Widow* for English National Opera and *Der Rosenkavalier* for Houston Grand Opera, the Holland Festival and Music Theatre, Amsterdam. Her musical designs include *On Your Toes* for Stuttgart Ballet, the company with which she created the designs for John Cranko's *Taming of the Shrew*, a production that has been seen on four continents, most recently in Moscow with the Bolshoi Ballet. Elisabeth Dalton is a Visiting Teacher for The Peter Williams Design for Dance Project.

1968 *The Sphinx*, MacMillan, Stuttgart Ballet

1969 *The Taming of the Shrew*, Cranko, Stuttgart Ballet, Stuttgart; *Daphnis and Chloë*, Cranko, Bayerische Staatsoper, Munich

1970 *Apollo*, Balanchine, Royal Ballet Touring Company, Theatre Royal, Nottingham (costumes by John Craxton); *Checkpoint*, MacMillan, Royal Ballet New Group, Opera House, Manchester; *Lilac Garden*, Tudor, Royal Ballet Touring Company, Theatre Royal, Nottingham

1974 *Lady and the Fool*, Cranko, Oslo

1975 *Romeo and Juliet*, Cranko, Teatro Municipal, Rio de Janeiro

1976 *Summertide*, Wright, Sadler's Wells Royal Ballet, Sadler's Wells, London

1977 *The Taming of the Shrew*, Cranko, Royal Ballet, Royal Opera House, London

1983 *Alice in Wonderland*, Helliwell, Northern Ballet Theatre

1990 *On Your Toes*, Balanchine, Stuttgart Ballet, Württemberg State Theatre

1991 *The Planets*, Haydée, Stuttgart Ballet, Württemberg State Theatre

1994 *Pineapple Poll*, Cranko, Ballet de Santiago, Santiago, Chile

Peter J. Davison

Peter J. Davison was a Design Assistant at the Royal Opera House from 1977 to 1986. Among his many opera designs are *Tosca* for the Hong Kong Arts Festival, *Der Rosenkavalier* and *Carmen* for English National Opera, *Capriccio* for Deutsche Staatsoper Berlin and *Katya Kabanova* for the New Zealand International Festival, Wellington. He has designed a number of productions for the Almeida Theatre, including *When We Dead Awaken*, *The Rules of the Game* and *All for Love*. His *Medea* for the Almeida transferred to the West End and then Broadway, earning him nominations for Tony, Drama Desk and Olivier Awards and, together with his design for *Le Cid* (Cottesloe Theatre, Royal National Theatre) won him the 1994 Martini/TMA Regional Theatre Best Designer Award. Other theatre designs include *Bed* and *The Beaux Stratagem* (Royal National Theatre) and *The White Devils* (RSC). His design for DV8's *Strange Fish* won the Time Out Award, 1992.

1992 *Strange Fish*, Newson, DV8 Physical
   Theatre
1995 *Edward II*, Bintley, Stuttgart Ballet
   (costumes by Jasper Conran)

Mstislav Doboujinsky

Born in Novgorod, Russia, 1875, Doboujinsky came to prominence as a contributor to Diaghilev's publication, *The World of Art*, and as a designer for the Moscow Art Theatre for productions including *A Month in the Country* (1909). He subsequently designed two productions for Diaghilev's Ballets Russes, *Les Papillons* and *Midas*. Through a long career he brought the style he had developed working with Diaghilev, steeped in Russian folk imagery and executed with extravagance, to other countries, living in Lithuania from 1925 and England and America from 1939. He died in New York in 1957.

1907 *Le Jeu de Robin et Marion* (dances),
   Fokine, Maryinsky Theatre, St Petersburg
1914 *Midas*, Fokine, Diaghilev's Ballets Russes,
   Théâtre National de l'Opéra, Paris; set for *Les
   Papillons*, Fokine, Diaghilev's Ballets Russes,
   Théâtre de Monte Carlo, Monte Carlo
   (costumes by Bakst)
1915 *The Fairy Doll*, Clustine, Pavlova
   Company
1934 *The Sleeping Beauty*, Petipa, National
   Ballet of Lithuania; *Raymonda*, Petipa,
   National Ballet of Lithuania
1935 *Coppélia*, Ivanov after Saint-Léon, Ballet
   de Monte Carlo
1936 Set for Act III of *Casse-Noisette*, Petipa
   (produced by Sergeyev), Sadler's Wells Ballet;
   in 1937 designed sets for Acts I and II
1941 *Ballet Imperial*, Balanchine, American
   Ballet
1942 *Russian Soldier*, Fokine, Ballet Theatre
1943 *Mademoiselle Angot*, Massine, Ballet
   Theatre
1944 *Graduation Ball*, Lichine, Ballet Theatre
1951 *Le Prisonnier du Caucase*, Skibine, Grand
   Ballet du Marquis de Cuevas
1957 *Coppélia*, Ivanov after Saint-Léon, Ballet
   Rambert

Peter Docherty

Peter Docherty was born in Blackpool. He studied Theatre Design at the Central School of Arts and Crafts and the Slade School of Fine Art. He has also designed for theatre and opera, including the musicals *Cole* (1968, Mermaid Theatre, directed by Alan Strachan and David Toguri), *Side by Side by Sondheim* (1976, London and New York, directed by Ned Sherrin) and numerous plays including *In Celebration* (1969, Royal Court Theatre, directed by Lindsay Anderson) and *The Play's the Thing* (1979, Greenwich Theatre, directed by Alan Strachan). Opera designs include *The Adventures of M. Brouček*, ENO, and *An Actor's Revenge*, English Music Theatre and Music Theatre of St Louis, both directed by Colin Graham. Both his designs and his paintings have been exhibited, including a one-man show at the Royal Festival Hall and are in many collections, including the Theatre Museum, V&A. As founding organiser of Action Against Aids he was responsible for putting on charity shows in 1986 and 1987. Formerly a guest lecturer at the Wimbledon School of Art, he is presently Senior Lecturer in Theatre Design at Central Saint Martins College of Art and Design and leading the Design for Performance Research Project.

1967 *Mogadon*, Worth, Royal Ballet's 'Ballet
   for All'; *Designs with Strings*, Taras, London
   Festival Ballet; *Le Corsaire*, Mazilier, London
   Festival Ballet
1968 *Ephemeron*, Darrell, Western Theatre
   Ballet
1970 *Herodias*, Darrell, Scottish Theatre Ballet;
   Four Portraits, Darrell, Scottish Theatre
   Ballet; *Divertissement*, Louther, London

Contemporary Dance Theatre; *Dvorak Variations*, Hynd, London Festival Ballet

1971 *Le Baiser de la Fée*, Hynd, Bayerische Staatsoper Ballet

1972 *In a Summer Garden*, Hynd, Sadler's Wells Royal Ballet, Sadler's Wells, London

1973 *Tales of Hoffmann*, Darrell, American Ballet Theatre; *Mozartiana*, Hynd, London Festival Ballet

1974 *Charlotte Brontë*, Hynd, Sadler's Wells Royal Ballet, Alhambra, Bradford; *Le Baiser de la Fée*, Hynd, London Festival Ballet; *The Soldier's Tale*, Louther, Television production

1975 *Valses Nobles et Sentimentales*, Hynd, New London Ballet; *Lyric Fantasies, Invention 1 and 2*, Louther, New London Ballet

1976 *Mary, Queen of Scots*, Darrell, Scottish Ballet; *The Fan* (later *The Sanguine Fan*), Hynd, London Festival Ballet, Théâtre de l'Opéra de Monte Carlo, Monte Carlo (commissioned by Princess Grace of Monaco); *The Nutcracker*, Hynd, London Festival Ballet

1978 *La Chatte*, Hynd, London Festival Ballet; *Francesca da Rimini*, Dollar, Asami Maki Ballet

1979 *Rosalinda*, Hynd, London Festival Ballet

1980 *Les Valses*, Hynd, Les Grandes Ballets Canadiens; *The Seasons*, Hynd, Houston Ballet; *Papillon*, Hynd, Sadler's Wells Royal Ballet, Grand Theatre, Leeds

1982 *Rosalinda*, Hynd, Houston Ballet

1983 *The Seasons*, Hynd, London Festival Ballet

1984 *Le Diable à Quatre*, Hynd, Bayerische Staatsoper Ballett; *Le Papillon*, Hynd, Bayerische Staatsoper Ballett

1985 *Der Facher*, Hynd, Bayerische Staatsoper Ballet; *Die Jahreszeiten*, Hynd, Bayerische Staatsoper Ballett; *Fanfare für Tanzer*, Hynd, Bayerische Staatsoper Ballett

1987 *Rosalinda* (redesigned), Hynd, Houston Ballet; *Rosalinda*, Hynd, Cincinnati Ballet

1988 *Hunchback of Notre Dame*, Hynd, Houston Ballet; *Three Tales on a Shoe String*, Louther, Dance Theatre Corporation; *Cages of Love*, Louther, Dance Theatre Corporation

1989 *Le Diable à Quatre*, Hynd, Ballet de Santiago, Chile

1990 *George and the Dragon*, Hamilton, Dance Unlimited; *Liaisons Amoureuses*, Hynd, Northern Ballet Theatre

1991 *More About Angels*, Hamilton, Dance Unlimited; *Even Cowgirls Get the Blues*, Jobe, Phoenix Dance

1992 *Rosalinda*, Hynd, Ballet West

1993 *The Sleeping Beauty*, Hynd after Petipa, English National Ballet

1994 *Die Lustige Witwe*, Hynd, Wiener Staatsopernballett

1995 *The Merry Widow*, Hynd, Ballet de Santiago, Chile

Robin Don

Robin Don was born in Scotland, and studied engineering and sculpture in Edinburgh. He served a ten-year 'apprenticeship' with Ralph Koltai before designing his first production, Picasso's *Four Little Girls* at the Open Space. Theatre productions include the Marowitz Shakespeares, *Anatol*, *Beautiful Thing* and, for the RSC, *Les Enfants du Paradis*. Opera commissions include *Mary, Queen of Scots* for Scottish Opera, and *Eugene Onegin* for the Aldeburgh Festival and then worldwide. He has designed a series of operas at the Sydney Opera House which were part of the British entry that

won the Golden Troika Award at the Prague Quadriennale. Robin Don's design for *Winter Guest* at the West Yorkshire Playhouse received a clutch of awards including the Critics' Circle Designer of the Year 1995 Award.

1970 *Lovedu (The People of the Rain Queen)*, Wells, Ploys Programme, Scottish Theatre Ballet, The Place, London

1972 *Totems*, Jones, Ballet Rambert, Jeannetta Cochrane Theatre, London

1977 *Mary, Queen of Scots*, opera, choreographed by Darrell, Scottish Opera

1983 *A Midsummer Marriage*, opera, choreographed by Gilbert, San Francisco Opera

1984 *The Boyfriend*, Old Vic, London

1988 *Ziegfeld*, Layton, London Palladium

1989 *Song and Dance*, von Laast, Palace Theatre, London

1991 *Macbeth*, Prokovsky, Ballet de Santiago, Chile

1992 *Macbeth*, Prokovsky, Scottish Ballet, Mercury Theatre, Colchester

Charles Dunlop

After training at the Central School of Art, Charles Dunlop began a career that has embraced design for both stage and screen. On seeing his design for *Spectrum*, Peter Williams sensed that his style 'evoked a certain period of Tchelitchev'. Dunlop ran an art gallery in London for some time, but now lives in Canada and works in America and Canada on film and television projects.

1967 *Family of Man*, Mittelholzer, London Contemporary Dance Theatre; *Spectrum*,

Roope, Western Theatre Ballet
1970 *Sleepers*, Hopps, Ploys Programme, Scottish Theatre Ballet, The Place, London; *The Dreamer*, Roope, Northern Dance Theatre
1972 *Summer Solstice*, Moreland, London Festival Ballet

Sir Jacob Epstein

Born in New York, 1880, he studied at the Art Student's League and subsequently at the Ecole des Beaux Arts in Paris. He settled in London in 1905, gaining prominence for his controversial figures designed for the British Medical Association's headquarters in the Strand. Returning to Paris he befriended many of the prominent artists of the time, including Picasso, Modigliani and Brancusi. He was a founding member of the London Group, established in 1913, the year of his first one-man show at the Twenty-One Gallery. Epstein was awarded a number of public commissions throughout his career, including 'St Michael and Lucifer' for Coventry Cathedral in 1957–8. He was knighted in 1954 and died in 1959.

1935 Curtain for *David*, Lester, Markova-Dolin Company

Alexandra Exter

Born in Kiev in 1882, Exter travelled to Paris in 1908 to study art at the Académie de la Grande Chaumière, where she mixed with Cubist painters such as Picasso, Braque and the Futurist, Marinetti. She founded her own studio in Moscow in 1918, where many artists

studied with her. From 1923 she produced fashion designs for the Atelier of Fashions, Moscow. After designing the set and costumes for the film *Aelita* (1924) she emigrated to Paris, continuing to work on stage designs (few of which were realised), fashion and interior design. She died in 1949.

1917 *Etudes de Bach*, Léonidov Ballet Company, Kiev
1923 *Ballet Satanique*, also known as *Les Diaboliques* and *The Satans* (not produced)
1924 Costumes, with Zak, Tchelitchev and others for *Suite des Danses*, Romanov, Russian Romantic Theatre, Paris (announced)
1932 Costumes with Zak, Blinsky and others for *Divertissement des Danses*, Nijinska, Théâtre de la Danse

Peter Farley

Born in Farnham, Surrey, Peter Farley's training spans West Surrey College of Art and Design (1972–3), Wimbledon School of Art (Theatre Design 1973–6, MA 1992) and presently Central Saint Martins College of Art and Design where he is undertaking a PhD investigating the collaborative process of dance design and its application within an educational context. He has worked as assistant designer to Yolanda Sonnabend and Barry Kay over a number of years. Recent design work outside the field of dance has included *The Slow Approach of Night* (directed by Lily Susan Todd). For eleven years he worked with Robin Duff of Meldrum, Chairman, and later President, of the Scottish Ballet. Besides theatre design, his work includes exhibition curation and design. He organised the 'Talking Theatre Design' conference in 1993.

He has taught theatre design at Wimbledon School of Art, The Slade School of Fine Art, The Royal Academy of Dramatic Art, The London Contemporary Dance School and Central Saint Martins College of Art and Design where he continues to teach. His doctoral research is undertaken as part of the Design for Performance Research Project.

1991 *Dark Horizons*, Hindle, Birmingham Royal Ballet, Sadler's Wells, London
1993 *The Nutcracker and the Hard Nut,* Pilobolus, Ballet du Rhin, Strasbourg Opera (with Yolanda Sonnabend)

Peter Farmer

Peter Farmer, born in Luton, trained at Central School of Art before embarking on a career as both painter and scenographer. He has been the subject of a number of solo shows at both the Mercury and Casson galleries in London. His long list of dance design credits show him to be equally adept at working with contemporary and classical companies. His long collaboration with London Contemporary Dance Theatre resulted in many notable designs, especially the high-octane multi-media environment for *Stages* (1971), while his affinity for established works was apparent in early commissions for *Giselle* and *The Dream*. This flexibility made Farmer an obvious choice to bring LCDT's *Troy Game* to the Covent Garden stage for the Royal Ballet. He recently designed Sir Peter Wright's farewell *Coppélia* for Birmingham Royal Ballet.

1964 *Agrionia*, Carter, London Dance Theatre
1965 *Giselle*, Coralli/Perrot/Petipa, Ballet Rambert

1966 *Giselle*, Coralli/Perrot/Petipa, Stuttgart Ballet; *The Dream*, Ashton, The Royal Ballet Touring Company, New Theatre, Oxford; *Beauty and the Beast*, Cranko, Western Theatre Ballet

1967 *Namouna*, Wright, Stuttgart Ballet; *Night Shadow*, Balanchine reproduced by Taras, London Festival Ballet, Teatro La Fenice, Venice; *The Sleeping Beauty*, Petipa, produced by Wright, Cologne

1968 *Giselle*, Coralli/Perrot, produced by Wright, The Royal Ballet Touring Company, Royal Opera House, London; *Danse Macabre*, Wright, Western Theatre Ballet; *Coppélia*, Carter after Saint-Léon, London Festival Ballet; *Meadow Lark*, Feld, London Festival Ballet

1970 *X*, Cohan, LCDT; *Cantabile*, Lapzeson, LCDT, The Place, London

1971 *Stages*, Cohan, LCDT, The Place, London (wigs and masks by Barbara Wilkes, film sequences and projections by Anthony McCall); *Consolation of the Rising Moon*, Cohan, LCDT, The Place, London; *Othello*, Darrell, New London Ballet

1973 *The Sleeping Beauty*, Petipa, MacMillan, Ashton and Lopokov, produced by MacMillan, The Royal Ballet, Royal Opera House, London; *Cinderella*, Stevenson, Festival Ballet

1974 *No Man's Land*, Cohan, LCDT, Sadler's Wells, London; *Troy Game*, North, LCDT, Royal Court Theatre, Liverpool; *Dressed to Kill*, North, LCDT, Nuffield Theatre, Southampton

1975 *Still Life*, North, LCDT, Shaw Theatre, London; *David–Goliath*, North/Sleep, LCDT; *Running Figures*, North, Ballet Rambert; *Arpège*, Wright, The Royal Ballet

Touring Company, Royal Shakespeare Theatre, Stratford-upon-Avon

1976 Costumes for *Pandora*, Morse, The Royal Ballet Touring Company, Royal Shakespeare Theatre, Stratford-upon-Avon; *Aurora's Wedding* (*The Sleeping Beauty*, Act III), Petipa and MacMillan, produced by Wright, The Royal Ballet Touring Company, Opernhaus, Zürich

1977 *Meeting and Parting*, North, LCDT, Sadler's Wells, London; *Soft Blue Shadows*, Prokovsky, Sadler's Wells Royal Ballet, Sadler's Wells, London; *Daydreams*, Prokovsky, Northern Ballet Theatre; *Les Sylphides*, Fokine, produced by Markova, Northern Ballet Theatre

1978 *Scriabin Preludes and Studies*, North, LCDT, Haymarket Theatre, Leicester

1979 *Cinderella*, de Warren, Northern Ballet Theatre; *Anna Karenina*, Prokovsky, Australian Ballet; *The Water's Edge*, North, Scottish Ballet; *Tristan and Iseult*, Darrell, New London Ballet; *January to June*, North, New London Ballet

1980 *The Three Musketeers*, Prokovsky, Australian Ballet, Sydney Opera House, Sydney; *The Nutcracker*, Prokovsky, Northern Ballet Theatre; *Troy Game*, North, The Royal Ballet, Royal Opera House, London; *Paquita*, Petipa, produced by Samsova, Sadler's Wells Royal Ballet, Pavilion Theatre, Bournemouth

1981 *The Storm*, Prokovsky, London Festival Ballet; *Verdi Variations*, Prokovsky, London Festival Ballet

1982 *Faust Divertimento*, Prokovsky, Northern Ballet Theatre

1983 *Brahms Love Songs*, Prokovsky, Northern Ballet Theatre

1985 *Othello*, de Warren, Northern Ballet

Theatre

1987 *The Picture of Dorian Grey*, Deane, Sadler's Wells Royal Ballet, Birmingham Hippodrome

1988 *Metamorphoses*, Cohan, LCDT; *Theme and Variations*, Balanchine, Sadler's Wells Royal Ballet, Birmingham Hippodrome

1989 *Divertimento No.15*, Balanchine, Sadler's Wells Royal Ballet, Birmingham Hippodrome

1991 *Winter Dreams*, MacMillan, The Royal Ballet, Royal Opera House, London; *Tales of Hoffmann*, Darrell, Hong Kong Ballet

1992 *Les Sylphides*, Fokine, produced by Samsova, Birmingham Royal Ballet

1993 *Street*, Hart, Birmingham Royal Ballet, Birmingham Hippodrome

1995 *Coppélia*, Wright after Petipa and Cecchetti, Birmingham Royal Ballet, Birmingham Hippodrome

Sophie Fedorovitch

Sophie Fedorovitch was born in Minsk, Russia, in 1893. After studying painting at the St Petersburg Academy in Moscow she moved to England in 1920 and began a long career designing for the dance alongside her work as a painter. She collaborated extensively with Sir Frederick Ashton, designing eleven of his ballets, including his first, *A Tragedy of Fashion*, in 1926. Perhaps their greatest triumph was the plotless *Symphonic Variations* (1946), though she was acclaimed for her work with other choreographers, including Antony Tudor and Andrée Howard. Fedorovitch designed a number of operas for the Covent Garden stage and theatre productions for the Royal

Shakespeare Company and at the Old Vic. She became a naturalised British subject in 1940 and was appointed a member of the artistic advisory panel of Sadler's Wells Ballet in 1951. She continued working until her death in London in 1953.

1925 *Les Nenophars*, James, Marie Rambert Studio Student Matinee, London
1926 *A Tragedy of Fashion or The Scarlet Scissors*, Ashton, Marie Rambert Dancers, London
1930/1 *Thumbelina* (not produced)
1932 *The Scorpions of Ysit*, de Valois, Vic-Wells Ballet, London
1933 *Les Masques*, Ashton, Ballet Club, London
1934 *Mephisto Valse*, Ashton, Ballet Club, London
1935 *Le Baiser de la Fée*, Ashton, Vic-Wells Ballet, Sadler's Wells, London; *Valentine's Eve*, Ashton, Ballet Rambert, London; *Douanes*, de Valois, Vic-Wells Ballet, Sadler's Wells, London
1936 *Nocturne*, Ashton, Vic-Wells Ballet, Sadler's Wells, London; *Prelude* and *Symphonie Russe*, Tudor, in *To and Fro*, Peter Farquharson Revue, Comedy Theatre, London
1937 *Lady into Fox*, Tudor, Ballet Rambert, London (not produced)
1938 *Horoscope*, Ashton, Vic-Wells Ballet, Sadler's Wells, London; *Valse Finale*, Gore, Ballet Rambert
1939 *Endymion*, Inglesby, Ballet de la Jeunesse Anglaise, London
1939/40 *Penny Royal*, a Ruritanian musical extravaganza (not produced)
1940 *Dante Sonata*, after Flaxman, Ashton, Sadler's Wells Ballet, Sadler's Wells, London; *La Fête Etrange*, Howard, London Ballet; *Concerto*, Lester, Arts Theatre Ballet, London

1941 *Orpheus and Eurydice*, de Valois, Sadler's Wells Ballet, New Theatre, London
1942 *The Great Gate of Kiev* (curtain-raiser to Mussorgsky's *Sorochinsky Fair*), De Viller, Jay Pomeroy Productions, London
1943 *Dorian Grey*, Helpmann (commissioned by Sadler's Wells Ballet but not produced)
1946 *Symphonic Variations*, Ashton, Sadler's Wells Ballet, Royal Opera House, London; *The Concerto Ballet* (from *Song of Norway*), Helpmann, Emile Littler Production, London
1947 *Valses Nobles et Sentimentales*, Ashton, Sadler's Wells Theatre Ballet, Sadler's Wells, London
1950 *Summer Interlude*, Somes, Sadler's Wells Theatre Ballet, Sadler's Wells, London
1952 *Clair de Lune*, Bartholin, Grand Ballet de Marquis de Cuevas (not produced)
1953 *Veneziana*, Howard, Sadler's Wells Ballet, Royal Opera House, London; *Orpheus and Eurydice*, opera by Gluck, choreography by Ashton, Sadler's Wells Ballet and Covent Garden Opera, London

David Fielding

David Fielding, born in Dukinfield, Cheshire, studied Theatre Design under Ralph Koltai at the Central School of Art and Design. Following a placement at Nottingham Playhouse on an Arts Council Bursary, Fielding soon established himself as a freelance designer. Early commissions include *The Magic Flute* for Scottish Opera, on which he worked alongside Maria Bjørnson who was designing the costumes. Whilst Head of Design at Theatre Royal, York, he designed a number of

productions including *Entertaining Mr Sloane* and *Hamlet*. He has worked with many of the world's opera companies and won both Olivier and *Evening Standard* awards for his work with English National Opera in 1985. He has subsequently established himself as a director/designer. His productions in this joint capacity include *The Hypochondriacs* (Citizens Theatre, Glasgow), *Soundbites* (ENO), and *Capriccio* and *Daphne* (Garsington Opera). Following his collaboration with the Pet Shop Boys, Fielding has produced designs for the singles and videos from their subsequent album, *Very!*

1991 Pet Shop Boys, World Tour
1993 *Fast and Dirty '93*, Mesmer and Castro, Second Stride Workshops

Rick Fisher

Rick Fisher has worked as a lighting designer for over a decade. From working with small touring companies such as The People Show, his work is now seen worldwide. Recent productions include *Machinal* (Royal National Theatre), *Hysteria* (Royal Court) and *Moonlight* (Almeida and Comedy Theatres) which together resulted in the award for Best Lighting Designer in the 1994 Laurence Olivier Awards. His work includes *All's Well that Ends Well* and *The Virtuoso* for the Royal Shakespeare Company, and *Peer Gynt* and *Black Snow* for the Royal National Theatre. Opera productions for which he has designed lighting include a number of works for Opera North and three seasons for Musica nel Chiostro, Batignano, Italy. His lighting design for *An Inspector Calls* on Broadway won both Tony and Drama Desk

Awards. His lighting for dance includes several shows for both The Kosh (including *A Matter of Chance*) and for Adventures in Motion Pictures, most recently their *Swan Lake* (1995).

Nicholas Georgiadis

Nicholas Georgiadis was born in Athens and as a young man studied and qualified as an architect. At the same time he had designed several projects for the theatre and submitted them to the Slade where he was given a British Council scholarship to the Theatre Design Class. Here his work was seen by Kenneth MacMillan and their work together on *Danses Concertantes* was the start of one of the most important collaborations in British ballet. In 1964 Rudolf Nureyev asked Georgiadis to design his first full-length ballet, *Swan Lake*, for the Vienna State Opera. A year later came MacMillan's full-length *Romeo and Juliet* for the Royal Ballet. Among the many other ballets that followed were MacMillan's *Manon* and *Mayerling*, Nureyev's *Don Quixote* for the Paris Opéra, *The Sleeping Beauty* for La Scala Ballet and *The Nutcracker* for the Royal Swedish Ballet. Nicholas Georgiadis has also designed many plays and operas and has exhibited his paintings worldwide. He was awarded a CBE in 1984.

1955 *Danses Concertantes*, MacMillan, Sadler's Wells Theatre Ballet, Sadler's Wells, London; *The House of Birds*, MacMillan, Sadler's Wells Theatre Ballet, Sadler's Wells, London
1956 *Noctambules*, MacMillan, Sadler's Wells Theatre Ballet, Royal Opera House, London
1957 *Winter's Eve*, MacMillan, American Ballet Theatre

1958 *The Burrow*, MacMillan, The Royal Ballet Touring Company, Royal Opera House, London; *Agon*, MacMillan, The Royal Ballet, Royal Opera House, London
1960 *The Invitation*, MacMillan, The Royal Ballet Touring Company, New Theatre, Oxford
1962 *Daphnis and Chloë*, Cranko, Stuttgart Ballet
1963 *Las Hermanas*, MacMillan, Stuttgart Ballet
1964 *Swan Lake*, Nureyev, Vienna State Opera Ballet, State Opera House, Vienna
1965 *Romeo and Juliet*, MacMillan, The Royal Ballet, Royal Opera House, London (revised 1978); *Song of the Earth*, MacMillan, Württemberg State Ballet Theatre, Stuttgart
1966 *The Sleeping Beauty*, Nureyev after Petipa, La Scala Ballet, La Scala, Milan
1967 *The Nutcracker*, Nureyev after Vainonen, Royal Swedish Ballet (The Royal Ballet, 1968)
1969 *Swan Lake*, MacMillan after Ivanov and Petipa, West Berlin State Opera Ballet
1972 *Raymonda*, Nureyev after Petipa, Zurich Opera Ballet, Stadttheater, Zurich
1974 *Manon*, MacMillan, The Royal Ballet, Royal Opera House, London
1978 *Mayerling*, MacMillan, The Royal Ballet, Royal Opera House, London; *Intimate Letters*, Seymour, Sadler's Wells Royal Ballet, Sadler's Wells, London
1979 *Danses Concertantes* (new designs), MacMillan, Sadler's Wells Royal Ballet, New Theatre, Cardiff
1982 *Orpheus*, MacMillan, The Royal Ballet; *The Tempest*, Nureyev, The Royal Ballet
1984 *Bach Suite*, Nureyev and Lancelot, Paris Opéra Ballet, Théâtre des Champs-Elysées, Paris

1985 *Washington Square*, Nureyev, Paris Opéra Ballet, Théâtre National, Paris
1986 *The Nutcracker*, Nureyev after Vainonen, Paris Opéra Ballet, Palais Garnier
1987 *The Sleeping Beauty*, MacMillan, American Ballet Theatre, Auditorium Theatre, Chicago
1989 *The Prince of the Pagodas*, MacMillan, The Royal Ballet, Royal Opera House, London
1991 *The Burrow* (new designs), MacMillan, Birmingham Royal Ballet, Birmingham Hippodrome

Natalia Gontcharova

Gontcharova was born in Ladyschino, Russia, in 1881. She met her future husband and fellow designer Mikhail Larionov in 1900 and together they led the 'rayonnisme' movement. Gontcharova worked closely with Malevich from 1906 to 1912 and exhibited in the second Blaue Reiter exhibition in 1912. The same year her work was seen in London in Roger Fry's Post-Impressionist exhibition. She and Larionov moved to Paris in 1914, where she created her first design for Diaghilev, *Le Coq d'Or*. Many commissions followed, both for Diaghilev and others, notably her design for the 1926 revival of *The Firebird*. Her designs outside of dance included *Tsar Sallam* for the National Theatre of Latvia (1932), and *La Vie Parisienne* for The Bat Theatre, New York (1933). She died in Paris in 1962.

1914 *Le Coq d'Or*, opera: choreographed by Fokine, Diaghilev's Ballets Russes, Paris Opéra, Paris
1915 *Liturgie*, Massine, Diaghilev's Ballets

Russes (begun but not completed); *The Invisible City of Kitezh* (not produced)

1916 *Triana,* Diaghilev's Ballets Russes (not produced); *España,* Diaghilev's Ballets Russes (not produced)

1917 Some costumes, though mainly by Larionov, for *Contes Russes,* Massine, Diaghilev's Ballets Russes; (with Bakst) *Sadko,* Fokine, Diaghilev's Ballets Russes, New York; *Triana,* Diaghilev's Ballets Russes (not produced)

1921 *Igrouchki,* Fokine, Palace Theatre, New York

1922 Additional costumes, largely designed by Benois, for *Aurora's Wedding,* Petipa, staged by Nijinska, Diaghilev's Ballets Russes, Théâtre National de l'Opéra, Paris; *Le Renard,* Nijinska, Diaghilev's Ballets Russes, Théâtre National de l'Opéra, Paris (set by Larionov)

1923 *Les Noces,* Nijinska, Diaghilev's Ballet Russes, Théâtre de la Gaîté-Lyrique, Paris

1924 *Night on the Bare Mountain,* Nijinska, Diaghilev's Ballets Russes, Monte Carlo

1926 *The Firebird,* Fokine, staged by Grigoriev and Tchernicheva, Diaghilev's Ballet Russes, London

1932 *Sur le Borsythène,* Lifar, Paris Opéra Ballet, Paris (with Larionov); *Bolero,* Nijinska, Théâtre de la Danse Nijinska, Paris

1933 *Voyage d'une Danseuse,* Romanov, Théâtre Chauve-Souris, New York

1935 *The Firebird,* Fokine, Ballets Russes de Monte Carlo, New York

1938 *Cendrillon (Cinderella),* Fokine, Colonel de Basil's Ballets Russe, London; *Bogatyri,* Massine, Ballet de Monte Carlo, New York

1940 *The Firebird,* Fokine, Original Ballet Russe, New York

1954 *Bolero,* Nijinska, Grand Ballet du Marquis de Cuevas, Théâtre Sarah Bernhardt, Paris; *The Firebird,* Fokine, staged by Grigoriev and Tchernicheva, Sadler's Wells Ballet, London

1958 *Ballade,* Massine, Théâtre d'Art du Ballet, Paris

Duncan Grant

Although born in Scotland in 1885, Grant was brought up in India. Studying at Westminster School of Art he lodged with his literary cousins, the Stracheys, completing his training in Paris during 1907. His enthusiasm for the Post-Impressionist painters brought him into contact with Roger Fry, later becoming director of Fry's Omega Workshops. As a painter he frequently exhibited with the London Group, while his decorative commissions included the murals for a chapel in Lincoln Cathedral. He circulated within the orbit of the 'Bloomsbury Group', which included not only the Stracheys and Fry but also his lifelong companion Vanessa Bell. He designed the costumes for Coppeau's *Pelléas and Mélisande* (1915/16) and in 1956 he designed English Opera Group's production of John Blow's *Venus and Adonis* at the Aldeburgh Festival. The Tate Gallery mounted a retrospective of Grant's work in 1959. He died in 1975.

1925 *The Postman,* Legat, Coliseum, London

1932 *The Enchanted Grove,* Doone, Vic-Wells Ballet, Sadler's Wells, London; *Swan Lake,* after Ivanov, Camargo Ballet Society, Savoy Theatre, London

Tim Hatley

Tim Hatley was born in Luton. He trained at Central Saint Martins College of Art and Design, graduating in 1989 with a First Class Honours degree. In the same year he was awarded a dance commission (*Roughcut* for Rambert Dance Company) as winner of the Linbury Prize for Stage Design. His designs for the theatre include two productions for Théâtre de Complicité (*Out of a House Walked a Man* and *The Three Lives of Lucie Chabrol*), *Richard III* for the RSC and *Stanley* for the Royal National Theatre. He has designed a number of operas, the most recent being *The Return of Ulysses* for Opera North (1995). In 1991 he was voted Best Designer in the Plays and Players Critics Awards and received a Time Out Award the following year for *Damned for Despair* at the Gate Theatre, directed by Stephen Daldry.

1990 *Roughcut,* Alston, Rambert Dance Company; *Flaming Desire,* Walsh, Extemporary Dance

1993 *Cinderella,* Gable, Northern Ballet Theatre

David Hockney

David Hockney was born in Bradford in 1937 and trained at the Bradford School of Art and at the Royal College of Art (1959–61). He made his name as an artist during the 1960s, having his first one-man exhibition at the Kasmin Gallery, London in 1963, followed by further solo shows in the next few years in New York, Amsterdam and Berlin. He travelled extensively between 1968 and 1971 and in 1974 was the subject of a film by Jack Hazan, *A Bigger Splash.* In 1975 he was invited to design the sets and costumes for Stravinsky's opera, *The Rake's Progress*, at Glyndebourne. This was followed by *The Magic Flute*, also for Glyndebourne, *Tristan and Isolde* in Los Angeles and *Turandot* in Chicago. For the Metropolitan Opera House, New York, he designed a new production of *Parade* and a Stravinsky triple bill.

1981 *Parade*, Massine, Metropolitan Opera House, New York; *L'Enfant et les Sortilèges*, Balanchine, Metropolitan Opera House, New York; *Le Sacre du Printemps*, Nijinsky, Metropolitan Opera House, New York; *Le Rossignol*, Romanov, Metropolitan Opera House, New York
1983 *Varii Capricci*, Ashton, The Royal Ballet, Royal Opera House, London (costumes by Ozzie Clarke)

Pamela Howard

Pamela Howard trained at Birmingham College of Art and the Slade School of Fine Art, London, where her tutors were Nicholas Georgiadis, Peter Snow and Peter Williams. Her many credits include work for the Royal Shakespeare Company, Royal National Theatre, West Yorkshire Playhouse, Birmingham Repertory Theatre and others. Television work includes *Border Warfare*, *Suffer Little Children* and *John Brown's Body*. Her design for John McGrath's *John Brown's Body* at the Tramway, Glasgow, was part of the British exhibit that won the Golden Triga Award for Best National Exhibit at the 1991 Prague Quadrennial International Exhibition. She continues to make a significant contribution to the understanding of stage design, founding and

directing an MA in Scenography that embraces European Scenography Centres in Prague, Barcelona and Utrecht as well as Central Saint Martins College of Art and Design in London. She has contributed to a number of journals and her volume in the *Theatre in Context* series, entitled *Scenography*, is to be published shortly. Her directorial work includes *Celestina* (workshop production, Almeida Theatre) and *Shakespeare's Universe* (Barbican Arts Centre).

1977 *War Music*, mixed media piece, Louther, Old Vic, London

John Hoyland

Born in Sheffield, John Hoyland studied at Sheffield College of Art (1951–6) and then at the Royal Academy Schools, London (1956–60). In 1958 he took an evening class at the Central School of Art under William Turnbull. He had begun exhibiting in 1958 at the Royal Academy Summer Show and commenced teaching in 1960. He is perhaps best known for his prints, silk screens, etchings and lithographs. Since the 1970s Waddington Galleries have mounted regular one-man exhibitions of his work and a retrospective was held at the Serpentine Gallery, London in 1979. He has combined his painting with teaching posts at both the Slade and Saint Martins School of Art.

1986 *Zanza*, Alston, Ballet Rambert, Alhambra Theatre, Bradford (assisted by Candida Cook)

Richard Hudson

Richard Hudson has designed numerous productions in Europe and America. His opera work includes *Die Meistersinger von Nürnberg* at the Royal Opera House, *The Force of Destiny* and *Figaro's Wedding* for English National Opera. Hudson's *The Rake's Progress* has been given at the Lyric Theatre, Chicago and the Saito Kinen Festival in Japan. In recognition of his designs for the 1988 season at the Old Vic, Hudson was awarded the 1988 Olivier Award. Among his many designs for theatre are *The Ends of the Earth*, *Volpone* and *The Misanthrope* for the Royal National Theatre; *The Cherry Orchard*, *A Clockwork Orange* and *Travesties* for the Royal Shakespeare Company, and the Broadway production of *La Bête*, for which Hudson received a nomination for a Tony Award. He recently gave a masterclass at Central Saint Martins College of Art and Design.

1983 *The White Goddess*, Corder, The Royal Ballet School, London; *St Anthony Variations*, Corder, Sadler's Wells Royal Ballet, The Big Top, Exeter
1984 *Wildlife*, Alston, Ballet Rambert, Theatre Royal, Brighton (assisted by Candida Cook)
1985 *Dangerous Liaisons*, Alston, Ballet Rambert, Gaumont Theatre, Southampton (assisted by Candida Cook)
1986 *Mignon*, directed by Richard Jones, Wexford Festival Opera, Eire

Jean Hugo

Jean Hugo, the grandson of Victor Hugo, was born in Paris in 1894. Essentially a painter, he did much work for the theatre and for ballet. His style was deceptively simple and many of his innovations later became standard elements of stage design. Both *Les Mariés* and *Roméo et Juliet* were conceived by Jean Cocteau, and Hugo brought to them a particular blend of humour and surrealism. He was a prolific illustrator and, on retiring to the Midi in France, was able to spend time painting, employing gouache to great effect, as he had done earlier in his life. He died in 1984. In 1994, the centenary of his birth was marked by a major exhibition of his work in Paris.

1921 Costumes for *Les Mariés de la Tour Eiffel*, Börlin, Ballets Suédois, Théâtre des Champs-Elysées, Paris
1924 *Roméo et Juliette*, Psota, Soirées de Paris, Théâtre de la Cigale, Paris
1935 *Les Cent Baisers*, Nijinska, Colonel de Basil's Ballet Russe, Royal Opera House, London
1946 *Les Amours de Jupiter*, Petit, Ballets des Champs-Elysées

Leslie Hurry

Born in London in 1909, Leslie Hurry studied at St John's Wood Art School and the Royal Academy Schools. Robert Helpmann saw the dramatic possibilities of Hurry's painting and chose him to design his 1942 ballet, *Hamlet*. He designed *Der Ring des Nibelungen* for the Royal Opera House, and went on to design regularly for the Old Vic, Stratford-upon-Avon and Stratford, Ontario. Among his notable theatre productions are *Tamburlaine the Great* (1951), *Venice Preserv'd* (1953) and *Cat on a Hot Tin Roof* (1958). His *Swan Lake* is one of the most enduring designs in the dance world and he continued to evolve his vision of the work over many productions. He died in 1978.

1942 *Hamlet*, Helpmann, Sadler's Wells Ballet, New Theatre, London
1943 *Swan Lake* (revised 1946 and 1949), after Petipa/Ivanov, produced by Sergeyev, revised 1946, Sadler's Wells Ballet, New Theatre, London
1951 *House of Cards*, Paltenghi, Ballet Rambert
1952 *Swan Lake*, Petipa, Ivanov, Ashton, produced by Sergeyev, revised by de Valois, Sadler's Wells Ballet, Royal Opera House, London
1960 Costumes for *Raymonda, Scène d'Amour*, Ashton, The Royal Ballet, Royal Opera House, London
1965 *Swan Lake*, Petipa, Ivanov, Ashton and de Valois, produced by Sergeyev, revised Ashton, The Royal Ballet, Royal Opera House, London
1971 *Swan Lake*, Petipa, Ivanov, Ashton, de Valois, Nureyev, Bruhn, production by Sergeyev, revised by de Valois in 1972, The Royal Ballet, Royal Opera House, London

Derek Jarman

Derek Jarman was born in 1942. After studying English, History and Art History at King's College, London, he trained at the Slade School of Art during the period 1963–7, where he was taught by Peter Williams, Peter Snow and Nicholas Georgiadis. As a painter he had several one-man shows and was given a retrospective by the ICA in 1984. He is most widely known as a film-maker, creating his first Super 8 shorts at the start of the 1970s before his first full-length work, *Sebastiane*, in 1976. Later films include *The Tempest* (1979), *Caravaggio* (1986) and *Edward II* (1991). He appeared in a number of films, including the role of Patrick Procktor in *Prick Up Your Ears* (Stephen Frears, 1987). His first design for dance was part of the *Collaborations 2* programme at the Jeannetta Cochrane Theatre and he later taught at Central Saint Martins as part of the Design for Dance Project. He died in 1994.

1968 *Throughway*, Popescu, *Collaborations 2*, Ballet Rambert/Central School of Art and Design, Jeannetta Cochrane Theatre, London; *Jazz Calendar*, Ashton, The Royal Ballet, Royal Opera House, London
1973 *Silver Apples of the Moon*, Spain, London Festival Ballet, New Theatre, Oxford
1980 *One*, Jobe, London Contemporary Dance Theatre, Arts Centre, Christ's Hospital, Horsham (assisted by Meaha)
1985 *Mouth of the Night*, Mantis Dance Company, London
1990 *Jazz Calendar*, Ashton, Birmingham Royal Ballet, Birmingham Hippodrome

Allen Jones

Allen Jones was born in Southampton. He studied at Hornsey College of Art (1955–9) and the Royal College of Art (1959–60). He exhibited at the Paris Biennale in 1961 and moved to New York in 1964. His work, embracing painting and sculpture as well as hybrid experiments involving multiple and shaped canvases, has been shown worldwide. Other activities include poster, stage and film design and a commission for the Pirelli calendar. He has written several essays on video and photography and a book on projected stage designs.

1989 *Cinema*, Alston, Ballet Rambert, Birmingham Repertory Theatre, Birmingham

1996 *Signed in Red*, Diamond, Dance Bites, The Royal Ballet, The Swan Theatre, Worcester

E. McKnight Kauffer

Born in Montana, USA, in 1890, E. McKnight Kauffer was employed as a scene painter prior to being trained in the field, both in California and Chicago. A move to Paris in 1913 was curtailed by the outbreak of World War One, which resulted in his move to London. Here he established himself as a commercial designer, working on books, brochures, textiles and murals. He was the subject of solo exhibitions in both England and America. His work for the stage included Milton's 1932 production of *Othello*, and Gielgud's production of Daviot's *Queen of Scots* (1934). His designs for *Checkmate* (1937) were lost in Holland during World War Two, requiring him to redesign the production in 1947. McKnight Kauffer moved back to the United States in 1940, where he continued to live until his death in 1954.

1932 Special curtain for a musical interlude during an evening of ballet, de Valois, Camargo Society, Savoy Theatre, London

1937 *Checkmate* (originally *Echec et Mat*), de Valois, Vic-Wells Ballet, Théâtre des Champs-Elysées, Paris, revised in 1947

Barry Kay

Born in Melbourne in 1932, Barry Kay studied at the Académie Julien in Paris and moved to London in 1956. His arrival coincided with the emergence of Western Theatre Ballet for whom he produced a number of designs as their Design Consultant. He designed plays for the Royal Shakespeare Company including *No Why* and *Measure for Measure* at the Old Vic, while his opera commissions included *Die Meistersinger von Nürnberg* (Royal Opera) and *The Tell-Tale Heart* (Netherlands Opera). He worked closely with two of the most prominent figures in the dance world, Kenneth MacMillan and Rudolf Nureyev. For the former he designed not only ballets but also one of the choreographer's drama productions, *Dance of Death*, at The Royal Exchange, Manchester. For Nureyev he worked as Production Designer on the film *Don Quixote* with the Australian Ballet in 1972. He died in 1985.

1957 Set for *Pulcinella*, West, Arts Theatre, London (costumes by Phyllida Law); *The Prisoners*, Darrell, Western Theatre Ballet; *Non-Stop*, Darrell, Western Theatre Ballet

1958 *Chiaroscuro*, Darrell, Western Theatre Ballet; *The Unicorn, the Gorgon and the Manticore*, opera, choreographed by Darrell, New Opera Company, Sadler's Wells

1960 *Bal de la Victoire*, Darrell, Western Theatre Ballet

1961 *Salade*, Darrell, Western Theatre Ballet

1964 *Images of Love*, MacMillan, The Royal Ballet, Royal Opera House, London; *Solitaire pas de deux*, MacMillan, Western Theatre Ballet; *Divertimento*, MacMillan, Western Theatre Ballet

1966 *Don Quixote*, Nureyev after Petipa, Vienna State Opera Ballet; *Raymonda*, Act III, Nureyev after Petipa, The Royal Ballet Touring Company, Suomen Kansallisoopera, Helsinki

1967 *The Sleeping Beauty*, MacMillan after Petipa, West German State Opera Ballet, Berlin; *Anastasia* (one-act version), MacMillan, West German State Opera Ballet, Berlin

1968 *Cain and Abel*, MacMillan, West German State Opera Ballet, Berlin

1970 *Don Quixote*, Nureyev after Petipa, Australian Ballet; *Miss Julie*, MacMillan, Stuttgart Ballet, Stuttgart

1971 *Anastasia* (three-act version), MacMillan, The Royal Ballet

1976 *The Four Seasons*, MacMillan, Paris Opéra Ballet; *Métaboles*, MacMillan, Paris Opéra Ballet

1978 *Solitaire*, MacMillan, Sadler's Wells Theatre Ballet

1981 *Isadora*, MacMillan, The Royal Ballet

1982 *Isadora Solos*, MacMillan, Sadler's Wells Royal Ballet, Teatro Olimpico, Rome

Ralph Koltai

Ralph Koltai, a former student at the Central School of Art and Design and a former Head of Theatre Design at the College, has designed over two hundred theatre, musical, opera and ballet productions since his work for the opera *Angélique* at the Fortune Theatre, London, in 1950. He was Associate Designer at the Royal Shakespeare Company for 22 years (1965–87), designing 25 productions for them, though he has worked with many other national companies and abroad. Recently he has designed *Madam Butterfly* for David Pountney in Tokyo, *My Fair Lady* (directed by Frank Dunlop) for an American tour and Lindsay Kemp's *Cruel Garden*. He has won many awards, including the Society of West End Theatre's Designer of the Year Award (twice – in 1978 for *Brandt* and in 1984 for *Cyrano de Bergerac*), the London Drama Critics Award in 1967 (*Little Murders, The Love Girl and the Innocent* and *As You Like It*) and the Individual Gold Medal at the Prague Quadrennial International Exhibition of Scenography in 1975. He was made a CBE in 1983 and elected a Fellow of the Academy of Performing Arts in Hong Kong in 1994. In 1996 Ralph Koltai was made an Honorary Fellow of The London Institute.

1958 *Two Brothers*, Morrice, Ballet Rambert
1959 *Hazaña*, Morrice, Ballet Rambert
1961 *A Place in the Desert*, Morrice, Ballet Rambert
1962 *Conflicts*, Morrice, Ballet Rambert
1963 *The Travellers*, Morrice, Ballet Rambert
1964 *Cul-de-Sac*, Morrice, Ballet Rambert
1965 *The Tribute*, Morrice, The Royal Ballet Touring Company, Royal Shakespeare Theatre, Stratford-upon-Avon; set for *Raymonda*, Nureyev after Petipa, Australian Ballet, Birmingham Theatre, Birmingham
1966 *Diversities*, Taylor, Ballet Rambert
1977 *Cruel Garden*, Bruce/Kemp, Ballet Rambert (with Lindsay Kemp)
1978 *Seven Deadly Sins*, Alston, English National Opera, London Coliseum (with Nadine Baylis)
1989 *Metropolis*, Jobe, directed by Jerome Savory, Piccadilly Theatre, London
1990 *The Planets*, Bintley, The Royal Ballet (costumes by Sue Blane)

Mikhail Larionov

Born in 1881 at Tiraspol, near Odessa, Larionov trained at the Moscow Institute of Painting, Sculpture and Architecture from 1898 until his expulsion in 1904. He came to Paris in 1914 with Natalia Gontcharova, the designer whom he met at the Institute in 1900 and who was to be his lifetime companion. Larionov soon became an integral part of the Diaghilev Ballet, not merely designing ballets, but advising on all aspects, even including the choreography, for which he is co-credited in *Le Chout* (1921). Mobilised in 1915, he rejoined Diaghilev later that year after sustaining a war wound. Designing various productions throughout the early part of the century, he and Gontcharova were largely forgotten until a resurgence of interest in their work was generated by Richard Buckle's 1954 Diaghilev Exhibition in Edinburgh. He died in 1964.

1915 *Soleil de Nuit*, Massine, Diaghilev's Ballets Russes, Grand Théâtre, Geneva; costumes and projections for *Histoires Naturelles*, Massine (not produced)
1916 *Kikimora*, Massine, Diaghilev's Ballets Russes, Teatro Eugenia-Victoria, San Sebastián
1916/17 Costumes, with Gontcharova, for *Les Contes Russes*, Massine, Diaghilev's Ballets Russes, Théâtre du Châtelet, Paris
1921 *Le Chout (Le Bouffon)*, Slavinsky and Larionov, Diaghilev's Ballets Russes, Théâtre de la Gaîté-Lyrique, Paris
1922 *Le Renard* , Nijinska, Diaghilev's Ballets Russes, Théâtre National de l'Opéra, Paris (costumes by Gontcharova)
1924 *Karaguez*, Bolm, Allied Arts, Chicago (not produced)

1929 *Le Renard*, Lifar, Diaghilev's Ballets Russes, Paris (with constructivist design and acrobats' costumes)
1930 *La Symphonie Classique*, Slavinsky, Opéra Ballet de Michel Benois, Paris
1932 *Sur le Borsythène*, Lifar, Paris Opéra Ballet, Paris (with Gontcharova)
1935 *Port Said*, Woizkowsky, Les Ballets de Léon Woizkowsky, European Tour

Marie Laurencin

Marie Laurencin, the painter, was born in Paris in 1885. She studied at the Académie Humbert with the intention of becoming a porcelain painter. Coming under the influence of the Cubist movement, she exhibited paintings at the Salon d'Automne and the Salon des Indépendants. As well as designing for the stage she produced a series of lithographs on dance and illustrated a number of books, including Lewis Carroll's *Alice in Wonderland*. She died in 1956.

1924 *Les Roses*, Massine, Soirées de Paris, Théâtre de la Cigale; *Les Biches*, Nijinska, Diaghilev's Ballets Russes, Monte Carlo
1927 Costumes for *L'Eventail de Jeanne*, Franck and Bourgat, Salon de Madame Jeanne Dubost (set by Pierre Legrain and René Moulaert)
1940 *Un Jour d'Eté*, Gantillon, Opéra Comique
1946 *Le Déjeuner sur l'Herbe*, Lidova, Ballet des Champs-Elysées

André Levasseur

Born in Paris, André Levasseur studied at the Ecole de la Haute Couture Parisienne and for several years was a designer for the couturier Christian Dior. In addition to his ballet designs, Levasseur created costumes for the *Fanfare pour le Prince* for the Rainier wedding in Monaco and a large number of costumes for the cabaret in Monte Carlo. He is currently living in France.

1952 *Piège de Lumière*, Taras, Grand Ballet du Marquis de Cuevas, Théâtre de l'Empire, Paris

1955 Costumes for *Les Noces Fantastiques*, Lifar, Paris Opéra; *Roméo et Juliette*, Skibine, Grand Ballet du Marquis de Cuevas, The Louvre courtyard, Paris

1956 Costumes for *Birthday Offering*, Ashton, Sadler's Wells Ballet, Royal Opera House, London (set by Fedorovitch from *Veneziana*)

1957 *La Péri*, Ashton, The Royal Ballet; *La Somnambule*, Balanchine, Grand Ballet de Marquis de Cuevas; *Capriccio for piano and orchestra*, Balanchine, New York City Ballet; *Jewels*, Balanchine, New York City Ballet; *Homage to a Princess*, Charnley, Festival Ballet, Holland Festival; *Entre Cour et Jardin*, Taras, Théâtre de Monte Carlo; *Suite New-Yorkaise*, Taras, Théâtre de Monte Carlo

1958 *La Valse*, Ashton, La Scala, Milan; *Theme and Variations*, Balanchine, American Ballet Theatre

1959 *La Valse*, Ashton, The Royal Ballet, Royal Opera House, London

1962 *Le Corsaire pas de deux*, Petipa, The Royal Ballet, Royal Opera House, London; *Raymonda pas de deux*, variations and coda, Ashton, The Royal Ballet, Royal Opera House, London

Andrew Logan

Andrew Logan was born and trained at the Oxford School of Architecture. Following his graduation in 1970 he had an exhibition at the ICA, London. Primarily a sculptor, he is also a jewellery maker for Zandra Rhodes and devised and continues to organise the Alternative Miss World Competition. He has exhibited his sculptures worldwide, having his first one-man exhibition at the New Arts Centre, London. Exhibitions include the 'Goddesses' exhibition at the Commonwealth Institute in 1984 and the Limelight exhibition in New York (1985). An interest in holography led to a travelling exhibition of holograms in 1982 and a sculpture mobile in a holography exhibition at the German Film Museum in Frankfurt in 1984.

1984 *The Mayfly*, Seymour, Nether Wallop Festival

1987 *Wolfi*, Seymour, Ballet Rambert

1988 *Bastet*, Seymour, Sadler's Wells Royal Ballet, Birmingham Hippodrome

Peter Logan

Peter Logan's fascination with sculpture and movement led to his participation in the experimental work being performed at The Place at the end of the 1960s. For his *Corridor* piece, Logan enlisted the help of both Derek Jarman (as the 'guest costume') and Richard Alston. From 1968 until 1978 he created sculptures that performed acrobatics, formal dances and a play, powered by electricity. Since 1978 his kinetic sculptures have been powered by the wind. His work has been seen in exhibitions and installations throughout the world, including the European Sculpture Garden in Seville, Spain as part of Expo '92.

1969 *Corridor and a Room for Robin Howard*, Explorations, The Place

1970 *Landscape*, choreography and design with Karl Brown, Ploys Programme, Scottish Theatre Ballet, The Place, London

1971 *St Thomas' Wake* (assemblage), Drew, Sadler's Wells Royal Ballet, Sadler's Wells, London

1986 *Red and Blue Crayons* – a dancing sculpture, Norwich Cathedral Cloisters

John Macfarlane

Born in Glasgow, Macfarlane studied at Glasgow School of Art 1966–70. As the recipient of the Leverhulme Travelling Scholarship in 1970 he spent two years studying and working in Italy and Greece. In 1972 he was awarded the Arts Council of Great Britain Trainee Theatre Design Bursary. He is both a scenographer and a painter and printmaker, exhibiting widely throughout Europe. His design work has been mainly concerned with dance and he has worked regularly with choreographers such as Jirí Kylián and Glen Tetley. He has designed *Giselle* and *La Ronde* for the Royal Ballet as well as *The Nutcracker* for Sir Peter Wright's Birmingham Royal Ballet. The first exhibition of his stage designs was held at the Marina Henderson Gallery, London 1986. In the late eighties, he started to design more for opera, and has worked for Köln, Geneva, Scottish, Brussels, Santa Fe and Paris.

1975 *Sinfonietta*, Ulrich, Köln Tanz Forum

1976 *Cradle* (retitled *The Sea Whisper'd Me*), Morrice, Ballet Rambert; *Requiem*, Ulrich, Köln Tanz Forum

1977 *Smiling Immortal*, Morrice, Ballet

Rambert; *Capriccio*, Ulrich, Köln Tanz Forum

1978 *De l'amour*, Burth, Zurich Opera House

1979 *Der Blaue Mantel*, Ulrich and Burth, Köln Tanz Forum; *Schemenstadt*, Burth, Zurich Opera House

1980 *Summer's End*, Tetley, Nederlands Dans Theater, The Hague; *Miraculous Mandarin*, Ulrich, Köln Tanz Forum; *Schwarzstrand*, Burth, Zurich Opera House

1981 *Forgotten Land*, Kylián, Stuttgart Ballet; *Summer's End*, Tetley, Boston Ballet; *Stravinsky's Firebird*, Tetley, Royal Danish Ballet, Copenhagen

1982 *Stravinsky's Firebird*, Tetley, television adaptation, Danmarks Radio; *Songs of the Wayfarer*, Kylián, Nederlands Dans Theater, The Hague; *Svadebka (Les Noces)*, Kylián, Nederlands Dans Theater, The Hague and Metropolitan Opera House, New York

1983 *Dreamtime*, Kylián, Nederlands Dans Theater, The Hague; *Wiegenlied*, Kylián, Wienerstaatsoper and Nederlands Dans Theater, The Hague

1984 *Lyric Suite*, Ulrich, Wienerstaatsoper, Vienna; *L'Enfant et les Sortilèges*, Kylián, Nederlands Dans Theater and Holland Festival

1985 *Giselle*, Petipa after Coralli and Perrot, produced by Wright, The Royal Ballet; *An Occasion for Some Revolutionary Gestures*, Wagoner, Ballet Rambert; *Dream Walk of the Shaman*, Tetley, Aterballetto, Reggio Emilia; *Piccolo Mondo*, Kylián, Scapino Ballet, Amsterdam; *Forgotten Land*, Kylián, The Joffrey Ballet, New York

1986 *The Soldier's Tale*, Kylián, Nederlands Dans Theater, The Hague

1987 *La Ronde*, Tetley, National Ballet of Canada, Toronto

1989 *Tagore*, Tetley, National Ballet of Canada, Toronto; *Tantz-Schul*, Kylián, Nederlands Dans Theater, The Hague; *Tantz-Schul*, Kylián, Théâtre National de l'Opéra de Paris; *La Ronde*, Tetley, television adaptation, Primedia Television, Toronto

1990 *The Nutcracker*, Wright, Birmingham Royal Ballet; *Piccolo Mondo*, Kylián, Grand Théâtre de Genève; *Forgotten Land*, Kylián, Grand Théâtre de Genève; *Forgotten Land*, Kylián, Scottish Ballet, Glasgow; *Tagore*, Tetley, San Francisco Ballet

1991 *Dialogues*, Tetley, Dance Theatre of Harlem, New York

1992 *Svadebka*, Kylián, Bayerisches Staatsballett, Munich

1993 *Nana's Lied*, Thomasson, San Francisco Ballet; *La Ronde*, Tetley, The Royal Ballet, London

1994 Set for *La Bayadère* (extract), Het National Ballet, Amsterdam

1995 *Swan Lake*, Barra, Bayerisches Staatsballett, Munich

Antony McDonald

After studying theatre design on the English National Opera Design Course, Antony McDonald was commissioned to design *Let's Make An Opera* for Welsh National Opera. Among his many theatre and opera credits, he designed *Hamlet* and *Richard II*, for the Royal Shakespeare Company, *Berenice* for the Royal National Theatre, *Chérubin* at the Royal Opera House, and *Billy Budd* for the English National Opera. He has also directed *The Birthday Party* (Glasgow Citizens, 1992) and *Escape at Sea* for Second Stride in 1993, for both of which he was also the designer. He has worked extensively with Second Stride since 1982.

1980 *Something to Tell*, Davies, London Contemporary Dance Theatre, Theatre Clywd, Mold

1981 *Some Fugues*, Spink, Ian Spink Group, Roehampton Institute, London; *Coolhaven*, Spink, Werkcentrum Dans, Rotterdam; *De Gas*, Spink, Ian Spink Group, York Arts Centre; design and photography for *Free Setting*, Davies, LCDT, Arts Centre, University of Warwick

1982 *Carnival*, Davies, Second Stride, Arts Centre, University of Warwick (with David Buckland); *Danse fra Pagoderms Rige*, Alston, Royal Danish Ballet, Royal Theatre, Copenhagen; *There Is No Other Woman*, Spink, Second Stride, Oxford Playhouse; *Second Turning*, Bannerman, LCDT, Ryerson Theatre, Toronto

1983 *Minor Characters*, Davies, Second Stride, Assembly Rooms, Edinburgh; *New Tactics*, Spink with director Tim Albery, Second Stride, Leeds Playhouse (with Craig Givens); *Secret Gardens*, Spink with McDonald, Tim Albery and Geraldine Pilgrim, ICA, London; *Canso Trobar*, Bannerman, LCDT, Arts Centre, University of Warwick; design and photography for *The Dancing Department*, Davies, LCDT, Apollo Theatre, Oxford

1984 *Further and Further into Night*, Spink, Second Stride, Gardner Centre, Brighton

1986 *Mercure*, Spink, Ballet Rambert, Sadler's Wells, London (with Catherine Felstead); *Bösendorfer Waltzes*, Spink, Second Stride, The Arnolfini, Bristol; *The Trojans: Fall of Troy*, opera, Spink, Opera North, Grand Theatre, Leeds (with Tom Cairns)

1987 Costumes for *John Somebody*, Newman, LCDT; *Weighing the Heart*, Spink, Second Stride, Gardner Centre, Brighton; *The Trojans: Trojans in Carthage*, opera, Spink,

Welsh National Opera, New Theatre, Cardiff
(with Tom Cairns)

1988 *Mates*, Gordon, Rambert Dance
Company; *Dancing and Shouting*, Spink,
Second Stride, Towngate Theatre, Basildon

1989 *Pulau Dewata*, Alston, Rambert Dance
Company; *Heaven Ablaze in his Breast*,
Spink, Second Stride

1991 *Lives of the Great Poisoners*, Spink, Second
Stride, The Arnolfini, Bristol

1993 *Escape at Sea*, Spink, Rubin and Page,
Second Stride, The Place, London; *Wanting
to Tell Stories*, Davies, Siobhan Davies Dance
Company, Gardner Centre, Brighton (set by
Buckland)

1994 *Fearful Symmetries*, Page, The Royal
Ballet, Royal Opera House, London

1996 *. . . now languorous, now wild*, Page, The
Royal Ballet, Royal Opera House, London

Norman McDowell

Norman McDowell, born in 1931, was one of a
rare breed, combining the skills of both dancer
and designer. As a dancer, trained at Sadler's
Wells Ballet School, he performed in ballets
from the classics through to creating the lead in
Jack Carter's *Witch Boy*. His design credits
include several dozen works for companies
throughout Europe, as well as *Swan Lake* for the
Argentinian company at the Teatro Colón. A
champion of new dance in Great Britain, he
founded and was director of London Dance
Theatre in 1964, introducing an ambitious
programme of new works with commissioned
scores and engaging established writers. The
company was disbanded after a year, and
McDowell went on to become Artistic Director

of London Festival Ballet in 1965. McDowell
continued to design for companies including
The Royal Ballet and Scottish Ballet throughout
the 1970s and died in London in 1980.

1952 *Past Recalled*, Carter, Ballet Workshop

1954 Costumes for *The Life and Death of Lola
Montez*, Carter, Ballet Workshop

1956 *Witch Boy*, Carter, Ballet der Lage Landen,
Amsterdam

1959 Costumes for *London Morning*, Carter,
London Festival Ballet

1961 *Grand Pas de Fiancées* (revised 1964),
Carter, London Festival Ballet

1964 *I Quattro Stagioni*, Carter, London Dance
Theatre

1966 *Noir et Blanc*, Lifar, reproduced by
Casenave, London Festival Ballet

1967 *The Sleeping Beauty*, Stevenson/Grey after
Petipa, London Festival Ballet; *Paquita*,
Mazilier and Petipa, London Festival Ballet

1973 Costumes for *Three Dances to Japanese
Music*, Carter, Scottish Theatre Ballet; *Vespri*,
Prokovsky, New London Ballet

1974 Costumes for *The Dancing Floor*, Carter,
Scottish Ballet

1975 *Shukumei*, Carter, The Royal Ballet
Touring Company, Royal Shakespeare
Theatre, Stratford-upon-Avon; *Impromptu for
Twelve*, Carter, Northern Dance Theatre

1976 *Lulu*, Carter, Sadler's Wells Royal Ballet,
Sadler's Wells, London

1977 *La Bayadère*, Sanchez after Petipa,
Northern Ballet Theatre; *Swan Lake*, Act III,
grand pas de deux, Petipa, Northern Ballet
Theatre; *Coppélia*, Petipa and Cecchetti,
reproduced with additions by Clegg,
Northern Ballet Theatre

Jock McFadyen

Jock McFadyen was born in Paisley, Scotland,
studying at Chelsea School of Art in the period
1973–7. He was appointed Artist-in-Residence
at the National Gallery, London in 1981. His
work takes its inspiration from contemporary
urban life, especially that of London's East End.
In 1989 he exhibited at the Scottish Gallery,
London and has had solo exhibitions
throughout Great Britain and been part of
many group exhibitions in Europe and the USA
since 1978. He is currently living and working
in London.

1992 *The Judas Tree*, MacMillan, The Royal
Ballet, Royal Opera House, London

Jean-Denis Malclès

Born in Paris, Jean-Denis Malclès designed
many plays for the Comédie Française and for
the Parisian theatre. In the 1950s he designed
several plays by Jean Anouilh including *La Valse
des Toréadors*.

1945 *La Fiancée du Diable*, Petit, Ballet des
Champs-Elysées.

1948 *Cinderella*, Ashton, Sadler's Wells Ballet,
Royal Opera House, London

Stephen Meaha

Born in London in 1956, Meaha was trained at
Wimbledon School of Art. He worked as Derek
Jarman's assistant on the film *The Tempest* and
for Tom Jobe's *One* for London Contemporary
Dance Theatre. He designed Pam Gems's *The

Treat and Gloria Theatre's *Lady Audley's Secret*, both of which were performed at the ICA, where he also designed Jonathan Gems's *The Secret of the Universe*. Meaha's long association with Nederlands Dans Theater as assistant included two commissions, as designer, from Kylián and Forsythe. In 1989 he began collaborating with William Tuckett, a partnership that resulted in three works before Meaha's death the following year.

1982 *Liquid Assets*, Jobe, London
 Contemporary Dance Theatre
1983 *Mental Model*, Forsythe, Nederlands Dans
 Theater, The Hague
1987 *Frankenstein!!*, Kylián, Nederlands Dans
 Theater, Scheveningen
1989 *Those Unheard*, Tuckett, Sadler's Wells
 Royal Ballet, Birmingham Hippodrome
1990 *Enclosure*, Tuckett, The Royal Ballet;
 Game, Tuckett, Sadler's Wells Royal Ballet,
 Birmingham Hippodrome

Oliver Messel

Oliver Messel was born in London in 1905, was educated at Eton and then studied at the Slade School of Fine Art (1922–4). He first designed costumes and masks for Diaghilev in 1925 and the following year for C.B. Cochran's revues. He designed many plays in London and New York up until the end of World War Two, including his first opera, *Francesca da Rimini* (Royal Opera, 1937), but his most memorable design was the 1946 *Sleeping Beauty* for the Sadler's Wells Ballet, that continued in the repertory for twenty-two years. He worked as a designer for many films, including *Suddenly Last Summer* (1960) and *Cleopatra* (1963). He was awarded a CBE in 1958 and retired to

Barbados in 1966, where he died in 1978.

1925 Masks for *Zéphyre et Flore*, Massine,
 Diaghilev's Ballets Russes
1932 Costumes for *The Miracle*, Massine,
 Lyceum Theatre, London
1937 *Francesca da Rimini*, Lichine, Original
 Ballet Russe, Royal Opera House, London
1942 *Comus*, Helpmann, Sadler's Wells Ballet,
 New Theatre, London
1946 *The Sleeping Beauty*, Petipa, staged by
 Sergeyev, Ashton, de Valois, revised 1952,
 Sadler's Wells Ballet, Royal Opera House,
 London; false proscenium, added to
 Whistler's design, for *The Rake's Progress*, de
 Valois, Vic-Wells Ballet, Sadler's Wells,
 London
1953 *Homage to the Queen*, Ashton, Sadler's
 Wells Ballet, Royal Opera House, London
1960 Partial redesign of 1946 production of
 The Sleeping Beauty, Petipa, staged by
 Wright, Royal Ballet, Royal Opera House,
 London
1976 Partial redesign of 1946 production of *The
 Sleeping Beauty*, Petipa, staged by Skeaping,
 American Ballet Theatre, Metropolitan
 Opera House, New York

John Minton

John Minton was born near Cambridge in 1917 and studied at the St John's Wood Art School and at the Atelier Colarossi in Paris. A conscientious objector, he entered the Pioneer Corps in 1941 and served for two years before leaving the army. He briefly shared the studio of Colquhoun and MacBryde during this time, his work displaying the influence of Picasso. He taught at Camberwell Arts School, Central School of Arts and Crafts and the Royal College

of Art. He began a long association with the Lefevre Gallery in 1945, having five solo exhibitions there and was elected a member of the London Group in 1949. Alongside his painting he worked on a number of stage designs, including a collaboration with Michael Ayrton on Gielgud's 1942 *Macbeth*. A familiar figure on the Soho scene, his sociability was mirrored by a melancholia that was in part responsible for his suicide in 1957.

Tanya Moiseiwitsch

Born in London, Tanya Moiseiwitsch was one of Jeannetta Cochrane's students at the Central School of Arts and Crafts in the early 1930s. Her career has spanned 50 years and over 200 productions ranging from Greek tragedy to musicals. In 1953, with Tyrone Guthrie, she designed the thrust stage for the Stratford (Ontario) Festival Theatre, regarded as a significant development in twentieth-century design. She has received many honours including a New York Drama Desk Award for Best Costumes in 1969 and a *Plays and Players* Design Award in 1976. She was awarded the CBE in 1976.

Motley

Motley was the 'stage name' of three friends; Margaret Harris, her sister Sophie Devine, and their friend Elizabeth Montgomery. Their first work for the stage was designing the costumes for John Gielgud's 1932 production of *Romeo and Juliet* for the OUDS and this led to a long stream of work for Gielgud during the 1930s including *Richard of Bordeaux*, *Hamlet* and

Romeo and Juliet at the New Theatre, and *The School for Scandal, The Three Sisters, Richard III* and *The Merchant of Venice* at the Queens. Their work at Michel St Denis' London Theatre Studio led eventually to the Motley School of Theatre Design, which flourishes to this day. In the 1940s they began to work for the Metropolitan Opera in New York and for Broadway where they dressed Mary Martin in the musicals *South Pacific* and *Peter Pan.* They worked for the Royal Shakespeare Company, the English National Opera and the Royal Court. In the cinema their best-known films are *The Loneliness of the Long Distance Runner* and *The Spy Who Came in from the Cold.* They wrote *Theatre Props* and *Designing and Making Stage Costumes,* with a foreword by Peggy Ashcroft. They retired in 1976.

Peter Mumford

After training in theatre design at the Central School of Art, Peter Mumford began a career in lighting design that embraces dance, theatre and opera. Recent lighting designs for the theatre include *Richard II, Volpone* and *Mother Courage* (all Royal National Theatre) and *The Winter Guest* (West Yorkshire Playhouse/ Almeida). Opera work includes *Fidelio* (Scottish Opera), *Simon Boccanegra* (Munich Staatsoper) and *The Return of Ulysses* (Opera North/Buxton Festival). His lighting designs for dance are numerous, including *Edward II* (Stuttgart Ballet), *Carmina Burana* and *Birthday Offering* (Birmingham Royal Ballet), *Sometimes I Wonder* (Richard Alston Dance Company) and *Mr Worldly Wise* (Royal Ballet). His work on *The Glass Blew In* (Siobhan Davies) and *Fearful Symmetries* (Royal Ballet) won him the

Laurence Olivier Award for Outstanding Achievement in Dance, 1995. In addition to his lighting work, Peter Mumford has worked for a number of years as a director for film and television.

John Napier

As the designer of the musicals *Cats, Starlight Express, Les Misérables, Miss Saigon* and *Sunset Boulevard,* John Napier's work is evident worldwide. He trained first at Hornsey College of Art and then at the Central School of Arts and Crafts under Ralph Koltai. He has designed many productions for the Royal Shakespeare Company and is currently an Associate Designer with them. With the National Theatre he designed the acclaimed production of Peter Shaffer's *Equus.* His opera credits include *Lohengrin* and *Macbeth* for the Royal Opera House. His contribution to design has been recognised in his two Society of West End Theatre Awards, a BAFTA and four Tony Awards. For Disney, he designed the futuristic *Captain Eo* video, whilst for Stephen Spielberg he designed the full-length film, *Hook.*

1967   *Inochi*, Toguri, Ballet Rambert/Central School of Art and Design
1969   *George Frideric*, Bruce, Ballet Rambert
1981   *Cats*, musical, choreographed by Lynne, New London Theatre, London
1984   *Starlight Express*, musical, choreographed by Philips, Apollo Victoria Theatre, London
1993   Set for *Sunset Boulevard*, musical, Goodwin, directed by Trevor Nunn, Adelphi Theatre, London (costumes by Anthony Powell)

Paul Nash

Paul Nash was born in London in 1889 and trained at the Slade School of Fine Art in 1910, having his first exhibition of drawings at the Carfax Gallery the following year. After a 1913 exhibition Roger Fry asked Nash to design for the Omega workshops. Injured during World War One, he established a reputation as a war artist. A prolific painter and illustrator for books, he also taught and wrote for various journals and compiled and edited the 1935 *Shell Guide to Dorset.* In 1924 he published designs for *A Midsummer Night's Dream.* He continued to paint and exhibit until his death in Boscombe in 1946.

1920   *The Truth About Russian Dancers,* Karsavina, London Coliseum

Lila de Nobili

Born in Lugano, Switzerland, Lila de Nobili is both a painter and designer for the theatre. Her designs for opera include Visconti's *La Traviata* at La Scala, Milan in 1955, Zeffirelli's *Rigoletto* for the Royal Opera, Covent Garden in 1964 and *Carmen* for Paris Opera. She also designed Hans Werner Henze's *Elegy for Young Lovers* for Glyndebourne in 1961. Her ballet designs have equally been seen across Europe. She is currently living in Paris.

1950   *Persephone*, Taras, Grand Ballet de Monte Carlo, Théâtre de Monte Carlo, Monte Carlo
1956   *Mario e il Mago*, Milloss, La Scala, Milan; *Sable*, Babilée, Ballets Jean Babilée, Théâtre des Champs-Elysées, Paris; *Les Saisons*, Gore, Ballets 56, Festival de Lyon-Charbonnières, Lyon

1958 *Ondine*, Ashton, The Royal Ballet, Royal
       Opera House, London
1968 Costumes with Rostislav Doboujinsky for
       The Sleeping Beauty, Ashton after Petipa,
       produced by Wright, The Royal Ballet, Royal
       Opera House, London (set by Henry
       Bardon)

Victor Pasmore

Born in Chelsham, Surrey, Victor Pasmore took
evening classes at the Central School of Arts
and Crafts from 1927 until 1931. His first one-
man show was in 1933 at the London Artist's
Association. He was one of the founder
members of the Euston Road School in 1937
and has subsequently exhibited internationally,
becoming master of painting in the Department
of Fine Art, Durham University in 1954. He has
taught at a number of art colleges, including the
Central School. From the late 1940s he shifted
towards pure abstraction, away from the natural
scenes he had previously painted.
Experimenting with moves away from the
canvas, first with collage and then reliefs, he
later returned to painting in the 1960s. In 1959
he was awarded a CBE.

1984 *Young Apollo*, Bintley, The Royal Ballet,
       Royal Opera House, London

Deanna Petherbridge

Born in Pretoria, South Africa, Deanna
Petherbridge first studied at the University of
Witwatersrand in her native country before
leaving for England in 1960. She moved once
more in 1967, spending five years in Greece

before travelling throughout the Middle East
and North Africa. She worked in a number of
media during this period, having her first solo
exhibition in 1973 at the Angela Flowers Gallery
in London. She was Artist-in-Residence at
Manchester City Art Gallery in 1982. In 1990
she received an Edwin Austin Abbey Memorial
Scholarship. She has written for a number of
journals on both art and architecture.

1984 *A Broken Set of Rules*, Page, The Royal
       Ballet, Royal Opera House, London
1987 *One by Nine*, Jackson, Sadler's Wells Royal
       Ballet, Sadler's Wells, London
1990 *Bloodlines*, Page, The Royal Ballet, Royal
       Opera House, London

Pablo Picasso

Born in Malaga, Spain, in 1881, Picasso is best
known as a painter, though both his hunger for
experimentation and an affinity for extending
the visual into the third dimension (as with his
collages) suggest that his work in the theatre
would have been an obvious extension of his
practice. Following the triumphs of the
exoticism of Benois and Bakst, Diaghilev's
choice of Picasso as designer indicated his
growing allegiance to the avant-garde that was
to continue through the 1920s. *Parade*,
confusing performers and scenery in the
costumes of the managers and music and 'noise'
in Erik Satie's assemblage of orchestral and
street sounds, was greeted with anger and
incomprehension. This confusion accompanied
subsequent experimentation in Picasso's dance
designs in the 1920s, though they are now
restaged as canonical works. He died in
Mougins in 1973.

1917 *Parade*, Massine, Diaghilev's Ballets
       Russes, Théâtre du Châtelet, Paris
1919 *Le Tricorne*, Massine, Diaghilev's Ballets
       Russes, Alhambra Theatre, London
1920 *Pulcinella*, Massine, Diaghilev's Ballets
       Russes, Théâtre National de l'Opéra, Paris
1921 *Cuadro flamenco* (traditional), Diaghilev's
       Ballets Russes, Théâtre de la Gaité-Lyrique,
       Paris
1923 *Trepar*, Nijinska, Diaghilev's Ballets Russes
       (not produced)
1924 *Mercure*, Massine, Comte Etienne de
       Beaumont's Soirées de Paris, Paris; curtain for
       Le Train Bleu, Nijinska, Diaghilev's Ballets
       Russes, Théâtre des Champs-Elysées, Paris
1947 *The Three-cornered Hat*, Massine, The
       Sadler's Wells Ballet, Covent Garden
1954 Backdrop for *Le Rendezvous*, Petit, Ballets
       des Champs-Elysées, Paris
1960 Backdrop for *L'Après-midi d'un Faune*,
       Lifar, Paris Opéra (design proposals rejected)
1962 *Icare*, Lifar, Paris Opéra

John Piper

John Piper, born in 1903, studied painting at the
Slade School and then travelled to Paris in 1933
to study the work of contemporary French
artists. He became a war artist during World
War Two and in 1946 worked with Benjamin
Britten on his opera *The Rape of Lucretia* in
what was to be the first of many collaborations
with the composer. In 1953 he designed
Gloriana, an opera composed by Britten in
honour of Queen Elizabeth II's coronation,
with choreography by John Cranko, with
whom he collaborated on a number of ballets.
He was awarded the title Companion of

Honour in 1972. A major retrospective of his work was held at the Tate Gallery, London in 1983–4. As a writer he succeeded John Betjeman as editor of the *Shell Guides*, writing and contributing to various volumes, including that for Oxfordshire, where he died in 1992.

1943 *The Quest*, Ashton, Sadler's Wells Ballet, New Theatre, London
1948 *Job*, de Valois, Sadler's Wells Ballet, Royal Opera House, London
1949 *Sea Change*, Cranko, Sadler's Wells Theatre Ballet, Gaiety Theatre, Dublin
1951 *Harlequin in April*, Cranko, Sadler's Wells Theatre Ballet, Sadler's Wells, London
1952 *Dancing*, Cranko, Kenton Theatre, Henley; *Umbrella*, Cranko, Kenton Theatre, Henley
1953 *The Shadow*, Cranko, Sadler's Wells Ballet, Royal Opera House, London
1955 *Cranks*, revue, Cranko
1957 Set for *The Prince of the Pagodas*, Cranko, Sadler's Wells Theatre Ballet, Royal Opera House, London (costumes by Desmond Heeley)
1958 *Reflection*, Cranko, Edinburgh Ballet, Edinburgh Festival; *Secrets*, Cranko, Edinburgh Festival Ballet, Edinburgh Festival

Anthony Powell

Born in Chorlton-cum-Hardy, Lancashire, Anthony Powell was educated in Manchester and went on to St Andrew's College, Dublin (1946–53). After doing National Service, Powell studied at the Central School of Art and Design (1955–8). For the next two years he was a costume designer at the Oxford Playhouse, before going freelance in 1960. He worked as an assistant to Beaton and Messel for a series of galas and theatre events in London in 1968, and was a consultant to Sabre Sportswear and Jantzen Swimwear during the 1960s. His many designs for the stage include *Women Beware Women* (RSC, Stratford-upon-Avon, 1961), *The Rivals* (Haymarket, London, 1966) and *Private Lives* (Queens Theatre, London, 1972). Opera designs include *Capriccio* for Glyndebourne Opera. His designs for *The Royal Hunt of the Sun* (1968) were the first of many for film, including *Tess* (1980) and *Indiana Jones and the Temple of Doom* (1983). Powell taught theatre design at Central Saint Martins from 1958 to 1971 and has undertaken numerous interior design commissions since 1978.

1993 Costumes for *Sunset Boulevard*, musical, Goodwin, directed by Trevor Nunn, Adelphi Theatre, London (set by John Napier)

Patrick Procktor

Born in Dublin, Procktor studied Russian at London University (1954–6) before training at the Slade (1958–62), where his tutors included Keith Vaughan. After National Service he worked as a Russian interpreter and took a variety of other employment while pursuing his painting, including positions as omelette chef and fashion model. He first exhibited in 1957 at the Redfern Gallery, where he held his first solo exhibition in 1963. He has taught at a number of art colleges including Camberwell School of Art and the Royal College of Art, where he was Lecturer in Painting (1968–72). He has designed a number of stage productions including *Saint's Day* by John Whiting for the Theatre Royal, Stratford, London and *Twelfth Night* for the Royal Court Theatre in 1968. He designed the British Pavilion for *Expo '67* in Montreal and contributed to *The Greatest Show on Earth* at the Coliseum, London in 1972.

1967 *Cage of God*, Carter, Western Theatre Ballet

Philip Prowse

Philip Prowse was born in Warwickshire. After studying at Malvern College of Art he went on to the Slade School of Fine Art (1956–9). During the 1960s he worked as a freelance designer, creating several productions at the Royal Opera House. Since 1970 Philip Prowse has been Associate Director of Glasgow Citizens Theatre where he has directed and designed numerous productions, including *Camino Real*, *Mary Stuart* and *Enrico IV*. He has also directed and designed productions for the National Theatre (*The Duchess of Malfi*, 1985) and the Royal Shakespeare Company (*A Woman of No Importance*, 1991). Opera productions include *The Threepenny Opera* (Opera North, 1982) and *The Pearl Fishers* (English National Opera and Opera North, 1982). He has taught at Central School of Art, Birmingham College of Art and is currently Head of Theatre Design at the Slade School of Fine Art.

1961 *Diversions*, MacMillan, The Royal Ballet, Royal Opera House, London; *Beauty and the Beast*, Cranko, Sadler's Wells Royal Ballet
1963 Costumes for *La Bayadère*, after Petipa, produced by Nureyev, The Royal Ballet, Royal Opera House, London
1964 *The Tempest*, Howard, London Dance Theatre

1965 *Circuit (Partita)*, Roy, London Dance
Theatre; *Laurentia* (divertissement),
Chaboukiani, reproduced by Nureyev, The
Royal Ballet, Royal Opera House, London

1970 *Tancredi and Clorinda*, Thorpe, Northern
Dance Theatre

1973 *The Nutcracker*, Ivanov/Darrell, Scottish
Theatre Ballet

1974 *Swan Lake*, Cauley, Zurich Opera Ballet,
Zurich

1980 *Miss Carter Wore Pink (Memories of an
Edwardian Childhood)*, Cauley, Northern
Ballet Theatre; *Chéri*, Darrell, Scottish Ballet

1981 *Swan Lake*, Petipa, Ivanov, Wright,
produced by Wright and Samsova, Sadler's
Wells Royal Ballet, Palace Theatre,
Manchester

1984 *The Sleeping Beauty*, Petipa and Wright,
produced by Wright, Sadler's Wells Royal
Ballet, Birmingham Hippodrome

1987 *Gloriana*, Corder, Sadler's Wells Royal
Ballet, Birmingham Hippodrome

1988 *Lazarus*, Cauley, Sadler's Wells Royal
Ballet

1995 *Carmina Burana*, Bintley, Birmingham
Royal Ballet, Birmingham Hippodrome

John B. Read

John B. Read is lighting consultant to the Royal
Ballet and has worked for most of the major
dance companies including Scottish Ballet,
London Festival Ballet, Nederlands Dans
Theater, Dutch National Ballet, Rambert
Dance Company, and London Contemporary
Dance Theatre. Among the many works he has
lit for the Royal Ballet are *The Tempest, Varii
Capricci, Fleeting Figures, The Nutcracker* and
Prince of the Pagodas. He has worked at Central
Saint Martins as both tutor and lighting design
consultant on The Peter Williams Design for
Dance Project.

Charles Ricketts

Born in 1866, Charles Ricketts, until his death
in 1931, was one of the most visible men of arts
and letters of his time. His publishing ventures
included *The Dial* magazine and The Vale Press
imprint, which produced 83 volumes in the
period 1896–1904. As art critic he published
three works, the import of which were sufficient
for him to be invited to fill the post of Director
of the National Gallery, London, an offer he
declined. The marriage of literary and visual
concerns was very much in evidence in his stage
designs for many of the leading dramatists of
the time, including Yeats, Wilde and Shaw.
Notable productions include *Saint Joan* (1924)
and *Henry VIII* (1925). Although acknowledging
the stage designs of Bakst as heralding 'the new
art of stage decoration', the exotic nature of
some of Ricketts's designs is informed as much
by his enthusiasm for oriental art as the direct
influence of the Russian designer.

1906 *Salome*, Literary Theatre Society

Bridget Riley

Bridget Riley was born in South London. She
trained at Goldsmith's College where she
studied drawing and at the Royal College of
Art. On leaving college she taught art at the
Convent of the Sacred Heart in Harrow and
worked in advertising for a time at the J. Walter
Thompson agency. Her career as a painter
progressed in 1959 after she attended Harry
Thubron's Summer School in Norfolk where
she met the painter and teacher Maurice de
Sausmarez. Her Op Art works of the early
1960s, championed by Anton Ehrenzweig, are
among the most memorable and arresting
images of the period. Initially working only in
black and white, she began experimenting with
colour in 1966. Riley won the International
Prize for Painting at the 34th Venice Biennale in
1968 and had a major exhibition at the
Hayward Gallery in 1971. She continues to
travel extensively and exhibit throughout the
world.

1983 *Colour Moves*, North, Ballet Rambert

Bob Ringwood

Bob Ringwood trained at Central Saint
Martins, before embarking on a career in stage
and film design. He designed three of the works
for Ballet Rambert's 'Dance for New
Dimensions' programme at the Young Vic. His
design for Peter Darrell's *Such Sweet Thunder*
(Scottish Ballet, 1979) assembled a whole
firmament of Hollywood stars, evident not only
on stage but in the credits which, for design
read 'Gowns by Adrian (assisted by Bob
Ringwood)'. Ringwood's career subsequently
embraced the world of films and among those
he has worked on are *The Draughtsman's
Contract* (directed by Peter Greenaway, 1982) as
Art Director, and the Batman films.

1973 *Magic Theatre – not for everyone*, Warren;
Interim 1, 2 and 3, Hassall; *Cantate*, Jones;
Dance for New Dimensions season, all Ballet
Rambert, The Young Vic, London

1979 *Such Sweet Thunder*, Darrell, Scottish
   Ballet

Bernadette Roberts

Bernadette Roberts trained at Central Saint
Martins College of Art and Design. Her designs
include *Necklaces* at the Cochrane Theatre,
Once Upon a War for National Youth Music
Theatre and *The Merry Widow* for Pavilion
Opera. She has worked as a designer for the
Arts Educational Schools Spring/Summer
Dance programmes and worked as a costume
designer for several productions, including *The
Television Programme* at the Gate Theatre in
Notting Hill.

1993 *Simple Symphony*, Hart, The Royal Ballet
   School, Royal Opera House, London

Jean Rosenthal

Jean Rosenthal, who was born in New York in
1912 and died there in 1969, is best known as a
lighting designer, particularly for the many
Broadway productions she worked on. Her
involvement with dance included long
associations with Balanchine, from the days of
the Ballet Society in 1946 through its
transformation into New York City Ballet in
1948 and from then until 1957. The following
year she began a long association with Martha
Graham and also worked with Jerome Robbins's
Ballets USA during the 1959–60 season.

1953 *Afternoon of a Faun*, Robbins, New York
   City Ballet, City Center, New York
1957 Set for *The Unicorn, the Gorgon and the
   Manticore*, Butler, New York City Ballet, City
   Center, New York (costumes by Robert
   Fletcher)

Leonard Rosoman

Born in London, Leonard Rosoman studied at
the University of Durham, the Royal Academy
Schools and Central School of Arts and Crafts.
In recognition of his growing stature as an artist
he was appointed Official War Artist to the
Admiralty in 1943. During the 1940s and 1950s
he was seen as part of the young English
Romantics group, which included John
Minton, Keith Vaughan and Prunella Clough.
The work produced during this period was the
subject of an exhibition at the Imperial War
Museum in 1989. Rosoman was the Chief
Designer of the acclaimed Diaghilev Exhibition
held in Edinburgh and London in 1954. He was
made ARA in 1960 and RA in 1970.

1949 *Pleasuredrome*, Hightower, Metropolitan
   Ballet Company, Coliseum, Harrow
1953 *Cyclasm*, Gore, Walter Gore Ballet, Princes
   Theatre, London

Loudon Sainthill

Born in Hobart, Tasmania, in 1919, Loudon
Sainthill studied at the Art School of
Melbourne Technical College, during which
time he met the Colonel de Basil Russian Ballet
Company, then touring Australia. He travelled
to Europe with the company in 1939 and was
given an exhibition at the Redfern Gallery. After
war service, Sainthill created designs for the
National Art Gallery of New South Wales

exhibition *A History of Costume from 4000BC to
1945AD*. His first stage design was *The Tempest*
(1951) at the Shakespeare Memorial Theatre,
Stratford-upon-Avon, followed the same year by
Coppélia for Sadler's Wells Ballet. His
subsequent commissions spanned theatre, film,
musicals and opera, including the Royal Opera's
Coq d'Or in 1954. His last designs, costumes for
The Four Musketeers, with sets by Sean Kenny,
were created in 1968. Sainthill was a visiting
teacher of Theatre Design at the Central School
of Art. He died in 1969.

1951 *Coppélia*, Ivanov/Cecchetti, reproduced by
   Sergeyev, Sadler's Wells Theatre Ballet,
   Sadler's Wells, London; *The Lyric Revue*,
   Globe Theatre, Hammersmith
1952 *Iles des Sirènes* [with Margot Fonteyn],
   Sadler's Wells, London
1956 *Jubilee Girl*, musical: choreographed by
   Darrell, Victoria Palace, London
1958 *Expresso Bongo*, musical; directed by
   Chappell, Saville Theatre, London;
   Cinderella, pantomime directed by
   Carpenter, Coliseum Theatre, London
1959 *Aladdin*, pantomime directed by
   Helpmann, Coliseum Theatre, London
1961 *Belle*, musical directed by Mankowitz,
   Strand Theatre, London
1962 *Sail Away*, musical directed by Coward,
   Savoy Theatre, London
1963 *Half a Sixpence*, musical directed by
   Dexter, Haymarket Theatre, London
1965 *Fielding's Music Hall Revue*, revue directed
   by Chappell, Prince Charles Theatre, London
1966 *Man of Magic*, musical directed by Ebert,
   Piccadilly Theatre, London (scenery by
   Michael Trangmar)
1967 *Canterbury Tales*, musical directed by
   Habunek, Phoenix Theatre, London (settings

by Derek Cousins)

1968 *The Four Musketeers*, musical directed by Coe, Theatre Royal, Drury Lane, London (settings by Sean Kenny)

Mathilde Sandberg

Mathilde Sandberg was born in Holland and studied Fashion Design at the Rietvelt Academy in Amsterdam and costume cutting with Nora Waugh at Central School of Art and Design in London. She worked first at Sadler's Wells Theatre and at the Royal Opera House, and then started the Costume Painting and Dye department at Wimbledon School of Art where she also taught on the Theatre Design course. She established her own business specialising in painting and dying costumes and has worked for a wide number of dance, theatre and opera companies as well as for television and film and for pop groups and musicals. She is a guest lecturer at the Slade School of Fine Art and at Central Saint Martins College of Art and Design.

1982 *Chanson*, Deane, The Royal Ballet, Royal Opera House, London

1983 *Riccordi*, Fernandez, Dance Umbrella

1984 *Fleeting Figures*, Deane, The Royal Ballet, Royal Opera House, London

Richard Smith

Richard Smith studied at Luton School of Art and, following National Service, at St Albans School of Art and the Royal College of Art. Following an RCA Scholarship for travel in Italy he was awarded a grant from the Harkness Fellowship of the Commonwealth Fund in 1959 which enabled him to spend the following two years in the USA. On his return to London he taught at St Martins School of Art for two years before returning to the States in 1963. Since 1961 he has had numerous one-man exhibitions both in Europe and the Americas. He was awarded a CBE in 1971 and has been living in New York since 1978, where he continues to evolve his three-dimensional approach to painting.

1984 *Wildlife*, Alston, Ballet Rambert

1985 *Dangerous Liaisons*, Alston, Ballet Rambert

Peter Snow

Peter Snow was born in Catford, London. He worked as a journalist for the South London Press in 1946 and began attending Goldsmith's School of Art, London, before he was called up for military service 1946–8. From 1948 to 1953 he studied painting at the Slade School of Fine Art, winning both a Malcolm Scholarship in Decorative Painting and Theatre Design and a Scholarship in Fine Art from the University of London. In 1957 he joined the staff of the Slade School of Fine Art where he continues to teach. His first major theatre project was the design of *Love's Labour's Lost* for the Shakespeare Festival in 1951, and his subsequent work, through to the re-design of Act III of *Coppélia* for Scottish Theatre Ballet in 1992, has embraced a variety of forms, including writing and designing multimedia productions. In 1970 he formed The Electric Theatre Company, London. He has exhibited extensively both as a painter as well as a theatre designer, most recently in a major retrospective (February 1995) at the Morley Gallery, London. In 1995, Peter Snow was appointed Visiting Professor at the Slade School of Fine Art.

1955 *Variations on a Theme of Purcell*, Ashton, Sadler's Wells Ballet, Royal Opera House, London

1962 *Encounters*, Holmes, Prince of Wales Theatre, London

1966 Backcloth for *Festina Lente,* Zolan, Ballets Minerva, London (costumes by Sandra Vane)

1967 *Observations*, Beale, Western Theatre Ballet

1979 *Coppélia*, after Petipa/Cecchetti; new choreography and produced by Wright, Sadler's Wells Royal Ballet, Royal Shakespeare Theatre, Stratford-upon-Avon

1992 *Coppélia*, Act III, Petipa and Wright, Scottish Ballet, Theatre Royal, Glasgow

Yolanda Sonnabend

Yolanda Sonnabend was born in Zimbabwe and was educated in Geneva. She studied painting and stage design at the Slade School of Fine Art and in 1960 was awarded the Boise travelling scholarship. She has taught on the theatre design course at Central School of Art and has been a visiting lecturer at Wimbledon School of Art and at the Slade. She has had one-man shows at the Whitechapel Art Gallery and at the Serpentine Gallery and her work is in a number of public collections including the British Theatre Museum, Victoria and Albert Museum, the National Portrait Gallery and the Library of Performing Arts, Lincoln Center, New York.

1957 *A Blue Rose*, Wright, Sadler's Wells Royal Ballet, Royal Opera House, London

1963 *Symphony*, MacMillan, The Royal Ballet,

Royal Opera House, London (redesigned 1975)

1964 *Orfeo*, opera, Darrell, Sadler's Wells New Opera Company; *Entwurfe für Tanzer,* Wright, Stuttgart Ballet, Württemberg State Theatre, Stuttgart

1975 *Rituals*, MacMillan, The Royal Ballet, Royal Opera House, London

1976 *Requiem* (Fauré), MacMillan, Stuttgart Ballet

1977 *Gloriana*, MacMillan, Royal Ballet, Royal Opera House, London

1978 *My Brother, My Sisters*, MacMillan, Stuttgart Ballet

1979 *Playground*, MacMillan, The Royal Ballet Touring Company, The Big Top, Edinburgh

1980 *My Brother, My Sisters*, MacMillan, The Royal Ballet, Royal Opera House, London

1981 *Three Pictures*, Corder, Sadler's Wells Ballet, Theatre Royal, Glasgow

1982 *L'Invitation au Voyage*, Corder, The Royal Ballet, Royal Opera House, London

1983 *Valley of Shadows*, MacMillan, The Royal Ballet, Royal Opera House, London

1984 Costumes for *Different Drummer*, MacMillan, The Royal Ballet; costumes for *The Seven Deadly Sins*, MacMillan, expanded version for Granada Television

1986 *Requiem* (Lloyd Webber), MacMillan, American Ballet Theatre

1987 *Swan Lake*, Petipa, Ivanov, additional choreography by Bintley, produced by Dowell, The Royal Ballet, Royal Opera House, London

1989 Costumes for *La Bayadère*, Makarova after Petipa; production by Makarova, The Royal Ballet, Royal Opera House, London

1993 *Fanfare*, Hart, The Royal Ballet, Royal Opera House, London; *The Nutcracker and the Hard Nut*, Pilobolus, Ballet du Rhin

1994 *Caught Dance*, Hart, The Royal Ballet, Haymarket Theatre, Leicester

Ian Spurling

Ian Spurling was born in South Australia in 1937, first studying in Adelaide before moving to England to continue his tuition at the Slade School of Fine Art. He designed for opera, including two Peter Maxwell Davies works for children, *The Two Fiddlers* and *Cinderella*, and created costumes for the late Freddie Mercury. His dance designs are typified by the exuberant costumes for MacMillan's perennial favourite, *Elite Syncopations*, another collaboration between choreographer and designer that began with the experimental *Seven Deadly Sins* for Western Theatre Ballet in 1961. His teaching included working with theatre design students at Central Saint Martins College of Art and Design on the annual Peter Williams Design for Dance Project. His designs for the tribute to Sir Peter Wright choreographed by Matthew Hart, *Sir Peter and the Wolf,* marked the start of what promised to become another enduring collaborative relationship. At the time of his death in 1996 he was working with Hart on a new production for English National Ballet.

1961 *The Seven Deadly Sins*, MacMillan, Western Ballet Theatre

1962 *Non Stop*, Darrell, Western Theatre Ballet; *Valse Eccentrique*, MacMillan, Western Theatre Ballet

1973 *The Seven Deadly Sins*, MacMillan, The Royal Ballet, Royal Opera House, London

1974 *Elite Syncopations*, MacMillan, The Royal Ballet, Royal Opera House, London

1978 *Elite Syncopations*, MacMillan, Sadler's Wells Royal Ballet; *6.6.78* (tribute to de Valois on her 80th birthday), MacMillan, Sadler's Wells Royal Ballet, Sadler's Wells, London

1979 *La Fin du Jour*, MacMillan, The Royal Ballet, Royal Opera House, London

1983 *The Winter Play*, Burrows, Sadler's Wells Royal Ballet, Birmingham Hippodrome

1988 *Soirée Musicale*, MacMillan, The Royal Ballet School, Royal Opera House, London

1991 *Danses Concertantes*, MacMillan, The Royal Ballet, Royal Opera House, London

1995 *Sir Peter and the Wolf*, Hart, The Royal Ballet School, Royal Opera House, London

Pavel Tchelitchev

Tchelitchev was born in Moscow in 1898 and died in Rome in 1957. Largely self-taught, although he took a series of lessons with Exter in Kiev during 1918, Tchelitchev's early artistic expression displayed a keen interest in the occult and astrology. This was filtered through the influence of Cubism and Constructivism, though his style tended more toward Surrealism after settling in Paris in 1923. He worked for Diaghilev during the 1920s and 1930s, and subsequently for Balanchine. Among his circle of associates were Gertrude Stein and Dame Edith Sitwell. As a painter, his best-known works are *Phenomena* (1936–8) and *Hide and Seek* (1940–2).

1919 *The Geisha*, Mardvanov's Theatre, Kiev (not produced)

1921 Ballets for weekly programmes of Viktor Zimin's Ballet Company, Istanbul

1922 *The Wedding Feast of the Boyars*, Romanov, Russian Romantic Ballet, Berlin; *The*

Sacrifice of Atoraga, Romanov, Russian Romantic Ballet, Berlin

1923 *Savonarola* (tragedy after Gobineau), Koenigsbiatzerstrasse Theater, Berlin

1924 Costumes with Exter, Zak and others for *Suite des Danses*, Romanov, Russian Romantic Theatre, Paris (announced)

1928 *Ode*, Massine, Diaghilev's Ballets Russes, Théâtre Sarah-Bernhardt, Paris (projections by Pierre Charbonnier)

1933 *L'Errante*, Balanchine, Les Ballets 1933, Paris

1936 *Orpheus and Eurydice*, Balanchine, American Ballet, New York; *Serenata: Magic*, Balanchine, Avery Memorial Theatre, Hartford, Connecticut

1938 *Nobilissima Visione (Saint Francis)*, Massine, Ballets Russes de Monte Carlo, London

1941 *Balustrade*, Balanchine, Original Ballet Russe, New York; *The Cave of Sleep*, Balanchine, American Ballet Caravan (not produced)

1942 *Concierto de Mozart*, Balanchine, Teatro Colón, Buenos Aires; *Apollon Musagète*, Balanchine, American Ballet, Buenos Aires

Rouben Ter-Arutunian

Born in Tiflis, Russia, Rouben Ter-Arutunian was educated in Berlin, studying design at the Reimann Art School, film music at the Musik Hochschule and art history and theatre arts at the Friedrich Wilhelm University. He studied painting and sculpture in Paris (Ecole des Beaux-Arts, Académie Julien and the Académie de la Grande Chaumière) before emigrating to the United States in 1951, becoming a US citizen in 1957. After working as a designer for both CBS and NBC television networks he became a freelance stage, film and television designer. His work as a designer is known internationally and includes numerous drama and opera commissions as well as a wide range of important dance works in both the classical and contemporary fields.

1955 *Souvenirs*, Bolender, New York City Ballet

1958 *The Seven Deadly Sins*, Balanchine, New York City Ballet

1961 *Visionary Recital*, Graham, Martha Graham Company

1962 *Pierrot Lunaire*, Tetley, Glen Tetley Company, New York

1963 *Time Out of Mind*, Macdonald, Joffrey Ballet

1964 Sets for *The Nutcracker*, Balanchine, New York City Ballet; *Ballet Imperial*, Balanchine, New York City Ballet

1965 *Harlequinade*, Balanchine, New York City Ballet; *Sargasso*, Tetley, Nederlands Dans Theater; *Field Mass*, Tetley, Nederlands Dans Theater

1966 *Ricercare*, Tetley, American Ballet Theatre

1967 *Firebird*, Macdonald, Harkness Ballet

1968 *Requiem Canticle*, Balanchine, New York City Ballet

1969 *Transitions*, Butler, Operhaus, Cologne

1970 *The Unicorn, The Gorgon and the Manticore*, Butler, Festival of the Two Worlds, Spoleto, Italy

1971 *Chronochromie*, Tetley, Hamburg State Opera Ballet

1972 *Laborintus*, Tetley, The Royal Ballet, Royal Opera House, London; *Chopiniana*, Fokine, New York City Ballet (not produced)

1973 *Voluntaries*, Tetley, Stuttgart Ballet; *Remembrances*, Joffrey, Joffrey Ballet

1974 *Dybbuk Variations*, Robbins, New York City Ballet; *Coppélia*, Danilov and Balanchine, after Saint-Léon

1976 *Union Jack*, Balanchine, New York City Ballet

1977 Set for *Vienna Waltzes*, Balanchine, New York City Ballet (costumes by Karinska)

1980 *Robert Schumann's Davidsbündlertänze*, Balanchine, New York City Ballet

1982 *Noah and the Flood*, Balanchine, New York City Ballet

Carl Toms

Carl Toms gained his first professional experience as an assistant to Oliver Messel. He soon established his name as a designer with commissions for drama, opera, ballet and film. His numerous credits include work for the National Theatre (*The Provok'd Wife* of 1981 earned Toms the Society of West End Theatre's award for Best Designer), the Royal Shakespeare Company and opera companies throughout the world. He was awarded an OBE in July 1969. In addition to his stage design, Carl Toms has redesigned theatre auditoria at both the Theatre Royal, Bath and the Richmond Theatre and was Design Consultant for the Investiture of HRH The Prince of Wales in 1969.

1959 *La Reja*, Cranko, Ballet Rambert; *Pièce d'Occasion*, Cranko, London Festival Ballet

1960 *New Cranks*, Cranko, Lyric Theatre, London

1963 *Swan Lake*, Petipa/Ivanov; Ashton, Nureyev, Fay, produced by Helpmann, The Royal Ballet, Royal Opera House, London; *Ballet Imperial*, Balanchine, Royal Ballet, Royal Opera House, London

1982 *Swan Lake*, Petipa, produced by Field, London Festival Ballet

1993 *Swan Lake*, after Gorsky and Messerer, staged by Struchkova, English National Ballet

Keith Vaughan

Born in Selsey Bill, Sussex, 1912, Vaughan worked in an advertising agency until the age of twenty-seven, when, realising that war was imminent, he moved to Surrey to spend a year painting. As a conscientious objector he was placed in a POW camp in Yorkshire as an assistant interpreter of German. His painting career flourished after the war with his first solo exhibition in 1946, the same year that he began sharing a flat with the artist John Minton. He taught at several art schools, including the Central School of Art. He was the subject of a retrospective exhibition at the Whitechapel Gallery, London, in 1962. Selections from the journals he had kept since 1939 were published in 1966. He died in 1977.

David Walker

After studying at the Central School of Arts and Crafts, David Walker worked alongside John Bury as costume designer for Joan Littlewood's productions during the 1960 season. He works in many genres, designing, among others, *Saratoga* and *London Assurance* for the Royal Shakespeare Company and *Man and Superman* for the National Theatre. He has designed for the Royal Opera (including *Così Fan Tutte*), English National Opera (including *La Traviata*)

and *Carmen* for the Metropolitan Opera House. Film design credits include *The Charge of the Light Brigade* and *Lady Caroline Lamb*. As a designer for dance he has worked with many leading companies throughout the world, having a particular affinity with nineteenth-century ballets.

1964 Costumes for *The Dream*, Ashton, The Royal Ballet, Royal Opera House, London (set by Henry Bardon)

1965 Costumes for *Cinderella*, Ashton, Sadler's Wells Ballet, Royal Opera House, London (set by Henry Bardon)

1966 Costumes for *Beatrix*, Carter, London Festival Ballet, Royal Festival Hall, London (set by Henry Bardon)

1971 *Giselle*, Skeaping after Perrot, Coralli, Petipa, London Festival Ballet

1977 *The Sleeping Beauty*, Sergeyev, Ashton, MacMillan and Lopokov after Petipa, produced by de Valois, The Royal Ballet, Royal Opera House, London

1979 *La Sylphide*, Schaufuss after Bournonville, London Festival Ballet

1981 *Napoli*, Bournonville, produced by Schaufuss, National Ballet of Canada

1982 *Cinderella*, Stevenson, English National Ballet; *Konservatoriet*, Bournonville, The Royal Ballet

1986 *The Dream*, Ashton, Sadler's Wells Royal Ballet

1987 *Cinderella*, Ashton, The Royal Ballet

1996 *Cinderella*, Corder, English National Ballet

Rex Whistler

Rex Whistler, born in 1905, studied at the Slade School of Fine Art and in Rome. He developed an instantly recognisable style of drawing which he used as a painter of murals, illustrator of books and designer for the theatre. Whistler illustrated the Cresset Press edition of Swift's *Gulliver's Travels* and among his murals are those in the refreshment room of the Tate Gallery. He made his name in the ballet world with his designs for de Valois's *The Rake's Progress*, still occasionally to be seen today, and went on to design Ashton's *The Wise Virgins*, a revival of *Le Spectre de la Rose*, ballets for the International Ballet as well as a number of plays. He was killed in action in 1944, during World War Two.

1932 *The Infanta's Birthday*, Spencer, Camargo Society, Adelphi Theatre, London

1935 *The Rake's Progress*, de Valois, Vic-Wells Ballet, Sadler's Wells, London (false proscenium by Oliver Messel added in 1946)

1940 *The Wise Virgins*, Ashton, Vic-Wells Ballet, Sadler's Wells, London

1941 *Les Sylphides*, Fokine, International Ballet, British Tour

1943 Set for *Everyman,* Inglesby, International Ballet, Lyric Theatre, London (costumes by William Chappell)

1944 *Le Spectre de la Rose*, Fokine, Sadler's Wells Ballet, New Theatre, London

Peter Whiteman

Peter Whiteman studied theatre design at Central School of Art and Design. He was the recipient of two Arts Council Bursaries for work at Sadler's Wells Theatre and Bristol Old Vic Theatre. He worked as a design assistant for Leslie Hurry, Alix Stone, Ralph Koltai and Yolanda Sonnabend. He has designed several operas in collaboration with the director Colin Graham, including *L'Incoronazione di Poppea* for English National Opera at the Coliseum. Theatre designs include *The Government Inspector* at Bristol Old Vic, *Peer Gynt* at Oxford Playhouse and *Funnyhouse of a Negro* at the Royal Court Theatre. His murals can be seen throughout the world; UK commissions include Cliveden House and Madame Tussauds. Further activities include work on numerous feature films, commercials, exhibition design and book illustrations, among them the covers for J.M. Dent's series of Joseph Conrad novels and short stories.

1992 *The Snow Princess*, Stevenson, Ballet de Santiago, Chile

Peter Williams

Peter Williams, born in 1914, was a student at Central School of Art and Design and ran his own business as a dress designer until the start of the war. In 1950 Williams became the founding editor of *Dance and Dancers*, a role he continued for thirty years. He served on dance committees for the British Council and for the Arts Council, was chairman of the Royal Ballet Benevolent Fund and founded the Dancers' Pension and Resettlement Fund, later The Dancers' Trust. His involvement with, and encouragment of, post-war British dance was immense. In recognition of his services he was awarded an OBE in 1971. A prolific contributor to his own and other dance magazines,

Williams's publications include a celebration of dance design. The Peter Williams Design for Dance Project, part of the theatre design course at Central Saint Martins College of Art and Design, was named in his honour in 1993 and creates an opportunity for young designers to work together with dance students and young musicians and present their work on the stage of The Cochrane Theatre. Peter Williams died in Cornwall in 1995.

1947 *Giselle*, Petipa, Metropolitan Ballet Company
1948 Set for *Selina*, Howard, Sadler's Wells Theatre Ballet, Sadler's Wells, London; *Designs with Strings*, Taras, Metropolitan Ballet Company, Scala Theatre, London; *Prince Igor*, Fokine, Metropolitan Ballet Company

Christopher Wood

Christopher Wood was born in Knowsley, Lancashire, in 1901. His schooling was interrupted for three and a half years when he caught polio at fourteen and he was nursed back to health by his mother. He studied architecture briefly and then moved to London where he began to paint, self-taught. While in Monte-Carlo in 1926 he was commissioned by Diaghilev, over better-established English painters such as Augustus John and Wyndham Lewis, to design *Romeo and Juliet*. The project did not come to fruition, however, as Diaghilev subsequently chose to use Ernst and Miró. A promising career was cut short by his early death at the age of twenty-nine in 1930. In 1938 the Redfern mounted an exhibition of virtually his complete output, some 530 watercolours,

oils and drawings.

1930 *Luna Park*, or *The Freaks*, Balanchine, Cochran's 1930 Revue, London Pavilion, London

Chiang Yee

Apart from his dates of birth and death (1903–77), it has proved impossible to obtain biographical information on this designer. His only known design is:

1942 *The Birds*, Helpmann, Sadler's Wells Ballet, New Theatre, London

Notes

Draped Life pp.34-40

[1] A medieval tight-sleeved body garment.

[2] Tanya Moiseiwitsch: designer of over two hundred productions in a career extending over fifty years.

[3] Tanya Moiseiwitsch, interview with the author, 26 March 1996.

[4] Examples of Ricketts's work were displayed at the exhibition *From Diaghilev to the Pet Shop Boys*, Lethaby Galleries, Central Saint Martins College of Art and Design, 1993.

[5] Peter Williams, interview with the author, 2 September 1992.

[6] Technical Education Board Minutes, LCC Archives, 109, 1903. Cited in Godfrey Rubens, *Richard William Lethaby*, Architectural Press Ltd, London, 1986, p.170.

[7] ibid. p.183

[8] Examples of Rex Whistler's work were displayed at the exhibition *From Diaghilev to the Pet Shop Boys*, 1993.

[9] Photographs of these productions can be viewed at The Theatre Museum, Victoria and Albert, London.

[10] Peter Williams, 'Prelude to an Anniversary', *Dance and Dancers*, Vol.27, No.4, April 1976, pp.25-9, 40.

[11] 'Jeannetta Cochrane 1882 – 1957', *The Opening of The Jeannetta Cochrane Theatre: One Man Show*, Theatre Programme, 12 November 1964.

[12] Peter Williams, interview with the author, 2 September 1992.

[13] Dennis Behl. *A Career in the Theater, The Stage Is All the World – The Theatrical Designs of Tanya Moiseiwitsch*. Catalogue, David and Alfred Smart Museum of Art, University of Chicago and The Washington Press, 1994.

[14] Nora Waugh's books include *Corsets and Crinolines, The Cut of Men's Clothes* and *The Cut of Women's Clothes*.

[15] Tanya Moiseiwitsch, interview with the author, 26 March 1996.

[16] 'Around the Art Schools: The LCC Central School of Arts and Crafts', *The Artist*, No.43, April 1952, pp.38-40.

[17] 'Jeannetta Cochrane 1882 – 1957', *The Opening of The Jeannetta Cochrane Theatre: One Man Show*, Theatre Programme, 12 November 1964.

[18] ibid.

[19] Tanya Moiseiwitsch, interview with the author, 26 March 1996.

[20] MS Notes on Art Education. The Athenaeum, Barnstaple, cited in Godfrey Rubens, op. cit.

[21] ibid.

[22] Tanya Moiseiwitsch, interview with the author, 26 March 1996.

[23] Peter Williams, op. cit.

[24] Pegeret Anthony, interview with the author, 26 March 1996.

[25] Peter Docherty, Designer, Senior Lecturer and Third Year Tutor; Peter Farley, Designer, Tutor and PhD Researcher; Dr Tim White, Tutor and Researcher; Norman Morrice, Director of Choreographic Studies, Royal Ballet School; David Drew, assistant to Norman Morrice; Susan Nash and Matthew Hamilton, lighting designers, choreographers, Directors of Dance Unlimited.

A Stage of Creation pp.41-9

[1] Norman Morrice, interview with Dr Tim White, London, 24 April 1995.

[2] ibid.

[3] Peter Williams, 'A Question of Time', *Dance and Dancers*, Vol.17, No.11, November 1966, pp.8-10, 40.

[4] Peter Williams, 'More Collaboration: Into the Arena', *Dance and Dancers*, Vol.19, No.5, May 1968, pp.13-16.

[5] Norman Morrice, interview with Dr Tim White, London, 24 April 1995.

[6] Norman Morrice and Ralph Koltai, video interview with Dr Tim White, London, October 1995.

[7] ibid.

[8] Open letter from F. S. Bromwich, General Administrator, The Mercury Theatre Trust Ltd, February 1967.

[9] ibid.

[10] Norman Morrice, interview with Dr Tim White, London, 24 April 1995.

[11] Alexander Bland, (pseudonym Nigel and Maude Gosling), 'Breezy Birth', *Observer*, London, 19 March 1967.

[12] Peter Williams, 'Visionary Cochrane', *Dance and Dancers*, Vol.18, No.5, May 1967, pp.18-19.

[13] ibid.

Design for Dance: The Story So Far pp.56-66

[1] Open letter from Pamela Howard, 27 July 1989.

[2] Norman Morrice, report to Peter Docherty, 1989.

[3] Matthew Hart, comments from dancers and choreographers, 1989.

[4] Peter Docherty, interview with the author, 4 April 1996.

[5] Publicity handout for *Design for Dance* exhibition, Bridge Gallery, Central Saint Martins College of Art and Design, January 1990.

[6] Norman Morrice, The Annual Design for Dance Project, Appraisal, 1990.

[7] Nicholas Dromgoole, 'Christina Hoyos and Design for Dance', *The Sunday Telegraph*, 13 March 1994.

[8] Sir Peter Wright, Introduction to Catalogue of *The Designers: Pushing the Boundaries – Advancing the Dance*. Design for Performance Research Project, London 1995.

[9] ibid.

[10] Norman Morrice, The Annual Design for Dance Project, Appraisal, 1990.

[11] Peter Docherty, Peter Williams Design for Dance Project, Student Seminar, Cochrane Theatre, 1994.

[12] Norman Morrice, The Annual Design for Dance Project, Appraisal, 1990.

Ballet. Monthly (irregular) Publication suspended November 1939–45. Known as *Ballet and Opera* 1948–9. Published by Ballet Publications, London, 1939–52

Beaton, Cecil, *Ballet.* A. Wingate, London, 1951

Beaumont, Cyril W., *Ballet Design: Past and Present.* The Studio, London, 1946

———, *Design for the Ballet.* The Studio, London, 1940

Buckle Richard (ed.), *The Diaghilev Exhibition* (catalogue). Edinburgh Festival Society, Edinburgh, 1954

———, *In Search of Diaghilev.* Sidgwick and Jackson, London, 1955

———, *Modern Ballet Design.* A.&C. Black, London, 1955

Castle, Charles, *Oliver Messel.* Thames and Hudson, London, 1986

Chappell, William, *Studies in Ballet.* J.Lehmann, London, 1948

Clarke, Mary and Crisp, Clement, *Design for Ballet.* Cassell and Collier Macmillan, London, 1978

———, *London Contemporary Dance Theatre: the first 21 years.* Photographs by Anthony Crickmay. Dance Books, London, 1989

Cooper, Douglas, *Picasso's Theatre.* Weidenfeld and Nicolson, London, 1968

Crisp, Clement, Sainsbury, Anya, and Williams, Peter, (eds) *Ballet Rambert: 50 years and on.* Scolar Press, 1976

Dance and Dancers (monthly). Hansom Books, London, 1950

Dance Collection of the New York Public Library. World Wide Web Address: http://honor.uc.wlu.edu:1020/-tr11506 log on as 'nypl'

Dance Now (quarterly). Dance Books, London, Spring 1992

Dance Theatre Journal (quarterly). Laban Centre for Movement and Dance, London, 1983

Diaghilev: Costumes and Designs of the Ballets Russes. Metropolitan Museum of Art, New York, 1978

Friedman, Martin, *Hockney Paints the Stage.* Thames and Hudson, London, 1983

Gadan, Francis and Maillard, Robert (eds), *A Dictionary of Modern Ballet.* Methuen, London, 1959

Goodwin, John, *British Theatre Design: The Modern Age.* Weidenfeld and Nicolson, London, 1989

Goodwin, Noël, *A Ballet for Scotland: the first ten years of the Scottish Ballet.* Canongate Publishing in association with Greenleaf Literary Enterprises, Edinburgh, 1979

Hurry, Leslie, *Leslie Hurry – Settings and Costumes for Sadler's Wells Ballets.* Introduction by Cyril W. Beaumont and Lillian Browse. Faber and Faber, London, 1967

Kochno, Boris, *Christian Bérard.* Introduction by John Russell and contributions from Jean Clair and Edmonde Charles-Roux. Thames and Hudson, London, 1988

Koegler, Horst (ed.), *The Concise Oxford Dictionary of Ballet.* Oxford University Press, 1977. Second Edition, London, 1982

Koltai, Ralph, 'Theatre design – the exploration of space', *Royal Society of Arts Journal* No.135, March 1987, pp.298–309

Larionov, Mikhail, *Les Ballets Russes: Serge Diaghilev et la décoration théâtrale.* With Natalia Gontcharova, and Pierre Vorms. revised edition, P. Vorms, Belvès Dordogne, 1955

Schouvaloff, Alexander and Borovsky, Victor, *Stravinsky on Stage.* Stainer and Bell, London, 1982

Schouvaloff, Alexander, *Set and Costume Designs for Ballet and Theatre: The Thyssen-Bornemisza Collection.* Sotheby's Publications, London, 1987

———, *Theatre on Paper.* Sotheby's Publications, London, 1990

Shaw, Phyllida and Allen, Keith (eds), *Make Space! Design for Theatre and Alternative Spaces.* Theatre Design Umbrella and The Society of British Theatre Designers, London, 1994

Sophie Fedorovitch 1893–1953: Memorial Exhibition of Designs for Ballet, Opera and Stage (exhibition catalogue). Victoria and Albert Museum, London, 1955

Sorley-Walker, Catherine and Woodcock, Sarah, *The Royal Ballet: a picture history.* Threshold Books, London, 1986

Spencer, Charles, *Cecil Beaton – Stage and Film Designs.* Academy Editions, London, 1975

———, *Léon Bakst.* Academy Editions, London, 1973

———, *The World of Serge Diaghilev.* Contributions by Philip Dyer and Martin Battersby. Penguin Books, Harmondsworth, 1979

Strong, Roy et al., *Designing for the Dancer.* Contributions from Ivor Guest, Richard Buckle, Barry Kay, Liz da Costa and Alexander Schouvaloff. Elron Press, London, 1981

The Dancing Times (monthly). First published in London, 1894. New series volume 1 in October 1910. Absorbed *Dancing and Ballroom* (July 1930), *Amateur Dancer* (April 1934) and *Ballet Annual* (1965)

The Designers: Pushing the Boundaries – Advancing the Dance (exhibition catalogue). Design for Performance Research Project, Central Saint Martins College of Art and Design, London, 1995

Thorpe, Edward, *Kenneth MacMillan: The Man and the Ballets.* Foreword by Dame Ninette de Valois, Hamish Hamilton, London, 1985

Whistler, Rex, *Designs for the Theatre.* B.T. Batsford, London and New York, 1950

Williams, Peter, *Masterpieces of Ballet Design.* Phaidon Press, Oxford, 1981

Woodcock, Sarah, *The Sadler's Wells Royal Ballet: now the Birmingham Royal Ballet.* Sinclair Stevenson, London, 1991

Journals are available for study at a number of sites, including The Theatre Museum, 1E Tavistock Street, London, WC2E 7PA (0171 836 7891) and the Laban Centre for Movement and Dance, Laurie Grove, New Cross, London SE14 6NW (0181 692 4070 ext.120). In both instances please ring to make an appointment.

The Scenographic Heritage

The list below refers only to artists featured in this book

Students of Jeannetta Cochrane

Ann Curtis
Peter Farmer
Ralph Koltai
Tanya Moiseiwitsch
Anthony Powell
David Walker
Peter Williams

Students of Ralph Koltai

Nadine Baylis
Maria Bjørnson
Peter Docherty
Charles Dunlop
David Fielding
John Napier
Bob Ringwood
Peter Whiteman

Students at Central Saint Martins

Nadine Baylis
Maria Bjørnson
Richard Bridgland
Lez Brotherston
Ann Curtis
Peter Docherty
Charles Dunlop
Peter Farley
Peter Farmer
David Fielding
Tim Hatley
Ralph Koltai
Tanya Moiseiwitsch
Peter Mumford
John Napier

Anthony Powell
Bob Ringwood
Bernadette Roberts
David Walker
Peter Whiteman
Peter Williams

Students of Peter Williams

Elisabeth Dalton
Peter Docherty
Pamela Howard
Derek Jarman
Peter Logan
Philip Prowse
Yolanda Sonnabend
Ian Spurling

Students of Nicholas Georgiadis

Terry Bartlett
Elisabeth Dalton
Peter Docherty
Pamela Howard
Derek Jarman
Peter Logan
Philip Prowse
Yolanda Sonnabend
Ian Spurling

Teachers at Central Saint Martins

Terry Bartlett
Nadine Baylis
Maria Bjørnson
Lez Brotherston
Jennifer Carey

Ann Curtis
Elisabeth Dalton
Peter J. Davison
Peter Docherty
Robin Don
Peter Farley
Peter Farmer
David Fielding
Rick Fisher
Tim Hatley
Pamela Howard
Richard Hudson
Derek Jarman
Ralph Koltai
Andrew Logan
John Macfarlane
Tanya Moiseiwitsch
Peter Mumford
John Napier
Anthony Powell
Philip Prowse
Paul Pyant
John B. Read
Bob Ringwood
Loudon Sainthill
Mathilde Sandberg
Peter Snow
Yolanda Sonnabend
Ian Spurling
Carl Toms
David Walker
Peter Williams

Nicholas Georgiadis is an Honorary Advisor to the MA Scenography Course
Patrick Caulfield and **Ralph Koltai** are Honorary Fellows of The London Institute

Contributors

Professor Margaret Buck Head of College, Central Saint Martins College of Art and Design.

Peter Docherty Designer, Project Director, Design for Performance and Third Year Tutor, BA (Hons) Theatre Design, Central Saint Martins College of Art and Design.

Sir John Drummond CBE Former Director of the Henry Wood Promenade Concerts, former Controller of BBC Radio Three, former Director of the Edinburgh Festival.

Peter Farley MA Designer and teacher. PhD Researcher, Design for Performance.

Rick Fisher Lighting Designer and Consultant, Peter Williams Design for Dance Project.

Nicholas Georgiadis CBE Designer and painter. Honorary Advisor, MA Scenography.

Matthew Hamilton Choreographer and artist. Artistic Director, Dance Unlimited. Consultant, Peter Williams Design for Dance Project.

Tim Hatley Designer and Visiting Teacher, Central Saint Martins College of Art and Design.

Marina Henderson Theatre design historian, writer and gallery owner.

Pamela Howard Designer. Artistic Director, MA Scenography.

Sue Merrett Editorial Assistant, *The Dancing Times*.

Philip Prowse Director and Designer. Head of Theatre Design, The Slade School of Fine Art. Associate Director, Citizens Theatre, Glasgow.

John B. Read Lighting Designer. Consultant, Peter Williams Design for Dance Project.

Yolanda Sonnabend Designer and artist. Lecturer in Theatre Design, The Slade School of Fine Art.

Malcolm Stewart MA Dance critic, Project Secretary, Design for Performance.

Dr Tim White Writer and teacher, Research Assistant, Design for Performance.

Peter Williams OBE Designer, Writer and Founding Editor of *Dance and Dancers*.

Index

All numerals in italics refer to illustrations